# Microcosm:
# College
# and the
# World

# Microcosm: College and the World

**Ann Wilkinson Connor**
*Foothill College*

**Gerald Kohs**
*Foothill College*

 HARCOURT BRACE JOVANOVICH, INC.
New York   Chicago   San Francisco   Atlanta

# LIBRARY
## University of Texas
### At San Antonio

© 1972 by Harcourt Brace Jovanovich, Inc.

All rights reserved. No part of this publication may be reproduced or transmitted in any form or by any means, electronic or mechanical, including photocopy, recording, or any information storage and retrieval system, without permission in writing from the publisher.

ISBN: 0-15-558600-9

Library of Congress Catalog Card Number: 70-184119

Printed in the United States of America

*COPYRIGHTS AND ACKNOWLEDGMENTS*

MORRIS ABRAM for "Violence and Power on Campus: A Debate" by Morris Abram, Seymour Lipset, Michael Rossman, and Michael Vozick.

ATHENEUM PUBLISHERS for quotation by Mark Rudd from *Up Against the Ivy Wall* by Jerry L. Avorn, Robert Friedman and Members of the Staff of the Columbia Daily Spectator. Copyright © 1968 by Members of the Board Associates. Reprinted by permission of Atheneum Publishers.

BEACON PRESS for "Stranger in the Village" from *Notes of a Native Son* by James Baldwin. Copyright © 1953, 1955 by James Baldwin. Reprinted by permission of Beacon Press.

ZUSANA BOROFF JUSTMAN for "Status-Seeking in Academe" by David Boroff.

CHANGE MAGAZINE for "Violence and Power on Campus: A Debate" by Morris Abram, Seymour Lipset, Michael Rossman, and Michael Vozick, *Change,* March–April 1969. For "Rochdale: The Ultimate Freedom" by Barrie Zwicker, *Change,* November–December 1969.

CITY LIGHTS BOOKS for lines from "Howl," Part I, from *Howl and Other Poems* by Allen Ginsberg. Copyright © 1956, 1959 by Allen Ginsberg. Reprinted by permission of City Lights Books.

BURTON R. CLARK for "The 'Cooling-Out' Function in Higher Education."

COLUMBIA UNIVERSITY PRESS for excerpt from page 87 of *The Reforming of General Education* by Daniel Bell, published by Columbia University Press, 1966.

COMMENTARY for excerpt from "Academic Industry" by Harold Taylor. Reprinted from *Commentary,* December 1964, by permission. Copyright © by the American Jewish Committee, 1964.

THE COURIER-JOURNAL, Louisville, Kentucky, for "Dr. Johns Wants Us to Do Our Own Thing" by Bill Peterson, *The Courier-Journal,* October 28, 1968.

J. M. DENT & SONS for excerpt from *Ghosts,* from *Ghosts, An Enemy of the People, The Warrior of Helgeland* by Henrik Ibsen. Trans. by R. Farquharson Sharp. Everyman's Library Edition.

(*Continued on Page 369*)

Bound by UNIVERSAL BOOKBINDERY., SAN ANTONIO, TEX. Date ................

*For*
*Allison Olivia,*
*Mary Kathleen,*
*and*
*Sherry Ann*

# Preface

The nature of the college has undergone intense examination during the past several years. There is disagreement as to whether this examination has led to beneficial change, or to any real change at all. But it is clear that much of the examination has sought to alter the old conception of the college as an ivory tower, removed from all but its own narrow and immediate concerns. Virtues and faults exist both within and outside the institution; it is the editors' conviction that one way to appreciate the former and correct the latter is to study their manifestations first at close hand, and then relate the familiar to more general and abstract issues.

The premise underlying this book is simple: that the college is a microcosm of the larger society, and that by examining a relatively small and familiar institution the reader may come to a better understanding of larger, more abstract ideas and issues. The editors have collected essays, stories, poems, and pictures which, when analyzed and compared, should help the reader make a connection between his immediate environment and matters which have always concerned thinking people. Each selection has been chosen on the basis of how well it fulfills two criteria: Is it lively and engaging in itself, and does it relate to issues beyond its immediate subject?

The book is in six sections. Each one but the last explores a separate aspect of the general theme. The Epilogue, "Dr. Johns Wants Us to Do Our Own Thing," defies classification.

*Ann Wilkinson Connor*
*Gerald Kohs*

# Contents

Preface     vii

## 1: PROLOGUE     3

Introduction     7
The Garden of Eden     9
The Garden of Love    *William Blake*     14
The Conversion of the Jews    *Philip Roth*     16
Cocksure Women and Hensure Men    *D. H. Lawrence*     33
Stranger in the Village    *James Baldwin*     40
There Are 00 Trees in Russia: The Function of Facts in
     Newsmagazines    *Otto Friedrich*     54
Report, Inference, and Judgment    *S. I. Hayakawa*     69
The Prince of Creation    *Susanne K. Langer*     70

## 2: PEOPLE     93

Introduction     97

A Dog in Brooklyn, A Girl in Detroit: Life Among the
     Humanities    *Herbert Gold*     98
The Talker    *Mona Van Duyn*     113
Theme for English B    *Langston Hughes*     115
Truth, Beauty and Sour Grapes, or: Is Gold Getting Rich
     Telling Us What Rotten Shape Society Is In?
     *Marion Dunham*     117
Of This Time, Of That Place    *Lionel Trilling*     122
Leslie Aumaire    *Harold Witt*     159
The Student As Nigger    *Jerry Farber*     163

There Is Nothing I Can't Use in My Teaching
  *Austin Warren*                                              174
Down & Back   *John Berryman*                                  176
Elegy for Jane   *Theodore Roethke*                            178


3: **INSTITUTIONS**                                            179

Introduction                                                   183
Carmen Ohio                                                    184
Status-Seeking in Academe   *David Boroff*                     185
Life in the Yellow Submarine: Buffalo's SUNY
  *Barbara Probst Solomon*                                     188
University Examinations in Egypt   *D. J. Enright*             198
The "Cooling-Out" Function in Higher Education
  *Burton R. Clark*                                            201
The Immigrant Experience   *Richard Olivas*                    213
Why We're Against the Biggees   *James S. Kunen*               217


4: **CHANGE**                                                  225

Introduction                                                   229
Top Scholars Urge Inquiry into Calcutta "Orgies"
  *The Times of India*                                         230
Port Huron Statement   *Students for a Democratic Society*     231
Violence and Power on Campus: A Debate   *Morris Abram,*
  *Seymour Lipset, Michael Rossman, and Michael Vozick*        246
Talking in Bed   *Philip Larkin*                               263
"Without Law, the University Is a Sitting Duck . . ."
  *Harris Wofford, Jr., and Theodore M. Hesburgh*              263
From Cornell: A Black Radical's Report on His Campus
  Struggles   *Michael Thelwell*                               271


5: **PROGRAMS AND PROPOSALS**                                  287

Introduction                                                   291
The Present Moment in Progressive Education
  *Paul Goodman*                                               293

An Interview with David Riesman  *Maria Wilhelm*  302

Toward an Ideal College  *Judson Jerome*  310

Nairobi College  *The Planning Committee of Nairobi College*  321

Space for Something Else: Bensalem  *Elizabeth Sewell*  327

Experiment at Berkeley  *Joseph Tussman*  334

Rochdale: The Ultimate Freedom  *Barrie Zwicker*  341


**6: EPILOGUE**  353

Dr. Johns Wants Us to Do Our Own Thing  *Bill Peterson*  358


**APPENDIX**  361

A Personal Bibliography on Higher Education  *Phillip Werdell*  363

# I

## PROLOGUE

A character in Henrik Ibsen's drama *Ghosts* remarks in Act II:

> It is not only what we have inherited from our fathers that exists again in us, but all sorts of old dead ideas and all kinds of old dead beliefs and things of that kind. They are not actually alive in us; but there they are dormant, all the same, and we can never be rid of them. Whenever I take up a newspaper and read it, I fancy I see ghosts creeping between the lines. There must be ghosts all over the world.

The reading selections in the Prologue are not "about" college; rather they attempt to grasp, if only momentarily, the "ghosts" Ibsen speaks of. The issues raised are those which, at some level (probably for many, a feeling level), concern the college student: his own individuality; his relation to society; the questions of his relationship to the authority figures—parents, teachers, bosses—in his life; his religious beliefs; his sexuality and his perceptions of sex roles; his ideas of superiority and inferiority, especially as they relate to prejudice, racial or otherwise; his certainty or uncertainty about the usefulness of knowledge. All of these issues will be dealt with directly in later chapters of the book. But the Prologue gives the student a chance to examine his feelings—to bring them to a level of consciousness where they *can* be examined—and to understand how his emotions relate to the processes of thinking and reasoning, how emotions can obstruct or distort thought. The student is not asked to give up immediately the old ideas and beliefs that have subjectively defined, shaped, and directed him; he is asked to make them available for objective, rational comparison with the same kinds of ideas, in different guises, that he will confront in this book, in his college, and in his world. (How, for example, can a student talk about revolution against the establishment unless he understands his own attitude toward authority and its basis?)

The first selection in the Prologue does, in a way, deal with education, but the Garden of Eden is not meant to represent an ideal campus; the story is included because it embodies cul-

7

tural beliefs of the Western world which are at least four thousand years old, ideas which may or may not be dead. William Blake's "The Garden of Love" was written during the Romantic period, when poets in England and revolutionaries in France and the American colonies were questioning what happens when beliefs are institutionalized and invested with power. A short story by Philip Roth and metaphorical, intensely personal essays by sex-advocate D. H. Lawrence and black-advocate James Baldwin deal with the dangers of being trapped by outdated ideas, beliefs, and roles. Otto Friedrich's essay examines the news media's role in the process of shaping beliefs. The chapter ends with a long essay by Susanne Langer, "The Prince of Creation," which suggests our inability to deal rationally with irrational events unless we learn to use language to examine and test against reality the myths we believe in.

# The Garden of Eden

*The story of Adam and Eve, the creation of man and the alienation of man from his god(s), has a counterpart in the literature of nearly all religions and cultures of the world. The narrative, found in Chapters Two and Three of Genesis, the first book of the Bible, may be four thousand years old or more. The story existed in the oral tradition of the Hebrews and was handed down by word of mouth for perhaps generations before being written down sometime after 1000 B.C. The text that follows is from the King James version of the Bible, first published in 1611. The translation was made from Hebrew, Aramaic, and Greek texts.*

And the Lord God formed man of the dust of the ground, and breathed into his nostrils the breath of life; and man became a living soul.

And the Lord God planted a garden eastward in Eden; and there he put the man whom he had formed.

And out of the ground made the Lord God to grow every tree that is pleasant to the sight, and good for food; the tree of life also in the midst of the garden, and the tree of knowledge of good and evil. . . .

And the Lord God took the man, and put him into the garden of Eden to dress it and to keep it.

And the Lord God commanded the man, saying, Of every tree of the garden thou mayest freely eat:

But of the tree of the knowledge of good and evil, thou shalt not eat of it: for in the day that thou eatest thereof thou shalt surely die.

And the Lord God said, It is not good that the man should be alone; I will make him an help meet for him.

And out of the ground the Lord God formed every beast of

the field, and every fowl of the air; and brought them unto Adam to see what he would call them: and whatsoever Adam called every living creature, that was the name thereof.

And Adam gave names to all cattle, and to the fowl of the air, and to every beast of the field; but for Adam there was not found an help meet for him.

And the Lord God caused a deep sleep to fall upon Adam, and he slept: and he took one of his ribs, and closed up the flesh instead thereof;

And the rib, which the Lord God had taken from man, made he a woman, and brought her unto the man.

And Adam said, This is now bone of my bones, and flesh of my flesh: she shall be called Woman, because she was taken out of Man.

Therefore shall a man leave his father and his mother, and shall cleave unto his wife: and they shall be one flesh.

And they were both naked, the man and his wife, and were not ashamed.

Now the serpent was more subtil than any beast of the field which the Lord God had made. And he said unto the woman, Yea, hath God said, Ye shall not eat of every tree of the garden?

And the woman said unto the serpent, We may eat of the fruit of the trees of the garden:

But of the fruit of the tree which is in the midst of the garden, God hath said, Ye shall not eat of it, neither shall ye touch it, lest ye die.

And the serpent said unto the woman, Ye shall not surely die:

For God doth know that in the day ye eat thereof, then your eyes shall be opened, and ye shall be as gods, knowing good and evil.

And when the woman saw that the tree was good for food, and that it was pleasant to the eyes, and a tree to be desired to make one wise, she took of the fruit thereof, and did eat, and gave also unto her husband with her; and he did eat.

And the eyes of them both were opened, and they knew that they were naked; and they sewed fig leaves together, and made themselves aprons.

And they heard the voice of the Lord God walking in the

garden in the cool of the day: and Adam and his wife hid themselves from the presence of the Lord God amongst the trees of the garden.

And the Lord God called unto Adam, and said unto him, Where art thou?

And he said, I heard thy voice in the garden, and I was afraid, because I was naked; and I hid myself.

And he said, Who told thee that thou wast naked? Hast thou eaten of the tree, whereof I commanded thee that thou shouldest not eat?

And the man said, The woman whom thou gavest to be with me, she gave me of the tree, and I did eat.

And the Lord God said unto the woman, What is this that thou hast done? And the woman said, The serpent beguiled me, and I did eat.

And the Lord God said unto the serpent, Because thou hast done this, thou art cursed above all cattle, and above every beast of the field; upon thy belly shalt thou go, and dust shalt thou eat all the days of thy life:

And I will put enmity between thee and the woman, and between thy seed and her seed; it shall bruise thy head, and thou shalt bruise his heel.

Unto the woman he said, I will greatly multiply thy sorrow and thy conception; in sorrow thou shalt bring forth children; and thy desire shall be to thy husband, and he shall rule over thee.

And unto Adam he said, Because thou hast hearkened unto the voice of thy wife, and hast eaten of the tree, of which I commanded thee, saying, Thou shalt not eat of it: cursed is the ground for thy sake; in sorrow shalt thou eat of it all the days of thy life;

Thorns also and thistles shall it bring forth to thee; and thou shalt eat the herb of the field;

In the sweat of thy face shalt thou eat bread, till thou return unto the ground; for out of it wast thou taken: for dust thou art, and unto dust shalt thou return.

And Adam called his wife's name Eve; because she was the mother of all living.

Unto Adam also and to his wife did the Lord God make coats of skins, and clothed them.

And the Lord God said, Behold, the man is become as one of us, to know good and evil: and now, lest he put forth his hand, and take also of the tree of life, and eat, and live for ever:

Therefore the Lord God sent him forth from the garden of Eden, to till the ground from whence he was taken.

So he drove out the man; and he placed at the east of the garden of Eden Cherubims, and a flaming sword which turned every way, to keep the way of the tree of life.

*SUGGESTIONS FOR DISCUSSION*

• "The Garden of Eden" might be described as an attempt by our early cultural ancestors to explain what life means. To an amazing extent, many of the assumptions of this narrative have never been seriously questioned, but have instead been accepted as prescriptions for social behavior. At least three basic questions related to your being in college are raised by the story:

> What is the nature of Man (male and female)?
> What is the nature of knowledge and education?
> What is the nature of language?

Are we still influenced by the thinking of our cultural ancestors with regard to the nature of Man and the differentiated roles of male and female? The nature of education? Of language?

All the readings in this book are in some way concerned with finding answers to these questions. They will provoke you to give a name to and justify what you believe, to examine your beliefs in the light of your college experience, and to question the value of those beliefs in today's world. Not all the questions raised in the Bible story have immediate or easy answers; in trying to make their experiences intelligible to themselves, our ancestors recognized their inability to find meaning in life without admitting to paradoxes.

• Keep the following questions in mind as you read through some of the text. (You probably will want to add questions of your own.) What is Man's basic nature? Is he born evil? (The term "Original Sin" was, in the Christian era, used in interpreting the "Garden of Eden" story, implying that Man *is* born evil.) If Man is not basically evil, is he basically good? Or is he born with a neutral nature, predisposed to neither good nor evil?

• If Man is not basically evil, where does the evil in the world come from? The Biblical story of Adam and Eve suggests that the serpent is the guide to, if not the source of, evil. If so, why was the serpent in Man's God-given utopia? (What is a utopia—a reality? A concept? A dream?) Would Man like to believe that he would not do evil on his own, but only if tempted? Why, in your opinion, was a serpent rather than another creature the tempter?

• Perhaps you do not believe in "evil." Can you define it? On what basis do you accept or reject the notion that evil exists today?

• How does Man develop a conscience that tells him certain things are right (good) and other things are wrong (evil)? What part do private religion, public morality, and law play in the development of the individual conscience? Has it been the role of authority figures (individuals or establishments) in our culture to establish "Thou shalt nots" and to see that they are enforced through punishment (jail, guilt, or both)?

• At what age do we expect a person to keep himself from doing evil because his conscience, or the threat of jail or guilt, dictates to him? Does guilt keep society's need for prisons at a minimum?

• Why are loss of innocence and gaining of knowledge seen as godly characteristics?

• The Bible story presents Man's "toil" and the pain of childbearing as punishments for his disobedience. Do we believe that work, productivity, and suffering have redeeming or therapeutic qualities? Do most people have a tendency to expect adults to work at "meaningful" rather than "joyful" jobs? (How, for example, do we regard the independent spirit who is happy making candles?)

• What implications for education do the various concepts of Man's basic nature hold? For instance, if Man is seen as basically evil, would our schools not be dedicated to restricting his activities and to rehabilitating him?

# The Garden of Love

*William Blake*

*William Blake—poet, mystic, humanitarian—was born in London in
1757 and lived most of his 80 years there, laboring as an engraver,
isolated from the culture of his times by poverty and paranoia (he was
reputedly mad). He classified many of his poems as* Songs of Innocence
*or* Songs of Experience.

I went to the Garden of Love,
And saw what I never had seen:
A Chapel was built in the midst,
Where I used to play on the green.

And the gates of this Chapel were shut,
And "Thou shalt not" writ over the door;
So I turn'd to the Garden of Love
That so many sweet flowers bore;

And I saw it was filled with graves,
And tomb-stones where flowers should be;
And Priests in black gowns were walking their rounds,
And binding with briars my joys & desires.

*SUGGESTIONS FOR DISCUSSION*

• How do you account for the shift of landscape in "The Garden of
Love"? What has taken place since the "I" (the persona, or voice of
the poem) last visited the garden? Do you take the chapel, gates, door,

flowers, graves, priests, and briars to be literal? If they are symbolic, rather than literal, what do they stand for?

• Why are "briars" used to bind the persona's "desires"? What joys and desires is he referring to? Why are the priests doing the "binding"?

• At what time in the persona's life do you think this poem was written? If you think of the "I" as an adult returning to the scene of his childhood, must you then interpret the poem as merely a wish for the uncomplex, irresponsible, innocent state of mind that childhood represents to an adult? Do you remember the first incident in your childhood that spoiled your picture of the world as ideally joyful?

• What relationships do you see between "The Garden of Eden" and "The Garden of Love"?

# The Conversion of the Jews

*Philip Roth*

*Philip Roth, born in 1933, is among the American writers of Jewish
background who have created fictional heroes struggling with their
historical, religious, and cultural pasts. Among Roth's best-known books
are* Goodbye, Columbus (*his first novel*) *and* Portnoy's Complaint.

"You're a real one for opening your mouth in the first place,"
Itzie said. "What do you open your mouth all the time for?"

"I didn't bring it up, Itz, I didn't," Ozzie said.

"What do you care about Jesus Christ for anyway?"

"I didn't bring up Jesus Christ. He did. I didn't even know
what he was talking about. Jesus is historical, he kept saying.
Jesus is historical." Ozzie mimicked the monumental voice of
Rabbi Binder.

"Jesus was a person that lived like you and me," Ozzie continued. "That's what Binder said—"

"Yeah? . . . So what! What do I give two cents whether he
lived or not. And what do you gotta open your mouth!" Itzie
Lieberman favored closed-mouthedness, especially when it came
to Ozzie Freedman's questions. Mrs. Freedman had to see Rabbi
Binder twice before about Ozzie's questions and this Wednesday
at four-thirty would be the third time. Itzie preferred to keep
*his* mother in the kitchen; he settled for behind-the-back sub-
tleties such as gestures, faces, snarls and other less delicate barn-
yard noises.

"He was a real person, Jesus, but he wasn't like God, and we
don't believe he is God." Slowly, Ozzie was explaining Rabbi

Binder's position to Itzie, who had been absent from Hebrew School the previous afternoon.

"The Catholics," Itzie said helpfully, "they believe in Jesus Christ, that he's God." Itzie Lieberman used "the Catholics" in its broadest sense—to include the Protestants.

Ozzie received Itzie's remark with a tiny head bob, as though it were a footnote, and went on. "His mother was Mary, and his father probably was Joseph," Ozzie said. "But the New Testament says his real father was God."

"His *real* father?"

"Yeah," Ozzie said, "that's the big thing, his father's supposed to be God."

"Bull."

"That's what Rabbi Binder says, that it's impossible—"

"Sure it's impossible. That stuff's all bull. To have a baby you gotta get laid," Itzie theologized. "Mary hadda get laid."

"That's what Binder says: 'The only way a woman can have a baby is to have intercourse with a man.' "

"He said *that,* Ozz?" For a moment it appeared that Itzie had put the theological question aside. "He said that, intercourse?" A little curled smile shaped itself in the lower half of Itzie's face like a pink mustache. "What you guys do, Ozz, you laugh or something?"

"I raised my hand."

"Yeah? Whatja say?"

"That's when I asked the question."

Itzie's face lit up. "Whatja ask about—intercourse?"

"No, I asked the question about God, how if He could create the heaven and earth in six days, and make all the animals and the fish and the light in six days—the light especially, that's what always gets me, that He could make the light. Making fish and animals, that's pretty good—"

"That's damn good." Itzie's appreciation was honest but unimaginative: it was as though God had just pitched a one-hitter.

"But making light . . . I mean when you think about it, it's really something," Ozzie said. "Anyway, I asked Binder if He could make all that in six days, and He could *pick* the six days He wanted right out of nowhere, why couldn't He let a woman have a baby without having intercourse."

"You said intercourse, Ozz, to Binder?"

"Yeah."

"Right in class?"

"Yeah."

Itzie smacked the side of his head.

"I mean, no kidding around," Ozzie said, "that'd really be nothing. After all that other stuff, that'd practically be nothing."

Itzie considered a moment. "What'd Binder say?"

"He started all over again explaining how Jesus was historical and how he lived like you and me but he wasn't God. So I said I under*stood* that. What I wanted to know was different."

What Ozzie wanted to know was always different. The first time he had wanted to know how Rabbi Binder could call the Jews "The Chosen People" if the Declaration of Independence claimed all men to be created equal. Rabbi Binder tried to distinguish for him between political equality and spiritual legitimacy, but what Ozzie wanted to know, he insisted vehemently, was different. That was the first time his mother had to come.

Then there was the plane crash. Fifty-eight people had been killed in a plane crash at La Guardia. In studying a casualty list in the newspaper his mother had discovered among the list of those dead eight Jewish names (his grandmother had nine but she counted Miller as a Jewish name); because of the eight she said the plane crash was "a tragedy." During free-discussion time on Wednesday Ozzie had brought to Rabbi Binder's attention this matter of "some of his relations" always picking out the Jewish names. Rabbi Binder had begun to explain cultural unity and some other things when Ozzie stood up at his seat and said that what he wanted to know was different. Rabbi Binder insisted that he sit down and it was then that Ozzie shouted that he wished all fifty-eight were Jews. That was the second time his mother came.

"And he kept explaining about Jesus being historical, and so I kept asking him. No kidding, Itz, he was trying to make me look stupid."

"So what he finally do?"

"Finally he starts screaming that I was deliberately simple-minded and a wise guy, and that my mother had to come, and this was the last time. And that I'd never get bar-mitzvahed if he could help it. Then, Itz, then he starts talking in that voice like a statue, real slow and deep, and he says that I better think over what I said about the Lord. He told me to go to his office and think it over." Ozzie leaned his body towards Itzie. "Itz, I thought it over for a solid hour, and now I'm convinced God could do it."

Ozzie had planned to confess his latest transgression to his mother as soon as she came home from work. But it was a Friday night in November and already dark, and when Mrs. Freedman came through the door she tossed off her coat, kissed Ozzie quickly on the face, and went to the kitchen table to light the three yellow candles, two for the Sabbath and one for Ozzie's father.

When his mother lit the candles she would move her two arms slowly towards her, dragging them through the air, as though persuading people whose minds were half made up. And her eyes would get glassy with tears. Even when his father was alive Ozzie remembered that her eyes had gotten glassy, so it didn't have anything to do with his dying. It had something to do with lighting the candles.

As she touched the flaming match to the unlit wick of a Sabbath candle, the phone rang, and Ozzie, standing only a foot from it, plucked it off the receiver and held it muffled to his chest. When his mother lit candles Ozzie felt there should be no noise; even breathing, if you could manage it, should be softened. Ozzie pressed the phone to his breast and watched his mother dragging whatever she was dragging, and he felt his own eyes get glassy. His mother was a round, tired, gray-haired penguin of a woman whose gray skin had begun to feel the tug of gravity and the weight of her own history. Even when she was dressed up she didn't look like a chosen person. But when she lit candles she looked like something better; like a woman who knew momentarily that God could do anything.

After a few mysterious minutes she was finished. Ozzie hung up the phone and walked to the kitchen table where she was beginning to lay the two places for the four-course Sabbath meal. He told her that she would have to see Rabbi Binder next Wednesday at four-thirty, and then he told her why. For the first time in their life together she hit Ozzie across the face with her hand.

All through the chopped liver and chicken soup part of the dinner Ozzie cried; he didn't have any appetite for the rest.

On Wednesday, in the largest of the three basement class-rooms of the synagogue, Rabbi Marvin Binder, a tall, handsome, broad-shouldered man of thirty with thick strong-fibered black hair, removed his watch from his pocket and saw that it was four o'clock. At the rear of the room Yakov Blotnik, the seventy-one-year-old custodian, slowly polished the large window, mumbling to himself unaware that it was four o'clock or six o'clock, Monday or Wednesday. To most of the students Yakov Blotnik's mumbling, along with his brown curly beard, scythe nose, and two heel-trailing black cats, made of him an object of wonder, a foreigner, a relic, towards whom they were alternately fearful and disrespectful. To Ozzie the mumbling had always seemed a monotonous, curious prayer; what made it curious was that old Blotnik had been mumbling so steadily for so many years, Ozzie suspected he had memorized the prayers and forgotten all about God.

"It is now free-discussion time," Rabbi Binder said. "Feel free to talk about any Jewish matter at all—religion, family, politics, sports—"

There was silence. It was a gusty, clouded November afternoon and it did not seem as though there ever was or could be a thing called baseball. So nobody this week said a word about that hero from the past, Hank Greenberg—which limited free discussion considerably.

And the soul-battering Ozzie Freedman had just received from Rabbi Binder had imposed its limitation. When it was Ozzie's turn to read aloud from the Hebrew book the rabbi had asked him petulantly why he didn't read more rapidly. He was showing no progress. Ozzie said he could read faster but that if he did he was sure not to understand what he was reading. Nevertheless, at the rabbi's repeated suggestion Ozzie tried, and showed a great talent, but in the midst of a long passage he stopped short and said he didn't understand a word he was reading, and started in again at a drag-footed pace. Then came the soul-battering.

Consequently when free-discussion time rolled around none

of the students felt too free. The rabbi's invitation was answered only by the mumbling of feeble old Blotnik.

"Isn't there anything at all you would like to discuss?" Rabbi Binder asked again, looking at his watch. "No questions or comments?"

There was a small grumble from the third row. The rabbi requested that Ozzie rise and give the rest of the class the advantage of his thought.

Ozzie rose. "I forget it now," he said, and sat down in his place. Rabbi Binder advanced a seat towards Ozzie and poised himself on the edge of the desk. It was Itzie's desk and the rabbi's frame only a dagger's-length away from his face snapped him to sitting attention.

"Stand up again, Oscar," Rabbi Binder said calmly, "and try to assemble your thoughts."

Ozzie stood up. All his classmates turned in their seats and watched as he gave an unconvincing scratch to his forehead.

"I can't assemble any," he announced, and plunked himself down.

"Stand up!" Rabbi Binder advanced from Itzie's desk to the one directly in front of Ozzie; when the rabbinical back was turned Itzie gave it five-fingers off the tip of his nose, causing a small titter in the room. Rabbi Binder was too absorbed in squelching Ozzie's nonsense once and for all to bother with titters. "Stand up, Oscar. What's your question about?"

Ozzie pulled a word out of the air. It was the handiest word. "Religion."

"Oh, now you remember?"

"Yes."

"What is it?"

Trapped, Ozzie blurted the first thing that came to him. "Why can't He make anything He wants to make!"

As Rabbi Binder prepared an answer, a final answer, Itzie, ten feet behind him, raised one finger on his left hand, gestured it meaningfully towards the rabbi's back, and brought the house down.

Binder twisted quickly to see what had happened and in the midst of the commotion Ozzie shouted into the rabbi's back what he couldn't have shouted to his face. It was a loud, toneless sound that had the timbre of something stored inside for about six days.

"You don't know! You don't know anything about God!"

The rabbi spun back towards Ozzie. "What?"

"You don't know—you don't—"

"Apologize, Oscar, apologize!" It was a threat.

"You don't—"

Rabbi Binder's hand flicked out at Ozzie's cheek. Perhaps it had only been meant to clamp the boy's mouth shut, but Ozzie ducked and the palm caught him squarely on the nose.

The blood came in a short, red spurt on to Ozzie's shirt front.

The next moment was all confusion. Ozzie screamed, "You bastard, you bastard!" and broke for the classroom door. Rabbi Binder lurched a step backwards, as though his own blood had started flowing violently in the opposite direction, then gave a clumsy lurch forward and bolted out the door after Ozzie. The class followed after the rabbi's huge blue-suited back, and before old Blotnik could turn from his window, the room was empty and everyone was headed full speed up the three flights leading to the roof.

If one should compare the light of day to the life of man: sunrise to birth; sunset—the dropping down over the edge—to death; then as Ozzie Freedman wiggled through the trapdoor of the synagogue roof, his feet kicking backwards bronco-style at Rabbi Binder's outstretched arms—at that moment the day was fifty years old. As a rule, fifty or fifty-five, reflects accurately the age of late afternoons in November, for it is in that month, during those hours, that one's awareness of light seems no longer a matter of seeing, but of hearing: light begins clicking away. In fact, as Ozzie locked shut the trapdoor in the rabbi's face, the sharp click of the bolt into the lock might momentarily have been mistaken for the sound of the heavier gray that had just throbbed through the sky.

With all his weight Ozzie kneeled on the locked door; any instant he was certain that Rabbi Binder's shoulder would fling it open, splintering the wood into shrapnel and catapulting his body into the sky. But the door did not move and below him he heard only the rumble of feet, first loud then dim, like thunder rolling away.

A question shot through his brain. "Can this be *me?*" For a thirteen-year-old who had just labeled his religious leader a bastard, twice, it was not an improper question. Louder and louder the question came to him—"Is it me? Is it me?"—until he discovered himself no longer kneeling, but racing crazily towards the edge of the roof, his eyes crying, his throat screaming, and his arms flying everywhichway as though not his own.

"Is it me? Is it me ME ME ME ME! It has to be me—but is it!"

It is the question a thief must ask himself the night he jimmies open his first window, and it is said to be the question with which bridegrooms quiz themselves before the altar.

In the few wild seconds it took Ozzie's body to propel him to the edge of the roof, his self-examination began to grow fuzzy. Gazing down at the street, he became confused as to the problem beneath the question: was it, is-it-me-who-called-Binder a bastard? or, is-it-me-prancing-around-on-the-roof? However, the scene below settled all, for there is an instant in any action when whether it is you or somebody else is academic. The thief crams the money in his pockets and scoots out the window. The bridegroom signs the hotel register for two. And the boy on the roof finds a streetful of people gaping at him, necks stretched backwards, faces up, as though he were the ceiling of the Hayden Planetarium. Suddenly you know it's you.

"Oscar! Oscar Freedman!" A voice rose from the center of the crowd, a voice that, could it have been seen, would have looked like the writing on scroll. "Oscar Freedman, get down from there. Immediately!" Rabbi Binder was pointing one arm stiffly up at him; and at the end of that arm, one finger aimed menacingly. It was the attitude of a dictator, but one—the eyes confessed all—whose personal valet had spit neatly in his face.

Ozzie didn't answer. Only for a blink's length did he look towards Rabbi Binder. Instead his eyes began to fit together the world beneath him, to sort out people from places, friends from enemies, participants from spectators. In little jagged starlike clusters his friends stood around Rabbi Binder, who was still pointing. The topmost point on a star compounded not of angels but of five adolescent boys was Itzie. What a world it was, with those stars below, Rabbi Binder below . . . Ozzie, who a moment earlier hadn't been able to control his own body, started to feel the meaning of the word control: he felt Peace and he felt Power.

"Oscar Freedman, I'll give you three to come down."

Few dictators give their subjects three to do anything; but, as always, Rabbi Binder only looked dictatorial.

"Are you ready, Oscar?"

Ozzie nodded his head yes, although he had no intention in the world—the lower one or the celestial one he'd just entered —of coming down even if Rabbi Binder should give him a million.

"All right then," said Rabbi Binder. He ran a hand through his black Samson hair as though it were the gesture prescribed for uttering the first digit. Then, with his other hand cutting a circle out of the small piece of sky around him, he spoke. "One!"

There was no thunder. On the contrary, at that moment, as though "one" was the cue for which he had been waiting, the world's least thunderous person appeared on the synagogue steps. He did not so much come out the synagogue door as lean out, onto the darkening air. He clutched at the doorknob with one hand and looked up at the roof.

"Oy!"

Yakov Blotnik's old mind hobbled slowly, as if on crutches, and though he couldn't decide precisely what the boy was doing on the roof, he knew it wasn't good—that is, it wasn't-good-for-the-Jews. For Yakov Blotnik life had fractionated itself simply: things were either good-for-the-Jews or no-good-for-the-Jews.

He smacked his free hand to his in-sucked cheek, gently. "Oy, Gut!" And then quickly as he was able, he jacked down his head and surveyed the street. There was Rabbi Binder (like a man at an auction with only three dollars in his pocket, he had just delivered a shaky "Two!"); there were the students, and that was all. So far it-wasn't-so-bad-for-the-Jews. But the boy had to come down immediately, before anybody saw. The problem: how to get the boy off the roof?

Anybody who has ever had a cat on the roof knows how to get him down. You call the fire department. Or first you call the operator and you ask her for the fire department. And the next thing there is great jamming of brakes and clanging of bells and shouting of instructions. And then the cat is off the roof. You do the same thing to get a boy off the roof.

That is, you do the same thing if you are Yakov Blotnik and you once had a cat on the roof.

When the engines, all four of them, arrived, Rabbi Binder had four times given Ozzie the count of three. The big hook-and-ladder swung around the corner and one of the firemen leaped from it, plunging headlong towards the yellow fire hydrant in front of the synagogue. With a huge wrench he began to unscrew the top nozzle. Rabbi Binder raced over to him and pulled at his shoulder.

"There's no fire . . ."

The fireman mumbled back over his shoulder and, heatedly, continued working at the nozzle.

"But there's no fire, there's no fire . . ." Binder shouted. When the fireman mumbled again, the rabbi grasped his face with both his hands and pointed it up at the roof.

To Ozzie it looked as though Rabbi Binder was trying to tug the fireman's head out of his body, like a cork from a bottle. He had to giggle at the picture they made: it was a family portrait —rabbi in black skullcap, fireman in red fire hat, and the little yellow hydrant squatting beside like a kid brother, bareheaded. From the edge of the roof Ozzie waved at the portrait, a one-handed, flapping, mocking wave; in doing it his right foot slipped from under him. Rabbi Binder covered his eyes with his hands.

Firemen work fast. Before Ozzie had even regained his balance, a big, round, yellowed net was being held on the synagogue lawn. The firemen who held it looked up at Ozzie with stern, feelingless faces.

One of the firemen turned his head towards Rabbi Binder. "What, is the kid nuts or something?"

Rabbi Binder unpeeled his hands from his eyes, slowly, painfully, as if they were tape. Then he checked: nothing on the sidewalk, no dents in the net.

"Is he gonna jump, or what?" the fireman shouted.

In a voice not at all like a statue, Rabbi Binder finally answered, "Yes, yes, I think so . . . He's been threatening to . . ."

Threatening to? Why, the reason he was on the roof, Ozzie remembered, was to get away; he hadn't even thought about jumping. He had just run to get away, and the truth was that he hadn't really headed for the roof as much as he'd been chased there.

"What's his name, the kid?"

"Freedman," Rabbi Binder answered. "Oscar Freedman."

The fireman looked up at Ozzie. "What is it with you, Oscar? You gonna jump, or what?"

Ozzie did not answer. Frankly, the question had just arisen.

"Look, Oscar, if you're gonna jump, jump—and if you're not gonna jump, don't jump. But don't waste our time, willya?"

Ozzie looked at the fireman and then at Rabbi Binder. He wanted to see Rabbi Binder cover his eyes one more time.

"I'm going to jump."

And then he scampered around the edge of the roof to the corner, where there was no net below, and he flapped his arms at his sides, swishing the air and smacking his palms to his trousers on the downbeat. He began screaming like some kind of engine. "Wheeeee . . . wheeeeee," and leaning way out over the edge with the upper half of his body. The firemen whipped around to cover the ground with the net. Rabbi Binder mumbled a few words to Somebody and covered his eyes. Everything happened quickly, jerkily, as in a silent movie. The crowd, which had arrived with the fire engines, gave out a long, Fourth-of-July fireworks oooh-aahhh. In the excitement no one had paid the crowd much heed, except, of course, Yakov Blotnik, who swung from the doorknob counting heads. "Fier und tsvansik . . . finf und tsvantsik . . . Oy, Gut!" It wasn't like this with the cat.

Rabbi Binder peeked through his fingers, checked the sidewalk and net. Empty. But there was Ozzie racing to the other corner. The firemen raced with him but were unable to keep up. Whenever Ozzie wanted to he might jump and splatter himself upon the sidewalk, and by the time the firemen scooted to the spot all they could do with their net would be to cover the mess.

"Wheeeee . . . wheeeee . . ."

"Hey, Oscar," the winded fireman yelled, "What the hell is this, a game or something?"

"Wheeeee . . . wheeeee . . ."

"Hey, Oscar—"

But he was off now to the other corner, flapping his wings fiercely. Rabbi Binder couldn't take it any longer—the fire engines from nowhere, the screaming suicidal boy, the net. He fell to his knees, exhausted, and with his hands curled together in front of his chest like a little dome, he pleaded, "Oscar, stop it, Oscar. Don't jump, Oscar. Please come down . . . Please don't jump."

And further back in the crowd a single voice, a single young voice, shouted a lone word to the boy on the roof.

"Jump!"

It was Itzie. Ozzie momentarily stopped flapping.

"Go ahead, Ozz—jump!" Itzie broke off his point of the star and courageously, with the inspiration not of a wise-guy but of a disciple, stood alone. "Jump, Ozz, jump!"

Still on his knees, his hands still curled, Rabbi Binder twisted his body back. He looked at Itzie, then, agonizingly, back to Ozzie.

"Oscar, Don't jump! Please, Don't jump . . . please please . . ."

"Jump!" This time it wasn't Itzie but another point of the star. By the time Mrs. Freedman arrived to keep her four-thirty appointment with Rabbi Binder, the whole little upside down heaven was shouting and pleading for Ozzie to jump, and Rabbi Binder no longer was pleading with him not to jump, but was crying into the dome of his hands.

Understandably Mrs. Freedman couldn't figure out what her son was doing on the roof. So she asked.

"Ozzie, my Ozzie, what are you doing? My Ozzie, what is it?"

Ozzie stopped wheeeeeing and slowed his arms down to a cruising flap, the kind birds use in soft winds, but he did not answer. He stood against the low, clouded, darkening sky—light clicked down swiftly now, as on a small gear—flapping softly and gazing down at the small bundle of a woman who was his mother.

"What are you doing, Ozzie?" She turned towards the kneeling Rabbi Binder and rushed so close that only a paper-thickness of dusk lay between her stomach and his shoulders.

"What is my baby doing?"

Rabbi Binder gaped up at her but he too was mute. All that moved was the dome of his hands; it shook back and forth like a weak pulse.

"Rabbi, get him down! He'll kill himself. Get him down, my only baby . . ."

"I can't," Rabbi Binder said, "I can't . . ." and he turned his handsome head towards the crowd of boys behind him. "It's them. Listen to them."

And for the first time Mrs. Freedman saw the crowd of boys, and she heard what they were yelling.

"He's doing it for them. He won't listen to me. It's them." Rabbi Binder spoke like one in a trance.

"For them?"

"Yes."

"Why for them?"

"They want him to . . ."

Mrs. Freedman raised her two arms upward as though she were conducting the sky. "For them he's doing it!" And then in a gesture older than pyramids, older than prophets and floods, her arms came slapping down to her sides. "A martyr I have. Look!" She tilted her head to the roof. Ozzie was still flapping softly. "My martyr."

"Oscar, come down, *please*," Rabbi Binder groaned.

In a startlingly even voice Mrs. Freedman called to the boy on the roof. "Ozzie, come down, Ozzie. Don't be a martyr, my baby."

As though it were a litany, Rabbi Binder repeated her words. "Don't be a martyr, my baby. Don't be a martyr."

"Gawhead, Ozz—*be* a Martin!" It was Itzie. "Be a Martin, be a Martin," and all the voices joined in singing for a Martindom, whatever *it* was. "Be a Martin, be a Martin . . ."

Somehow when you're on a roof the darker it gets the less you can hear. All Ozzie knew was that two groups wanted two new things: his friends were spirited and musical about what they wanted; his mother and the rabbi were even-toned, chanting, about what they didn't want. The rabbi's voice was without tears now and so was his mother's.

The big net stared up at Ozzie like a sightless eye. The big, clouded sky pushed down. From beneath it looked like a gray corrugated board. Suddenly, looking up into that unsympathetic sky, Ozzie realized all the strangeness of what these people, his friends, were asking: they wanted him to jump, to kill himself;

they were singing about it now—it made them that happy. And there was an even greater strangeness: Rabbi Binder was on his knees, trembling. If there was a question to be asked now it was not "Is it me?" but rather "Is it us? . . . Is it us?"

Being on the roof, it turned out, was a serious thing. If he jumped would the singing become dancing? Would it? What would jumping stop? Yearningly, Ozzie wished he could rip open the sky, plunge his hands through, and pull out the sun; and on the sun, like a coin, would be stamped JUMP or DON'T JUMP.

Ozzie's knees rocked and sagged a little under him as though they were setting him for a dive. His arms tightened, stiffened, froze, from shoulders to fingernails. He felt as if each part of his body were going to vote as to whether he should kill himself or not—and each part as though it were independent of *him*.

The light took an unexpected click down and the new darkness, like a gag, hushed the friends singing for this and the mother and rabbi chanting for that.

Ozzie stopped counting votes, and in a curiously high voice, like one who wasn't prepared for speech, he spoke.

"Mamma?"

"Yes, Oscar."

"Mamma, get down on your knees, like Rabbi Binder."

"Oscar—"

"Get down on your knees," he said, "or I'll jump."

Ozzie heard a whimper, then a quick rustling, and when he looked down where his mother had stood he saw the top of a head and beneath that a circle of dress. She was kneeling beside Rabbi Binder.

He spoke again. "Everybody kneel." There was the sound of everybody kneeling.

Ozzie looked around. With one hand he pointed towards the synagogue entrance. "Make *him* kneel."

There was a noise, not of kneeling, but of body-and-cloth stretching. Ozzie could hear Rabbi Binder saying in a gruff whisper, ". . . or he'll *kill* himself," and when next he looked there was Yakov Blotnik off the doorknob and for the first time in his life upon his knees in the Gentile posture of prayer.

As for the firemen—it is not as difficult as one might imagine to hold a net taut while you are kneeling.

Ozzie looked around again; and then he called to Rabbi Binder.

"Rabbi?"

"Yes, Oscar."

"Rabbi Binder, do you believe in God?"

"Yes."

"Do you believe God can do Anything?" Ozzie leaned his head out into the darkness. "Anything?"

"Oscar, I think—"

"Tell me you believe God can do Anything."

There was a second's hesitation. Then: "God can do Anything."

"Tell me you believe God can make a child without intercourse."

"He can."

"Tell me!"

"God," Rabbi Binder admitted, "can make a child without intercourse."

"Mamma, you tell me."

"God can make a child without intercourse," his mother said.

"Make *him* tell me." There was no doubt who *him* was.

In a few moments Ozzie heard an old comical voice say something to the increasing darkness about God.

Next, Ozzie made everybody say it. And then he made them all say they believed in Jesus Christ—first one at a time, then all together.

When the catechizing was through it was the beginning of evening. From the street it sounded as if the boy on the roof might have sighed.

"Ozzie?" A woman's voice dared to speak. "You'll come down now?"

There was no answer, but the woman waited, and when a voice finally did speak it was thin and crying, and exhausted as that of an old man who has just finished pulling the bells.

"Mamma, don't you see—you shouldn't hit me. He shouldn't hit me. You shouldn't hit me about God, Mamma. You should never hit anybody about God—"

"Ozzie, please come down now."

"Promise me, promise me you'll never hit anybody about God."

He had asked only his mother, but for some reason every one kneeling in the street promised he would never hit anybody about God.

Once again there was silence.

"I can come down now, Mamma," the boy on the roof finally said. He turned his head both ways as though checking the traffic lights. "Now I can come down . . ."

And he did, right into the center of the yellow net that glowed in the evening's edge like an overgrown halo.

## SUGGESTIONS FOR DISCUSSION

• How much of Ozzie's rooftop escape do you consider to be rebellion specifically against the rigidity of the rabbi's teaching, and how much of it as rebellion (perhaps not fully understood by Ozzie) against his environment in general? What are the main elements of that environment (Ozzie's "establishment")? Who are the authority figures? With what rules and regulations is Ozzie expected to comply? What freedoms does he have? What beliefs or traditions are expected to be upheld? Who are Ozzie's allies or friends? Do they hold the same beliefs?

• Is Ozzie's approach to the truth or fact as presented in the Bible more rational than Rabbi Binder's? Can you explain why the rabbi (the word in Hebrew means "teacher") could not, or would not, talk directly to Ozzie's point? Do you think a teacher should discuss something he does not believe in?

• Both Rabbi Binder and Ozzie resort to unusual behavior (for them as characters, and for them as representatives of teacher and pupil) when the question between them cannot be settled by intellectual dialogue. Ozzie's behavior is both more dramatic and more effective than the rabbi's: it wins converts. Why was the communication at the verbal level ineffective, and why was the nonverbal communication (Ozzie's rooftop behavior) effective? How many Jews did Ozzie really convert? Can you account for Ozzie's sense of Peace and Power on the rooftop? For his clear grasp of his own identity ("ME ME ME ME!")? Have you ever had a similar experience, on or off a rooftop, inside or outside a school?

• In many ways, Roth is concerned with the quality of mind of his characters. What lines in the story best describe the way the rabbi "thinks"? The mother? Yakov?

• In his essay "Stranger in the Village," the contemporary black writer James Baldwin states: "People are trapped in history and history is trapped in them." How does this relate to the major characters in Roth's story: to Ozzie, to the rabbi, to Ozzie's mother, to Yakov, to Ozzie's friend Itzie? If they are all in some way "trapped" and "trapping," is it the same way for each?

• To what degree does Ozzie represent the typical kid-hero of American fiction, movies, and TV who sets out to bug his elders and winds up revealing truth ("and a little child shall lead them")? Huck Finn, is, of course, the classic example. Can you name others and compare them with Ozzie?

• Although Ozzie may be "typical," is he a stereotype? Are other characters in the story stereotypes?

# Cocksure Women
# and Hensure Men

## D. H. Lawrence

*D. H. (David Herbert) Lawrence, an Englishman, wrote many novels, including* Sons and Lovers, Women in Love, *and* Lady Chatterley's Lover, *dealing with the complexity of male-female relations in a society with institutionalized sex roles. He also wrote poems, plays, scathing letters, and highly personal essays like the one included here, first published in 1928. He lived a restless life, traveling a great deal, living for a while in the United States. He died in France, in 1930, at the age of 44.*

It seems to me there are two aspects to women. There is the demure and the dauntless. Men have loved to dwell, in fiction at least, on the demure maiden whose inevitable reply is: Oh, yes, if you please, kind sir! The demure maiden, the demure spouse, the demure mother—this is still the ideal. A few maidens, mistresses and mothers *are* demure. A few pretend to be. But the vast majority are not. And they don't pretend to be. We don't expect a girl skilfully driving her car to be demure, we expect her to be dauntless. What good would demure and maidenly Members of Parliament be, inevitably responding: Oh, yes, if you please, kind sir!—Though of course there are masculine members of that kidney.—And a demure telephone girl? Or even a demure stenographer? Demureness, to be sure, is outwardly becoming, it is an outward mark of femininity, like bobbed hair. But it goes with inward dauntlessness. The girl who has got to make her way in life has got to be dauntless, and if she has a pretty, demure manner with it, then lucky girl. She kills two birds with two stones.

With the two kinds of femininity go two kinds of confidence: there are the women who are cocksure, and the women who are hensure. A really up-to-date woman is a cocksure woman. She doesn't have a doubt nor a qualm. She is the modern type. Whereas the old-fashioned demure woman was sure as a hen is sure, that is, without knowing anything about it. She went quietly and busily clucking around, laying the eggs and mothering the chickens in a kind of anxious dream that still was full of sureness. But not mental sureness. Her sureness was a physical condition, very soothing, but a condition out of which she could easily be startled or frightened.

It is quite amusing to see the two kinds of sureness in chickens. The cockerel is, naturally, cocksure. He crows because he is *certain* it is day. Then the hen peeps out from under her wing. He marches to the door of the hen-house and pokes out his head assertively: *Ah ha! daylight, of course, just as I said!*—and he majestically steps down the chicken ladder towards *terra firma,* knowing that the hens will step cautiously after him, drawn by his confidence. So after him, cautiously, step the hens. He crows again: *Ha-ha! here we are!*—It is indisputable, and the hens accept it entirely. He marches towards the house. From the house a person ought to appear, scattering corn. Why does the person not appear? The cock will see to it. He is cocksure. He gives a loud crow in the doorway, and the person appears. The hens are suitably impressed, but immediately devote all their henny consciousness to the scattered corn, pecking absorbedly, while the cock runs and fusses, cocksure that he is responsible for it all.

So the day goes on. The cock finds a tit-bit, and loudly calls the hens. They scuffle up in henny surety, and gobble the tit-bit. But when they find a juicy morsel for themselves, they devour it in silence, hensure. Unless, of course, there are little chicks, when they most anxiously call the brood. But in her own dim surety, the hen is really much surer than the cock, in a different way. She marches off to lay her egg, she secures obstinately the nest she wants, she lays her egg at last, then steps forth again with prancing confidence, and gives that most assured of all sounds, the hensure cackle of a bird who has laid her egg. The cock, who is never so sure about anything as the hen is about the egg she has laid, immediately starts to cackle like the female of his species. He is pining to be hensure, for hensure is so much surer than cocksure.

Nevertheless, cocksure is boss. When the chicken-hawk appears in the sky, loud are the cockerel's calls of alarm. Then the hens scuffle under the verandah, the cock ruffles his feathers on guard. The hens are numb with fear, they say: Alas, there is no health in us! How wonderful to be a cock so bold!—And they huddle, numbed. But their very numbness is hensurety.

Just as the cock can cackle, however, as if he had laid the egg, so can the hen bird crow. She can more or less assume his cocksureness. And yet she is never so easy, cocksure, as she used to be when she was hensure. Cocksure, she is cocksure, but uneasy. Hensure, she trembles, but is easy.

It seems to me just the same in the vast human farmyard. Only nowadays all the cocks are cackling and pretending to lay eggs, and all the hens are crowing and pretending to call the sun out of bed. If women to-day are cocksure, men are hensure. Men are timid, tremulous, rather soft and submissive, easy in their very henlike tremulousness. They only want to be spoken to gently. So the women step forth with a good loud *cock-a-doodle-do!*

The tragedy about cocksure women is that they are more cocky, in their assurance, than the cock himself. They never realise that when the cock gives his loud crow in the morning, he listens acutely afterwards, to hear if some other wretch of a cock dare crow defiance, challenge. To the cock, there is always defiance, challenge, danger and death on the clear air; or the possibility thereof.

But alas, when the hen crows, she listens for no defiance or challenge. When she says *cock-a-doodle-do!* then it is unanswerable. The cock listens for an answer, alert. But the hen knows she is unanswerable. *Cock-a-doodle-do!* and there it is, take it or leave it!

And it is this that makes the cocksureness of women so dangerous, so devastating. It is really out of scheme, it is not in relation to the rest of things. So we have the tragedy of cocksure women. They find, so often, that instead of having laid an egg, they have laid a vote, or an empty ink-bottle, or some other absolutely unhatchable object, which means nothing to them.

It is the tragedy of the modern woman. She becomes cocksure, she puts all her passion and energy and years of her life into some effort or assertion, without ever listening for the denial which she ought to take into count. She is cocksure, but she is a hen all the time. Frightened of her own henny self, she rushes to mad lengths about votes, or welfare, or sports, or business: she is marvellous, out-manning the man. But alas, it is all fundamentally disconnected. It is all an attitude, and one day the attitude will become a weird cramp, a pain, and then it will collapse. And when it has collapsed, and she looks at the eggs she has laid, votes, or miles of typewriting, years of business efficiency—suddenly, because she is a hen and not a cock, all she has done will turn into pure nothingness to her. Suddenly it all falls out of relation to her basic henny self, and she realises she has lost her life. The lovely henny surety, the hensureness which is the real bliss of every female, has been denied her: she had never had it. Having lived her life with such utmost strenuousness and cocksureness, she has missed her life altogether. Nothingness!

## SUGGESTIONS FOR DISCUSSION

• Describe in your own words the types of women labeled by Lawrence as "hensure" and "cocksure," and the types of men to whom he applies the same terms. Do you think his classifications are adequate, or are his established types too limited?

• Do you believe that women are destined solely to bear and rear children? Is there anything about women, other than their ability to breast-feed, that makes them better suited than men for the role of nurturing children? Is it a "tragedy," as Lawrence contends, if women do not fulfill egg-laying/chick-hatching roles? Or would you agree with Betty Rollin, a *Look* magazine senior editor, who has said, "Motherhood is in trouble, and ought to be. A rude question is long overdue: who needs it?" In an article debunking "The Motherhood Myth," she quotes Dr. Robkin, a New York psychiatrist, who observes: "Women don't need to be mothers any more than they need spaghetti. But if you're in a world where everyone is eating spaghetti, thinking they need it and want it, you will think so too."

• Why is housework considered "henny" or "unmanly"? Why is it "unmanly" for a man to take over in the family kitchen, and enjoy it, but acceptable for him to cook if he is camping or employed as a chef in a restaurant? Are there other household chores that are considered exclusively "woman's work"? Or "the man's job"?

• How many professional women, besides teachers, do you know well? Would you want your surgeon to be a woman? Your airline pilot? Would you vote for a woman for President?

• How much do you know about the development of children in societies where the natural mother does not have the primary responsibility for child-rearing, or in societies where children are turned over to professional *amahs,* or where children are reared by the tribal family or in nurseries supported by the entire society?

• Kate Millett, in her book *Sexual Politics,* describes the American system of sexual relationships as one based on dominance and subordination:

> What goes largely unexamined, often even unacknowledged (yet it is institutionalized nonetheless) in our social order is the birthright priority whereby males rule females . . . this is so because our society . . . is a patriarchy. The fact is evident at once if one recalls that the military, industry, technology, universities, science, political office, and finance —in short, every avenue to power within the society, including the coercive force of the police, is entirely in male hands. As the essence of politics is power, such realization cannot fail to carry impact. What lingers of supernatural authority, the Deity, "His" ministry, together with the ethics and values, the philosophy and art of our culture— its very civilization—as T. S. Eliot once observed, is of male manufacture.

(Kate Millett, incidentally, spends 56 pages of her book reviewing the novels of D. H. Lawrence and faulting his cultural contribution to the case of the subordinate female.)

• Do you agree or disagree that it is the male's "birthright" to rule the female? Can you argue with Miss Millett's contention that the "birthright" of male supremacy has become institutionalized in our society? Think back on the Garden of Eden story: Why was Eve created? What justified her God-ordered subservient role after both she and Adam had sinned?

• Kate Millett is considered by some to be a Women's Liberation stereotype. Lawrence would undoubtedly call her "cocksure" and "unfulfilled." Do you think of any one type of woman in connection with the Women's Liberation Movement? What type?

• Consider this description of Women's Liberation by Marlene Dixon, a professor of sociology at McGill University:

The three major groups which make up the new women's movement—working women, middle class married women and students—bring very different kinds of interests and objectives to women's liberation. Working women are most concerned with the economic issues of guaranteed employment, fair wages, job discrimination and child care. Their most immediate oppression is rooted in industrial capitalism and felt directly through the vicissitudes of an exploitative labor market.

Middle class women, oppressed by the psychological mutilation and injustice of institutionalized segregation, discrimination and imposed inferiority, are most sensitive to the dehumanizing consequences of severely limited lives. Usually well educated and capable, these women are rebelling against being forced to trivialize their lives, to live vicariously through husbands and children.

Students, as unmarried middle class girls, have been most sensitized to the sexual exploitation of women. They have experienced the frustration of one-way relationships in which the girl is forced into a "wife" and companion role with none of the supposed benefits of marriage. Young women have increasingly rebelled not only against passivity and dependency in their relationships but also against the notion that they must function as sexual objects, being defined in purely sexual rather than human terms, and being forced to package and sell themselves as commodities on the sex market.

Do Professor Dixon's views refute the Women's Liberation stereotype?

• Professor Dixon also comments on male chauvinism as a form of racism:

Indeed, the phenomenon of male chauvinism can only be understood when it is perceived as a form of racism, based on stereotypes drawn from a deep belief in the biological inferiority of women. The so-called "black analogy" is no analogy at all; it is the same social process that is at work, a process which both justifies and helps perpetuate the exploitation of one group of human beings by another.

The very stereotypes that express the society's belief in the biological inferiority of women recall the images used to justify the oppression of blacks. The nature of women, like that of slaves, is depicted as dependent, incapable of reasoned thought, childlike in its simplicity and warmth, martyred in the role of mother, and mystical in the role of sexual partner. In its benevolent form, the inferior position of women results in paternalism; in its malevolent form, a domestic tyranny which can be unbelievably brutal.

Keep in mind Professor Dixon's remarks about paternalism in its "benevolent" and "malevolent" forms when you read the essay by Baldwin.

# Stranger in the Village

*James Baldwin*

*James Baldwin, born in 1924, grew up in the Harlem ghetto which is the setting for many of his essays and novels. This autobiographical piece, however, is set in Switzerland; Baldwin draws parallels between his alienation in a foreign village and the black man's alienation in America. His long essay "The Fire Next Time," published in 1963, greatly disturbed many thinking whites, but not sufficiently for Baldwin. He now is living in Paris, in self-imposed exile from his native land. "Stranger in the Village" was written in 1955.*

From all available evidence no black man had ever set foot in this tiny Swiss village before I came. I was told before arriving that I would probably be a "sight" for the village; I took this to mean that people of my complexion were rarely seen in Switzerland, and also that city people are always something of a "sight" outside of the city. It did not occur to me—possibly because I am an American—that there could be people anywhere who had never seen a Negro.

It is a fact that cannot be explained on the basis of the inaccessibility of the village. The village is very high, but it is only four hours from Milan and three hours from Lausanne. It is true that it is virtually unknown. Few people making plans for a holiday would elect to come here. On the other hand, the villagers are able, presumably, to come and go as they please—which they do: to another town at the foot of the mountain, with a population of approximately five thousand, the nearest place to see a movie or go to the bank. In the village there is no movie house, no bank, no library, no theater; very few radios, one jeep, one station wagon; and, at the moment, one typewriter, mine, an invention which the woman next door to me here had never seen. There are about six hundred people living here, all Catholic—I conclude this from the fact that the Catholic church is open all year round, whereas the Protestant chapel, set off on a hill a little removed from the village, is open only in the summertime when the tourists arrive. There are four or five hotels, all closed now, and four or five *bistros,* of which, however, only two do any business during the winter. These two do not do a great deal, for life in the village seems to end around nine or ten o'clock. There are a few stores, butcher, baker, *épicerie,* a hardware store, and a money-changer—who cannot change travelers' checks, but must send them down to the bank, an operation which takes two or three days. There is something called the *Ballet Haus,* closed in the winter and used for God knows what, certainly not ballet, during the summer. There seems to be only one schoolhouse in the village, and this for the quite young children; I suppose this to mean that their older brothers and sisters at some point descend from these mountains in order to complete their education—possibly, again, to the town just below. The landscape is absolutely forbidding, mountains towering on all four sides, ice and snow as far as the eye can reach. In this white wilderness, men and women and children move all day, carrying washing, wood, buckets of milk or water, sometimes skiing on Sunday afternoons. All week long boys and young men are to be seen shoveling snow off the rooftops, or dragging wood down from the forest in sleds.

The village's only real attraction, which explains the tourist season, is the hot spring water. A disquietingly high proportion of these tourists are cripples, or semicripples, who come year after year—from other parts of Switzerland, usually—to take the waters. This lends the village, at the height of the season, a rather terrifying air of sanctity, as though it were a lesser Lourdes. There is often something beautiful, there is always something awful, in the spectacle of a person who has lost one of his faculties, a faculty he never questioned until it was gone, and who struggles to recover it. Yet people remain people, on crutches or indeed on deathbeds; and wherever I passed, the first summer I was here, among the native villagers or among the lame, a wind passed with me—of astonishment, curiosity, amusement, and outrage. That first summer I stayed two weeks and never intended to return. But I did return in the winter, to work; the village offers, obviously, no distractions whatever and has the further advantage of being extremely cheap. Now it is winter again, a year later, and I am here again. Everyone in the village knows my name, though they scarcely ever use it, knows that I come from America—though, this, apparently, they will never really believe: black men come from Africa—and everyone knows that I am the friend of the son of a woman who was born here, and that I am staying in their chalet. But I remain as much a stranger today as I was the first day I arrived, and the children shout *Neger! Neger!* as I walk along the streets.

It must be admitted that in the beginning I was far too shocked to have any real reaction. In so far as I reacted at all, I reacted by trying to be pleasant—it being a great part of the American Negro's education (long before he goes to school) that he must make people "like" him. This smile-and-the-world-smiles-with-you routine worked about as well in this situation as it had in the situation for which it was designed, which is to say that it did not work at all. No one, after all, can be liked whose human weight and complexity cannot be, or has not been, admitted. My smile was simply another unheard-of phenomenon which allowed them to see my teeth—they did not, really, see my smile and I began to think that, should I take to snarling, no one would notice any difference. All of the physical characteristics of the Negro which had caused me, in America, a very different and almost forgotten pain were nothing less than miraculous —or infernal—in the eyes of the village people. Some thought my hair was the color of tar, that it had the texture of wire, or the texture of cotton. It was jocularly suggested that I might let it all grow long and make myself a winter coat. If I sat in the sun for more than five minutes some daring creature was certain to come along and gingerly put his fingers on my hair, as though he were afraid of an electric shock, or put his hand on my hand, astonished that the color did not rub off. In all of this, in which it must be conceded there was the charm of genuine wonder and in which there was certainly no element of intentional unkindness, there was yet no suggestion that I was human: I was simply a living wonder.

I knew that they did not mean to be unkind, and I know

it now; it is necessary, nevertheless, for me to repeat this to myself each time that I walk out of the chalet. The children who
shout *Neger!* have no way of knowing the echoes this sound
raises in me. They are brimming with good humor and the more
daring swell with pride when I stop to speak with them. Just the
same, there are days when I cannot pause and smile, when I
have no heart to play with them; when, indeed, I mutter sourly
to myself, exactly as I muttered on the streets of a city these
children have never seen, when I was no bigger than these children are now: *Your* mother *was a nigger.* Joyce is right about
history being a nightmare—but it may be the nightmare from
which no one *can* awaken. People are trapped in history and
history is trapped in them.

There is a custom in the village—I am told it is repeated
in many villages—of "buying" African natives for the purpose of
converting them to Christianity. There stands in the church all
year round a small box with a slot for money, decorated with a
black figurine, and into this box the villagers drop their francs.
During the *carnaval* which precedes Lent, two village children
have their faces blackened—out of which bloodless darkness their
blue eyes shine like ice—and fantastic horsehair wigs are placed
on their blond heads; thus disguised, they solicit among the
villagers for money for the missionaries in Africa. Between the
box in the church and the blackened children, the village
"bought" last year six or eight African natives. This was reported to me with pride by the wife of one of the *bistro* owners
and I was careful to express astonishment and pleasure at the
solicitude shown by the village for the souls of black folk. The
*bistro* owner's wife beamed with a pleasure far more genuine
than my own and seemed to feel that I might now breathe more
easily concerning the souls of at least six of my kinsmen.

I tried not to think of these so lately baptized kinsmen, of
the price paid for them, or the peculiar price they themselves
would pay, and said nothing about my father, who having taken
his own conversion too literally never, at bottom, forgave the
white world (which he described as heathen) for having saddled
him with a Christ in whom, to judge at least from their treatment of him, they themselves no longer believed. I thought of
white men arriving for the first time in an African village,
strangers there, as I am a stranger here, and tried to imagine the

astounded populace touching their hair and marveling at the color of their skin. But there is a great difference between being the first white man to be seen by Africans and being the first black man to be seen by whites. The white man takes the astonishment as tribute, for he arrives to conquer and to convert the natives, whose inferiority in relation to himself is not even to be questioned; whereas I, without a thought of conquest, find myself among a people whose culture controls me, has even, in a sense, created me, people who have cost me more in anguish and rage than they will ever know, who yet do not even know of my existence. The astonishment with which I might have greeted them, should they have stumbled into my African village a few hundred years ago, might have rejoiced their hearts. But the astonishment with which they greet me today can only poison mine.

And this is so despite everything I may do to feel differently, despite my friendly conversations with the *bistro* owner's wife, despite their three-year-old son who has at last become my friend, despite the *saluts* and *bonsoirs* which I exchange with people as I walk, despite the fact that I know that no individual can be taken to task for what history is doing, or has done. I say that the culture of these people controls me—but they can scarcely be held responsible for European culture. America comes out of Europe, but these people have never seen America, nor have most of them seen more of Europe than the hamlet at the foot of their mountain. Yet they move with an authority which I shall never have; and they regard me, quite rightly, not only as a stranger in their village but as a suspect latecomer, bearing no credentials, to everything they have—however unconsciously—inherited.

For this village, even were it incomparably more remote and incredibly more primitive, is the West, the West onto which I have been so strangely grafted. These people cannot be, from the point of view of power, strangers anywhere in the world; they have made the modern world, in effect, even if they do not know it. The most illiterate among them is related, in a way that I am not, to Dante, Shakespeare, Michelangelo, Aeschylus, Da Vinci, Rembrandt, and Racine; the cathedral at Chartres says something to them which it cannot say to me, as indeed would New York's Empire State Building, should anyone here ever see it. Out of their hymns and dances come Beethoven and Bach. Go back a few centuries and they are in their full glory—but I am in Africa, watching the conquerors arrive.

The rage of the disesteemed is personally fruitless, but it is also absolutely inevitable; this rage, so generally discounted, so little understood even among the people whose daily bread it it, is one of the things that makes history. Rage can only with difficulty, and never entirely, be brought under the domination of the intelligence and is therefore not susceptible to any arguments whatever. This is a fact which ordinary representatives of the *Herrenvolk,* having never felt this rage and being unable to imagine it, quite fail to understand. Also, rage cannot be hidden, it can only be dissembled. This dissembling deludes the thoughtless, and strengthens rage and adds, to rage, contempt. There are, no doubt, as many ways of coping with the resulting complex of tensions as there are black men in the world, but no black man can hope ever to be entirely liberated from this internal warfare—rage, dissembling, and contempt having inevitably accompanied his first realization of the power of white men. What is crucial here is that, since white men represent in the black man's world so heavy a weight, white men have for black men a reality which is far from being reciprocal; and hence all black men have toward all white men an attitude which is designed, really, either to rob the white man of the jewel of his naïveté, or else to make it cost him dear.

The black man insists, by whatever means he finds at his disposal, that the white man cease to regard him as an exotic rarity and recognize him as a human being. This is a very charged and difficult moment, for there is a great deal of will power involved in the white man's naïveté. Most people are not naturally reflective any more than they are naturally malicious, and the white man prefers to keep the black man at a certain human remove because it is easier for him thus to preserve his simplicity and avoid being called to account for crimes committed by his forefathers, or his neighbors. He is inescapably aware, nevertheless, that he is in a better position in the world than black men are, nor can he quite put to death the suspicion that he is hated by black men therefore. He does not wish to be hated, neither does he wish to change places, and at this point in his uneasiness he can scarcely avoid having recourse to those legends which white men have created about black men, the most usual effect of which is that the white man finds himself enmeshed, so to speak, in his own language which describes hell, as well as the attributes which lead one to hell, as being as black as night.

Every legend, moreover, contains its residuum of truth, and the root function of language is to control the universe by describing it. It is of quite considerable significance that black men remain, in the imagination, and in overwhelming numbers in fact, beyond the disciplines of salvation; and this despite the fact that the West has been "buying" African natives for centuries. There is, I should hazard, an instantaneous necessity to be divorced from this so visibly unsaved stranger, in whose heart, moreover, one cannot guess what dreams of vengeance are being nourished; and, at the same time, there are few things on earth more attractive than the idea of the unspeakable liberty which is allowed the unredeemed. When, beneath the black mask, a human being begins to make himself felt one cannot escape a certain awful wonder as to what kind of human being it is. What one's imagination makes of other people is dictated, of course, by the laws of one's own personality and it is one of the ironies of black-white relations that, by means of what the white man imagines the black man to be, the black man is enabled to know who the white man is.

I have said, for example, that I am as much a stranger in this village today as I was the first summer I arrived, but this is not quite true. The villagers wonder less about the texture of my hair than they did then, and wonder rather more about me. And the fact that their wonder now exists on another level is reflected in their attitudes and in their eyes. There are the children who make those delightful, hilarious, sometimes astonishingly grave overtures of friendship in the unpredictable fashion of children; other children, having been taught that the devil is a black man, scream in genuine anguish as I approach. Some of the older women never pass without a friendly greeting, never pass, indeed, if it seems that they will be able to engage me in conversation; other women look down or look away or rather contemptuously smirk. Some of the men drink with me and suggest that I learn how to ski—partly, I gather, because they cannot imagine what I would look like on skis—and want to know if I am married, and ask questions about my *métier*. But some of the men have accused *le sale nègre*—behind my back—of stealing wood and there is already in the eyes of some of them that peculiar, intent, paranoiac malevolence which one sometimes surprises in the eyes of American white men when, out walking their Sunday girl, they see a Negro male approach.

There is a dreadful abyss between the streets of this village and the streets of the city in which I was born, between the children who shout *Neger!* today and those who shouted *Nigger!* yesterday—the abyss is experience, the American experience. The syllable hurled behind me today expresses, above all, wonder: I am a stranger here. But I am not a stranger in America and the same syllable riding on the American air expresses the war my presence has occasioned in the American soul.

For this village brings home to me this fact: that there was a day, and not really a very distant day, when Americans were scarcely Americans at all but discontented Europeans, facing a great unconquered continent and strolling, say, into a market-place and seeing black men for the first time. The shock this spectacle afforded is suggested, surely, by the promptness with which they decided that these black men were not really men but cattle. It is true that the necessity on the part of the settlers of the New World of reconciling their moral assumptions with the fact—and the necessity—of slavery enhanced immensely the charm of this idea, and it is also true that this idea expresses, with a truly American bluntness, the attitude which to varying extents all masters have had toward all slaves.

But between all former slaves and slave-owners and the drama which begins for Americans over three hundred years ago at Jamestown, there are at least two differences to be observed. The American Negro Slave could not suppose, for one thing, as slaves in past epochs had supposed and often done, that he would ever be able to wrest the power from his master's hands. This was a supposition which the modern ear, which was to bring about such vast changes in the aims and dimensions of power, put to death; it only begins, in unprecedented fashion, and with dreadful implications, to be resurrected today. But even had this supposition persisted with undiminished force, the American Negro slave could not have used it to lend his condition dignity, for the reason that this supposition rests on another: that the slave in exile yet remains related to his past, has some means—if only in memory—of revering and sustaining the forms of his former life, is able, in short, to maintain his identity.

This was not the case with the American Negro slave. He is unique among the black men of the world in that his past was taken from him, almost literally, at one blow. One wonders what on earth the first slave found to say to the first dark child he bore. I am told that there are Haitians able to trace their ancestry back to African kings, but any American Negro wishing to go back so far will find his journey through time abruptly arrested by the signature on the bill of sale which served as the entrance paper for his ancestor. At the time—to say nothing of the circumstances—of the enslavement of the captive black man who was to become the American Negro, there was not the remotest possibility that he would ever take power from his master's hands. There was no reason to suppose that his situation would ever change, nor was there, shortly, anything to indicate that his situation had ever been different. It was his necessity, in the words of E. Franklin Frazier, to find a "motive for living under American culture or die." The identity of the American Negro comes out of this extreme situation, and the evolution of this identity was a source of the most intolerable anxiety in the minds and the lives of his masters.

For the history of the American Negro is unique also in this: that the question of his humanity, and of his rights therefore as a human being, became a burning one for several generations of Americans, so burning a question that it ultimately became one of those used to divide the nation. It is out of this argument that the venom of the epithet *Nigger!* is derived. It is an argument which Europe has never had, and hence Europe quite sincerely fails to understand how or why the argument arose in the first place, why its effects are so frequently disastrous and always so unpredictable, why it refuses until today to be entirely settled. Europe's black possessions remained—and do remain—in Europe's colonies, at which remove they represented no threat whatever to European identity. If they posed any problem at all for the European conscience, it was a problem which remained comfortingly abstract: in effect, the black man, *as a man,* did not exist for Europe. But in America, even as a slave, he was an inescapable part of the general social fabric and no American could escape having an attitude toward him. Americans attempt until today to make an abstraction of the Negro, but the very nature of these abstractions reveals the tremendous effects the presence of the Negro has had on the American character.

When one considers the history of the Negro in America it is of the greatest importance to recognize that the moral beliefs of a person, or a people, are never really as tenuous as life—which is not moral—very often causes them to appear; these create for them a frame of reference and a necessary hope, the hope being that when life has done its worst they will be enabled to rise above themselves and to triumph over life. Life would scarcely be bearable if this hope did not exist. Again, even when the worst has been said, to betray a belief is not by any means to have put oneself beyond its power; the betrayal of a belief is not the same thing as ceasing to believe. If this were not so there would be no moral standards in the world at all. Yet one must also recognize that morality is based on ideas and that all ideas are dangerous—dangerous because ideas can only lead to action and where the action leads no man can say. And dangerous in this respect: that confronted with the impossibility of remaining faithful to one's beliefs, and the equal impossibility of becoming free of them, one can be driven to the most inhuman excesses. The ideas on which American beliefs are based are not, though Americans often seem to think so, ideas which originated in America. They came out of Europe. And the establishment of democracy on the American continent was scarcely as radical a break with the past as was the necessity, which Americans faced, of broadening this concept to include black men.

This was, literally, a hard necessity. It was impossible, for one thing, for Americans to abandon their beliefs, not only because these beliefs alone seemed able to justify the sacrifices they had endured and the blood that they had spilled, but also because these beliefs afforded them their only bulwark against a moral chaos as absolute as the physical chaos of the continent it was their destiny to conquer. But in the situation in which Americans found themselves, these beliefs threatened an idea which, whether or not one likes to think so, is the very warp and woof of the heritage of the West, the idea of white supremacy.

Americans have made themselves notorious by the shrillness and the brutality with which they have insisted on this idea, but they did not invent it; and it has escaped the world's notice that those very excesses of which Americans have been guilty imply a certain, unprecedented uneasiness over the idea's life and power, if not, indeed, the idea's validity. The idea of white supremacy rests simply on the fact that white men are the creators of civilization (the present civilization, which is the only one that matters; all previous civilizations are simply "contributions" to our own) and are therefore civilization's guardians and defenders. Thus it was impossible for Americans to accept the black man as one of themselves, for to do so was to jeopardize their status as white men. But not so to accept him was to deny his human reality, his human weight and complexity, and the strain of denying the overwhelmingly undeniable forced Americans into rationalizations so fantastic that they approached the pathological.

At the root of the American Negro problem is the necessity of the American white man to find a way of living with the Negro in order to be able to live with himself. And the history of this problem can be reduced to the means used by Americans—lynch law and law, segregation and legal acceptance, terrorization and concession—either to come to terms with this necessity, or to find a way around it, or (most usually) to find a way of doing both these things at once. The resulting spectacle, at once foolish and dreadful, led someone to make the quite accurate observation that "the Negro-in-America is a form of insanity which overtakes white men."

In this long battle, a battle by no means finished, the unforeseeable effects of which will be felt by many future generations, the white man's motive was the protection of his identity; the black man was motivated by the need to establish an identity. And despite the terrorization which the Negro in America endured and endures sporadically until today, despite the cruel and totally inescapable ambivalence of his status in his country, the battle for his identity has long ago been won. He is not a visitor to the West, but a citizen there, an American; as American as the Americans who despise him, the Americans who fear him, the Americans who love him—the Americans who became less than themselves, or rose to be greater than themselves by virtue of the fact that the challenge he represented was inescapable. He is perhaps the only black man in the world whose relationship to white men is more terrible, more subtle, and more meaningful than the relationship of bitter possessed to uncertain possessor. His survival depended, and his development depends, on his ability to turn his peculiar status in the Western world to his own advantage and, it may be, to the very great advantage of that world. It remains for him to fashion out of his experience that which will give him sustenance, and a voice.

The cathedral at Chartres, I have said, says something to the people of this village which it cannot say to me; but it is important to understand that this cathedral says something to me which it cannot say to them. Perhaps they are struck by the power of the spires, the glory of the windows; but they have known God, after all, longer than I have known him, and in a different way, and I am terrified by the slippery bottomless well to be found in the crypt, down which heretics were hurled to death, and by the obscene, inescapable gargoyles jutting out of the stone and seeming to say that God and the devil can never be divorced. I doubt that the villagers think of the devil when they face a cathedral because they have never been identified with the devil. But I must accept the status which myth, if nothing else, gives me in the West before I can hope to change the myth.

Yet, if the American Negro has arrived at his identity by virtue of the absoluteness of his estrangement from his past, American white men still nourish the illusion that there is some means of recovering the European innocence, of returning to a state in which black men do not exist. This is one of the greatest errors Americans can make. The identity they fought so hard to protect has, by virtue of that battle, undergone a change: Americans are as unlike any other white people in the world as it is possible to be. I do not think, for example, that it is too much to suggest that the American vision of the world—which allows so little reality, generally speaking, for any of the darker forces in human life, which tends until today to paint moral issues in glaring black and white—owes a great deal to the battle waged by Americans to maintain between themselves and black men a human separation which could not be bridged. It is only now beginning to be borne in on us—very faintly, it must be admitted, very slowly, and very much against our will—that this vision of the world is dangerously inaccurate, and perfectly useless. For it protects our moral high-mindedness at the terrible expense of weakening our grasp of reality. People who shut their eyes to reality simply invite their own destruction, and anyone who insists on remaining in a state of innocence long after that innocence is dead turns himself into a monster.

The time has come to realize that the interracial drama acted out on the American continent has not only created a new black man, it has created a new white man, too. No road whatever will lead Americans back to the simplicity of this European village where white men still have the luxury of looking on me as a stranger. I am not, really, a stranger any longer for any American alive. One of the things that distinguishes Americans from other people is that no other people has ever been so deeply involved in the lives of black men, and vice versa. This fact faced, with all its implications, it can be seen that the history of the American Negro problem is not merely shameful, it is also something of an achievement. For even when the worst has been said, it must also be added that the perpetual challenge posed by this problem was always, somehow, perpetually met. It is precisely this black-white experience which may prove of indispensable value to us in the world we face today. This world is white no longer, and it will never be white again.

## SUGGESTIONS FOR DISCUSSION

• Can you identify Baldwin's intended audience?

• What makes Baldwin a "stranger" in the Swiss village he visits, beyond the explanation, in the first paragraph, that no black man had ever set foot there before? What makes him a religious and cultural "stranger"?

• How does he use his "tourist" experience to introduce the subject of the black man being a "stranger" in America—of which he is a native son?

• Baldwin, in the tenth paragraph, seems to shift suddenly from the subtopic of White Culture to that of Black Rage. But the two subtopics are not really unrelated. How does Baldwin relate them? Do you think his explanation of Black Rage as "absolutely inevitable" is justified in his essay? From your own experience, do you feel that Black Rage is justified?

• What happens if you are black and live in a culture where God is repeatedly depicted, through centuries of treasured art, as white? What would happen if you were white and lived in a culture where

God was depicted as black? Or red? Would you accept the model and feel inferior? Would you try and become, through your behavior and attitudes, the "color" of the god? Or would you reject the model and the moral values it represents? What if you are female and God is male?

• What does Baldwin mean when he says "There are few things on earth more attractive than the idea of the unspeakable liberty which is allowed the unredeemed"? How does envy relate to prejudice? Baldwin touches on the myth of the sexual prowess of the black male. Do his remarks suggest that a latent and perhaps unrecognized paranoia is involved in much racial prejudice? If men did not regard their wives as property that might be taken away, would they be as fearful of competition? Does the same fear of loss of property motivate them to distrust well-educated blacks in a "white" business? Do most white men regard being passed over for a promotion more ego-shattering if the superior job is given to a black or to a Mexican-American rather than to another white? On the other hand, do most white Americans admire the culture heroes who have connived or fought their way to the top? Do movies and TV shows tend to promote this admiration?

• Baldwin says that "The idea of white supremacy" is "the very warp and woof of the heritage of the West." Discuss this idea in relation to what you know about the historical treatment of the American Indian, the Mexican-American, the Oriental American, and the Puerto Rican American.

• "Thus it was impossible for Americans to accept the black man as one of themselves, for to do so was to jeopardize their status as white men. But not so to accept him was to deny his human reality, his human weight and complexity, and the strain of denying the overwhelmingly undeniable forced Americans into rationalizations so fantastic that they approached the pathological." Is there anything in the essay that suggests that the effects of prejudice have left Baldwin "pathological," perhaps even paranoid?

• Is there a hopeful note to Baldwin's essay? Can you think of concrete ways in which his abstract solutions can be effective?

# There Are 00 Trees in Russia:
# The Function of Facts in Newsmagazines

*Otto Friedrich*

*Otto Friedrich here examines another area of how we know what we know, since much of what we say we believe is based on what the news media tell us. Friedrich has been a journalist for twenty years; he has worked with the United Press, the* New York Daily News, *and* Newsweek, *among others. This article was first published in* Harper's *magazine.*

"Of course I'm sure—I read it in *Newsweek*." For several years, this slogan appeared in large advertisements all over the country. The advertisements usually showed no people, simply some scene of affluence and presumed influence, a board room or a golf club. From some unseen figure of authority came a huge white cartoon-style balloon filled with the crushing rejoinder, "Of course I'm sure—I read it in *Newsweek*."

The theory behind the advertisements was probably sound. Since *Newsweek* has fewer reporters, writers, and editors than its omniscient rival, *Time,* since it has a smaller circulation and less influence than *Time,* its chief claim to attention is that it makes a reasonable effort at fairness in summarizing the week's events. By boasting of its congeries of columnists, *Newsweek* manages to imply that everything else it publishes is the simple factual truth. Its recent ads promise a magazine "where you can always distinguish fact from opinion." One of them, portraying Walter Lippmann next to Washington bureau chief Benjamin Bradlee, emphasizes the special qualities of the latter: "The facts he gets are often 'firsts'—are always *facts.*"

*Time,* of course, has never admitted the validity of these accusing insinuations from its smaller *Doppelgänger. Time* has always opposed the idea of mere objectivity, and it acknowledges a certain bias in favor of democracy, free enterprise, and the enlightened human spirit. But it insists that its experienced staff simply distills the facts of the news into the truth. Earlier this year, one weekly Publisher's "Letter," which normally serves as a medium of self-congratulation, sadly criticized the Soviet Union for expelling *Time's* Moscow correspondent: "Soviet officials have never been able to understand or accept or even get accustomed to our kind of reporting." What the Soviets couldn't understand, *Time* went on, was that "our stories on the Soviet Union come from a wide array of sources available to our writers and editors in New York and to our correspondents elsewhere around the world." Thus *Time's* kind of reporting doesn't depend primarily on having a reporter at the scene of the event. "From these many sources . . ." *Time* concluded, "we will continue to report frankly and deeply on the Soviets despite last week's reading-out of our correspondent." (There is still one other smaller and less interesting newsmagazine, but *Time* and *Newsweek* understandably ignore the Brobdingnagian claims of the *U.S. News & World Report,* which purports to be "America's Class newsmagazine.")

Despite the competing claims of *Time* and *Newsweek,* they have a certain identity of both purpose and technique. Not only is the basic function of the two magazines almost the same, but the editor, national editor, and foreign editor of *Newsweek* are all alumni of *Time,* and there is a kind of all-purpose newsweekly office jargon that involves phrases like "the cosmic stuff" and "give it some global scope."

To anyone who has ever tried to work with these concepts and techniques, the newsmagazines' easy equation of facts, news, and truth can be rather disturbing. A reporter doesn't have to be a philosopher to know that "the facts" do not necessarily represent the truth, and that neither one of them necessarily represents the news. That men should live at peace with one another might be described as truth, but it is not a fact, nor is it news. That a certain number of children were born yesterday in Chicago is a fact, and the truth, but not news. Journalism involves an effort to discover, select, and assemble certain facts in a way that will be not only reasonably true but reasonably interesting—and therefore reasonably salable. Because of the eagerness with which an anxious and uninformed public buys anything which promises "the real story," it is easy for editors to forget these distinctions and boast about producing the facts and the truth in the name of freedom of the press and "an informed electorate."

## THE FETISH OF THE FACTS

Behind this forgetfulness lies an enduring and endearing myth of American journalism, the myth of the police reporter and the city editor. Like all myths, it once had a certain reality. When I first went to work on the Des Moines *Register,* I was the police reporter, and I turned in my copy to a dour assistant city editor who spoke with a cutting Missouri accent and didn't believe in anything. No three-paragraph story about a minor burglary was immune to his questions about the number of floors in the burgled house, the denomination of the stolen bills, or the location of the shards of glass from the broken window. Of all possible answers, the least acceptable was "I guess so." "Let's not guess, let's know," he would retort. Sometimes I had to telephone him a half-dozen times from my bare, yellow-walled cubicle in the police station to verify trivial details in trivial stories. The copy that he finally sent to the composing room was, as nearly as possible, the facts.

Quite a few years have passed since then, and I no longer expect reporters to know the answers to questions about their stories. I have grown accustomed to their complaints that the facts in question can't be discovered, and to their further complaints about being questioned at all. They have some justification, for what happens in the U.S. Senate or the French cabinet simply can't be covered like a mugging on Sixth Street in Des Moines. The facts are more elusive, and, in a way, less important, for the physical details of who spoke to whom are relatively meaningless until they are put into perspective by an act of judgment and a point of view. In other words, the legendary police reporter and the legendary city editor no longer exist as criteria; their talents and techniques are irrelevant to most of the major news stories.

The newspapers and news agencies acknowledge this. Later

editions of newspapers correct the factual mistakes and the misjudgments caused by the need for speed in getting out the first edition; a wire service revises a story with the euphemistic confession of error: "First lead and correct." It is among magazine editors, many of whom have never worked for newspapers or wire services, much less seen the inside of a police station, that the myth of "reporting the facts" remains strongest. Since a magazine must go to press several days, or even weeks, before it appears on the newsstands, and since it remains on display for at least a week, errors and all, magazine editors have developed a fetish about absolute accuracy on the most inconsequential facts, a fetish that even makes "the facts" a substitute for reality. To be sure that you can be sure because you read it in *Newsweek* (or *Time* or, for that matter, *The New Yorker* and a number of other magazines), there has come into existence an institution unknown to newspapers: the checker.

The checker, or researcher, is usually a girl in her twenties, usually from some Eastern college, pleasant-looking but not a *femme fatale*. She came from college unqualified for anything, but looking for an "interesting" job. After a few years, she usually feels, bitterly and rightly, that nobody appreciates her work. Her work consists of assembling newspaper clippings and other research material early in the week and then checking the writer's story at the end of the week. The beginning of the week is lackadaisical, and so is the research, but toward the end, when typewriters clack behind closed doors and editors snap at intruders, there are midnight hamburgers and tears in the ladies' room. For the checker gets no credit if the story is right, but she gets the blame if it is wrong. It doesn't matter if the story is slanted or meretricious, if it misinterprets or misses the point of the week's news. That is the responsibility of the editors. What matters—and what seems to attract most of the hostile letters to the editors—is whether a championship poodle stands thirty-six or forty inches high, whether the eyes of Prince Juan Carlos of Spain are blue or brown, whether the population of some city in Kansas is 15,000 or 18,000.

The first question about this fetish of facts, which no newsmagazine ever questions, is whether these facts, researched and verified at such enormous trouble and expense, really matter. Obviously, there is an important difference between saying that

Charles de Gaulle accepts Britain's entry into the Common Market, which a number of prominent reporters used to report, and saying that de Gaulle opposes Britain's entering the Common Market, which mysteriously turned out to be the case. But how much does it really matter whether a newsmagazine reports that de Gaulle is sixty-seven or sixty-eight years old, six feet one or six feet two, that he smokes Gauloises or Chesterfields, that he eats a brioche or a melon for breakfast, that Madame de Gaulle puts fresh roses or does not put fresh roses on his desk every day? Judging by the legend of the police reporter and the city editor, and judging by the amount of space the newsmagazines devote to such minutiae, it matters very much to provide "the facts" and "provide them straight." Despite the public statements of principle, however, the men who usually care the least about such details are the men who actually write and edit the newsmagazines.

## HAWKS WHEEL OVER CYPRUS

There is an essential difference between a news story, as understood by a newspaperman or a wire-service writer, and the newsmagazine story. The chief purpose of the conventional news story is to tell what happened. It starts with the most important information and continues into increasingly inconsequential details, not only because the reader may not read beyond the first paragraph but because an editor working on galley proofs a few minutes before press time likes to be able to cut freely from the end of the story. A newsmagazine is very different. It is written and edited to be read consecutively from beginning to end, and each of its stories is designed, following the critical theories of Edgar Allan Poe, to create one emotional effect. The news, what happened that week, may be told in the beginning, the middle, or the end; for the purpose is not to throw information at the reader but to seduce him into reading the whole story, and into accepting the dramatic (and often political) point being made.

In beginning a story, the newsmagazine writer often relies on certain traditional procedures of his special craft. They change little from year to year, but, for purposes of examination, we might select the first three issues of *Time* and *Newsweek* last May.

"Flowers were in bloom on the crumbling towers of St. Hilarion, and hawks turned soundlessly high above Kyrenia." This is

*Time*'s beginning for a story on civil strife in Cyprus. The "weather lead" is always a favorite because it creates a dramatic tone; because, by so obviously avoiding the news, it implicitly promises the reader more important things to come.

Then there is the "moving-vehicle lead," most often a description of a plane landing. In one of these May issues, *Time* began a story this way: "One foggy morning in Berlin, a yellow Mercedes from the Soviet zone drew up at the tollgate at the Heerstrasse crossing point." *Newsweek*'s beginning was almost identical: "Shortly after 5 o'clock in the morning a heavily shrouded black Mercedes bearing license tags issued by the Allied Control Commission in Germany rolled quietly into the no man's land between the Western and Russian sectors of Berlin." (There is no real contradiction between the black Mercedes and the yellow Mercedes, for the magazines were focusing on two different vehicles involved in an exchange of spies.)

Another favorite is the "narrative" opening involving an unidentified person: "The hooded, gambler eyes tracked the jurors as they filed into the courtroom" (*Newsweek,* on the trial of Roy Cohn); or the provocative quote involving an unidentified object: " 'She's in there,' pointed one proud Pinkerton. 'She's the most magnificent thing I've ever seen' " (*Time,* on the appearance of Michelangelo's Pietà at the New York World's Fair). Occasionally, the newsmagazine writer just gets bored with it all: "There was a sense of *déjà vu* about the whole affair—an uncanny paramnesic feeling that all of this had happened before" (*Time,* on the May Day Parade in Moscow).

The writer had some reason to be bored. Presumably assigned to write a full-page lead story on the week's events in Eastern Europe, he had only two things to say—that nothing much had happened at the May Day Parade, and that the Romanians were playing off the Russians against the Chinese for their own benefit. In elaborating on this, he engaged in some characteristic newsmagazine equivocation: "Dej is playing a double game in the Sino-Soviet conflict, one that could lead to plenty of trouble—or perhaps to a certain amount of freedom." But though the story has nothing much to say, it absolutely bristles with the facts that newsmagazines use as a substitute for reality. It tells us what Khrushchev was wearing (a Homburg) and what he had been eating lately (cabbage rather than meat). It tells us how to pronounce the name of Romania's Galati steel combine (Galatz) and what its rolling mill cost ($42 million). It gives us a figure for Romanian industrial growth (15 per cent) and a translation for the name of the Romanian Communist newspaper *Scînteia* (*Spark*). And to persuade us that the activity in Romania is important, the story reports as alphabetical fact that "every Communist from Auckland to Zanzibar took note of it."

As a rule, facts are not scattered around so indiscriminately, like sequins ornamenting some drab material, for their main function in a newsmagazine story is to illustrate a dramatic thesis. When *Newsweek* begins a story on an African "summit conference," for example, it is apt to open with a variation of the moving-vehicle lead, which might be called the crowd-gathering lead: "Some came in sleek Italian suits from the Via Condotti . . ." Did any African premier really wear clothing from the Via Condotti? The problem would never arise on an ordinary newspaper, since it doesn't particularly matter where the African statesmen buy their clothes. But since the newsmagazine writer starts with a dramatic concept—the African leaders are a self-indulgent lot—he needs a dramatic concept to illustrate it.

An even more characteristic opening dramatized *Time*'s cover story on Henry Cabot Lodge:

> In the early-morning gloom of Saigon's muggy pre-monsoon season, an alarm clock shrills in the stillness of a second-floor bedroom at 38 Phung Khac Khoan Street. The Brahmin from Boston arises, breakfasts on mango or papaya, sticks a snub-nosed .38-cal. Smith & Wesson revolver into a shoulder holster, and leaves for the office.

This is a fine example of the well-trained virtuoso at work, not only disguising the subject of the story but combining a series of insignificant facts into a cadenza of exotic weather, breakfast food, strange street names, and gunplay. The author was so pleased with the results that he went on repeating himself for three paragraphs, which disclosed that the temperature that day was ninety degrees, with 90 per cent humidity, that Lodge's moving vehicle was a Checker Marathon sedan, that the U.S. Embassy building is located at 39 Nam Nghi Boulevard, and that Lodge's office desk contains yet another gun, a .357 Smith & Wesson Magnum. There are two reasons for this inundation of minutiae. The first—based on the theory that knowledge of lesser facts implies knowledge of major facts—is to prove that *Time* knows everything there is to know about Lodge. The second—based on the theory that a man who carries a gun is tough and aggressive—is to dramatize the basic thesis, that Lodge would be a good Republican candidate for President.

## IN SEARCH OF THE ZIP

But what does the specific fact itself matter? Does it matter whether Lodge carries a .38-cal. Smith & Wesson or a Luger or a pearl-handled derringer? Does it make any difference whether he lives on the second floor of 38 Phung Khac Khoan Street or the third floor of some other building? The newsmagazines have provided their own answer by evolving a unique system which makes it theoretically possible to write an entire news story without any facts at all. This is the technique of the "zip." It takes various forms: Kuming (a deliberate misspelling of "coming" to warn copy editors, proofreaders, and printers not to use the word itself), or TK, meaning To Kum, or, in the case of statistics, 00 (the number of zeros is purely optional). This technique enables the writer to ignore all facts and concentrate on the drama. If he is describing some backward country, for example, he can safely write that 00 per cent of its people are ravaged by TK diseases. It obviously doesn't matter too much whether the rate of illiteracy is 80 per cent or 90 per cent. Any statistic will sound equally authoritative. It is the checker who is responsible for facts, and she will fill in any gaps.

Filling in the "zips" is sometimes costly. One former newsmagazine writer, for example, recalls some problems that arose when he was writing a cover story on General Naguib, then the President of Egypt. Naguib, he wrote, was such a modest man that his name did not appear among the 000 people listed in *Who's Who in the Middle East*. Moreover, Naguib disliked luxury and had refused to live in the royal palace, surrounded by an 00-foot-high wall. A cable—as the writer tells the story—duly went to the Cairo stringer. There was no answer. Indignant at the stringer's fecklessness, the editors changed the copy so that neither of the missing facts was needed. A week later, came a cable saying something like this:

AM IN JAIL AND ALLOWED SEND ONLY ONE CABLE SINCE WAS ARRESTED WHILE MEASURING FIFTEEN FOOT WALL OUTSIDE FAROUKS PALACE AND HAVE JUST FINISHED COUNTING THIRTY-EIGHT THOUSAND FIVE HUNDRED TWENTYTWO NAMES WHOS WHO IN MIDEAST

When both the writer and the researcher accept this as a game, the search for the key fact can become pure fantasy. On one occasion, for example, a newsmagazine editor wrote into a piece of copy: "There are 00 trees in Russia." The researcher took a creative delight in such an impossible problem. From the Soviet government, she ascertained the number of acres officially listed as forests; from some Washington agency she ascertained the average number of trees per acre of forests. The result was a wholly improbable but wholly unchallengeable statistic for the number of trees in Russia.

In the normal case of the 00, however, someone calls a government agency to get the official answer. The results are sometimes equally strange. One *Newsweek* researcher recalls the story of the Sudanese army, which a writer had described as "the 00-man Sudanese army." No newspaper clippings could fill in the figure, and telephone calls to the Sudanese Embassy in Washington indicated that nobody there could either. The Sudanese may well have been surprised that anybody should want to know such a figure. As the weekly deadline approached, an editor finally instructed the checker to make "an educated guess," and the story appeared with a reference to something like "the 17,000-man Sudanese army." There were no complaints. The *Newsweek* story duly reached Khartoum, where the press complaisantly reprinted it and commented on it. Digests of the Khartoum press returned to Washington, and one day a Sudanese Embassy official happily telephoned the *Newsweek* researcher to report that he finally was able to tell her the exact number of men in the Sudanese army: seventeen thousand.

## DOCUMENTING THE DREAM

Once you go beyond the Des Moines police station, you find yourself dealing more and more with some equivalent of the Sudanese Embassy. The "facts," which are supposed to form the basis of the news, are often simply unknown. Yet in any week's issue of any magazine of journalism, you can find the most impressive statistics—00 per cent of the people of Brazil are illiterate, or the per capita income of the Burmese is $00.00.

Newsmagazine writers are very skilled in the popular sport of statistics. With the cooperation of various partisan sources, they make comparative projections of the American and Russian gross national product in 1970—when nobody has more than a vague estimate of what these figures will be even in 1965. The birth-control lobby issues horrendous statistics about the number of human beings who will be living on every cubic yard of earth in the year 2000, and yet all such projections are based heavily on the estimated future populations of China and India, estimates that vary even today by hundreds of millions. All over the world, in fact, most estimates of population, illiteracy, illness, industrial growth, or per capita income are little more than wild guesses. "Let's not guess, let's know," the assistant city editor in Des Moines used to say, expressing a characteristically American desire for certainty. At one point during one of the periodic crises in Laos, however, an American correspondent bitterly complained to a Laotian government spokesman that he had spoken to sixteen government officials and got sixteen different versions of the facts. The Laotian was bewildered. It seemed perfectly natural to him, he said, that if you spoke to sixteen different officials you would get sixteen different answers.

The Laotian was wise in acknowledging and answering the first fundamental question about the fetish of facts: Does it really matter which "fact" is to be officially certified as "true"? He was equally wise in acknowledging and answering a second question: Does anyone really know which "fact" is "true"? He was equally wise in raising a third question, and implying an answer: Every man sees the "facts" according to his own interests.

Governments and business corporations have long acknowledged this by employing public-relations men and "information officers" to make sure that any facts make them look virtuous. *Time* once quoted a French spokesman's poetic definition of his job: *"Mentir et dementir"* (to lie and to deny). And in the world of newsmagazines, seeking the certainty of unascertainable facts, official government statistics carry a surprising weight. On one occasion, for instance, I was writing a story about the economic problems of Sicily, and I wrote that approximately 30 per cent of the inhabitants were unemployed, which I believed to be roughly true. When I saw the story in print, I read that something like 8 per cent of the Sicilians were unemployed. In other words, one of Europe's poorest areas was scarcely worse off than the United States—but this was the official statistic that the Italian government had given to the researcher. "After all," as one of the researchers once said, "we have to protect ourselves."

The basic purpose of the newsmagazines' facts, however, is not to report the unemployment statistics in Sicily, or the shopping habits of African statesmen, but to provide an *appearance* of documentation for what are essentially essays. The *Time* cover story on Lodge, for example, with its fact-choked lead, eventually arrives at the question of whether the Republicans might nominate Goldwater because no Republican can defeat President Johnson anyway. "This defeatist attitude is pretty silly," comments *Time, The Weekly Newsmagazine.* "Sure as his political moves have been, Johnson could still stumble politically. And healthy as the President may seem, there is always that dread possibility of disablement or worse. The Republican nomination is therefore nothing to give away for the mere asking." After that Olympian declaration, the *Time* story goes on to outline the Lodge supporters' hopes for their candidate's triumphant return to the United States. "A foolish fantasy?" *Time* wonders. "Perhaps. But that is one of the most enchanting things about U.S. politics: dreams can and do come true."

Unfortunately, the perils of prophecy are high. The week after the Lodge story, which assumed that the Ambassador would sweep onward from a victory in the Oregon primary, *Time* had to rush out with a cover story that began, a little hysterically: "Battling Nelson did it! Battered, bloodied, beaten, taunted, hooted, and laughed at during bitter, frustrating months, Republican Nelson Rockefeller never gave up, never stopped swinging." This story, too, concluded with a warning to Republicans not to accept defeat: "Nelson Rockefeller doesn't think like that—and in Oregon he demonstrated that perhaps it is a pretty poor way of thinking." No man waits for *Time,* however, and when Barry Goldwater finally won the Republican nomination, the editors declared that it had been inevitable: "Goldwater won the presidential nomination by arduously cultivating support at the precinct and county levels . . . What helped clinch it for Goldwater was the fact that a strong conservative tide was running in the U.S., fed by a deep disquiet at the grass roots over the role of an ever-expanding Government. Goldwater and the tide came together, and the one could not have succeeded without the other."

On a less exalted plane, the typical newsmagazine story almost invariably reaches a point where the writer drops the factual ballast and summarizes his views on the importance of the week's events. And there is nothing wrong about this. In view of the general inadequacy of American newspapers and the ignorance of the American public, an informed evaluation of the week's news is something to be commended. Yet if the reality were candidly admitted, it would antagonize the newsmagazine readers. The English, who read newspapers on a scale that should shame most Americans, appreciate magazines that frankly comment on a body of presumed knowledge, such as *The Economist, The New Statesman,* or *The Spectator.* Most Americans, however, taught to believe that they should assimilate the "facts" for themselves, reject such American counterparts as *The New Republic* and *The Nation.* They accept the newsmagazines not as magazines of commentary or interpretation but as magazines which will tell them yet more facts, "the real story."

## NEWS BREAK OR NEWS LEAK?

Here is the flaw in the newsmagazines' equation of fact and truth. For if you assume that nobody really knows or cares how many men there are in the Sudanese army, as newsmagazine editors do every time they use the term "00," you acknowledge the hypocrisy of your claim to be simply reporting the facts; then you take on the sacerdotal role of providing not the facts but "the truth." (It is worth noting that newsmagazine reporters chronically complain that their "files"—the reports they send in—are ignored when the final story is written.) Apart from the size of the Sudanese army, what is really going on in the Sudan? Apart from the number of trees growing on the steppes, what is really going on in Russia? Or in London and Paris and Washington?

It is in the major political capitals, where the major news is made, that the myth of the police reporter in pursuit of the facts has become particularly irrelevant. A skillful police reporter turned loose in the Pentagon not only wouldn't be able to get the right answer, he wouldn't even be able to find the person who knew the answer. The officials of the State Department or the Quai d'Orsay speak only to people they know well. And the reporter who persuades himself that he represents the so-called "Fourth Estate" very often becomes an unofficial and perhaps unconscious spokesman for the government he is assigned to cover. At the very least, the capital correspondent thinks he is the intermediary divinely chosen to interpret the activities of politicians to the electorate; quite often, he acquires a vocation to educate and inspire the politicians themselves; rarely does he realize that in representing a "Fourth Estate" he serves the government as an instrument for leaks, propaganda, and outright lies. After all, if you're having a candlelit dinner with a Secretary of State, isn't it the better part of valor to assume that anything he tells you is "the truth"?

The situation remains much the same from one Administration to another, but one incident that still seems most illustrative occurred a few years ago. At a time when no Berlin crisis was visible in the daily press, the Washington bureau manager of a newsmagazine telephoned his superiors to say that a major Berlin crisis was imminent. Having had access to the President, he reported that "the only thing on the President's desk" was a melodramatic plan to evacuate U. S. dependents from Berlin, to mobilize reserves, and to behave as though war were imminent. This was a little puzzling since the Russians apparently hadn't done anything about Berlin recently, but the newsmagazine was so impressed by the President's supposed anxiety that it printed a major story about the supposed "emergency plan." When that issue appeared, the President was reported to have telephoned an executive of the magazine and asked how he could jeopardize the national interest with such an article. He even announced publicly that he was calling in the FBI to investigate the Pentagon to see who had leaked such a dangerous story to the magazine. The editors, who had thought they were acting for rather than against the national interest, were very much embarrassed. But the FBI somehow never succeeded in finding or punishing the culprit who had leaked the story.

It remained for the *New York Times,* one of the last redoubts of independent journalism in Washington, to suggest that the

President had called in the FBI to investigate the leaking of a highly tentative "emergency plan" so that the Russians would think it was a real emergency plan. Not long after this, the President was on the air, urging Americans to build bomb shelters because of the impending Berlin crisis. And the newsmagazine, which spends tens of thousands of dollars every year to verify the per capita income of nonexistent peasants in Thailand, was left wiping the pie off its face. It could only wipe in dignified silence. For unlike the daily newspaper, which can publish a political "leak" one day and the official denial the next, the newsmagazine purports to tell not just the facts but the inside, authoritative, "real" story, and thus it remains peculiarly vulnerable to inside, authoritative, real propaganda. It cannot deny what it has authoritatively told as the truth without denying itself.

## MY OWN DE GAULLE

And yet the myth survives—we must report the facts. Every statement must be checked and double-checked. One day in March of 1958, when it seemed that France was drifting toward chaos, a newsmagazine editor assigned me to write a generally sympathetic story about Charles de Gaulle and his views on France's future. Our Paris bureau chief was an ardent Gaullist and sent a long file to explain de Gaulle's policies. And since I had long been an admirer of de Gaulle, I felt no misgivings about writing an article outlining the hopeful prospects for a Gaullist France. But there was nothing in the Paris file and nothing in de Gaulle's own writing that seemed to provide an adequate summary of the Gaullist contempt for the Fourth Republic. And so I ended with a note of typical newsmagazine rhetoric, that France's main problem was to remake itself. This, I concluded, "involves a change in outlook and atmosphere, an end to the meanness, corruption, and squabbling that have darkened the past decade." When I saw the published version, I saw to my surprise that my own rhetoric had somehow become de Gaulle's rhetoric. "This, he adds," it said, referring to de Gaulle, " 'involves a change in outlook and atmosphere . . .' " And so on. When I asked the researcher how my words had become de Gaulle's words, she said that the quotation marks had been added by an editor, who had answered her protests by saying, "Well, that's his idea, isn't it? He *could* have said it."

So the matter rested, for a few weeks, and then I went on vacation. During my vacation, the army and the mob seized control of Algiers, and France shook, and de Gaulle announced his readiness to return to power, and the researcher sent me a page torn from the New York *Herald Tribune,* quoting de Gaulle on every known issue. And what was his view on the basic condition of France? France must remake itself, he said, and this "involves a change in outlook and atmosphere, an end to the meanness, corruption, and squabbling that have darkened the past decade."

By now, I can only assume that this statement is a documented "fact," like the "fact" that there are 00 men in the Sudanese army and 00 trees in Russia. Until some Laotian, who never met a Des Moines police reporter, suggests that neither facts nor news is necessarily the truth.

*SUGGESTIONS FOR DISCUSSION*

• Friedrich discusses "the easy equation of facts, news, and truth" practiced by some journalists. Does he define his terms and differentiate between them? Are his definitions indisputable?

• Does it matter that such an "easy equation" is used? If so, why is it important to distinguish clearly between facts and truth, facts and news, and news and truth? Are the newsmagazines that use the "easy equation" entirely to blame for using it?

• Do you have any way of checking the accuracy of Friedrich's report?

• Does your local paper or your campus paper practice an "easy equation of facts, news, and truth"? What about the TV news in your area?

• According to a *Time-Life* report, the average American is exposed to between 650 and 1,600 ads a day, and he ignores 85 percent of them completely. Considering that he may not have ignored 15 percent of them, or 240 ads a day, what does such a statistic suggest about the way we formulate our ideas? Do the magazine ads and TV commercials create "truths" or capitalize on our hidden desires? Is it a truth, for example, that blondes have more fun, or do we only wish so, and therefore purchase a blonde-making product?

# Report, Inference,
# and Judgment

## S. I. Hayakawa

*The following excerpts are from S. I. Hayakawa's book* Language in
Thought and Action, *first published in 1949. The book gained him a
national reputation as a semanticist, and he subsequently became a
popular public lecturer and a teacher at San Francisco State College.
He currently is the controversial president of San Francisco State.*

For the purposes of the interchange of information, the basic
symbolic act is the report of what we have seen, heard, or felt:
"There is a ditch on each side of the road." "You can get those at
Smith's hardware store for $2.75." Then there are reports of re-
ports: "The longest waterfall in the world is Victoria Falls in
Rhodesia." . . . Reports adhere to the following rules: first, they
are *capable of verification;* second, they *exclude,* as far as possible,
*inferences* and *judgments.* . . .

An *inference,* as we shall use the term, is *a statement about
the unknown made on the basis of the known.* We may *infer* from
the handsomeness and cut of a woman's clothes her wealth or
social position; we may *infer* from the character of the ruins the
origin of the fire that destroyed the building. . . . Inferences may
be carelessly or carefully made. They may be made on the basis
of a great background of previous experience with the subject
matter or no experience at all. . . .

By *judgments,* we shall mean *all expressions of the writer's
approval or disapproval of the occurrences, persons or objects he
is describing.*

# The Prince of Creation

*Susanne K. Langer*

*Susanne Langer, born in 1895, has had a distinguished teaching and writing career. Now Professor Emeritus of Philosophy, Mrs. Langer's books include* An Introduction to Symbolic Logic, Philosophy in a New Key, Feeling and Form, The Problem of Art, *and* Philosophical Sketches. *"The Prince of Creation" was written during World War II.*

The world is aflame with man-made public disasters, artificial rains of brimstone and fire, planned earthquakes, cleverly staged famines and floods. The Prince of Creation is destroying himself. He is throwing down the cities he has built, the works of his own hand, the wealth of many thousand years in his frenzy of destruction, as a child knocks down its own handiwork, the whole day's achievement, in a tantrum of tears and rage.

What has displeased the royal child? What has incurred his world-shattering tantrum?

The bafflement of the magnificent game he is playing. Its rules and its symbols, his divine toys, have taken possession of the player. For this global war is not the old, hard, personal fight for the means of life, *bellum omnium contra omnes,* which animals perpetually wage; this is a war of monsters. Not mere men but great superpersonal giants, the national states, are met in combat. They do not hate and attack and wrestle as injured physical creatures do; they move heavily, inexorably, by strategy and necessity, to each other's destruction. The game of national states has come to this pass, and the desperate players ride their careening animated toys to a furious suicide.

These moloch gods, these monstrous states, are not natural beings; they are man's own work, products of the power that makes him lord over all other living things—his mind. They are not of the earth, earthy, as families and herds, hives and colonies are, whose members move and fight as one by instinct and habit until a physical disturbance splits them and the severed parts reconstitute themselves as new organized groups. The national states are not physical groups; they are social symbols, profound and terrible.

They are symbols of the new way of life, which the past two centuries have given us. For thousands of years, the pattern of daily life—working, praying, building, fighting, and raising new generations—repeated itself with only slow or unessential changes. The social symbols expressive of this life were ancient and familiar. Tribal gods or local saints, patriarchs, squires, or feudal lords, princes and bishops, raised to the highest power in the persons of emperors and popes—they were all expressions of needs and duties and opinions grounded in an immemorial way of life. The average man's horizon was not much greater than his valley, his town, or whatever geographical ramparts bounded his community. Economic areas were small, and economic problems essentially local. Naturally in his conception the powers governing the world were local, patriarchal, and reverently familiar.

Then suddenly, within some two hundred years, and for many places far less than that, the whole world has been transformed. Communities of different tongues and faiths and physiognomies have mingled; not as of old in wars of conquest, invading lords and conquered population gradually mixing their two stocks, but by a new process of foot-loose travel and trade, dominated by great centers of activity that bring individuals from near and far promiscuously together as a magnet draws filings from many heaps into close but quite accidental contact. Technology has made old horizons meaningless and localities indefinite. For goods and their destinies determine the structure of human societies. This is a new world, a world of persons, not of families and clans, or parishes and manors. The proletarian order is not founded on a hearth and its history. It does not express itself in a dialect, a local costume, a rite, a patron saint. All such traditions by mingling have canceled each other, and disappeared.

Most of us feel that since the old controlling ideas of faith and custom are gone, mankind is left without anchorage of any sort. None of the old social symbols fit this modern reality, this shrunken and undifferentiated world in which we lead a purely economic, secular, essentially homeless life.

But mankind is never without its social symbols; when old ones die, new ones are already in process of birth; and the new gods that have superseded all faiths are the great national states. The conception of them is mystical and moral, personal and devotional; they conjure with names and emblems, and demand our constant profession and practice of the new orthodoxy called "Patriotism."

Of all born creatures, man is the only one that cannot live by bread alone. He lives as much by symbols as by sense report, in a realm compounded of tangible things and virtual images, of actual events and ominous portents, always between fact and fiction. For he sees not only actualities but meanings. He has, indeed, all the impulses and interests of animal nature; he eats, sleeps, mates, seeks comfort and safety, flees pain, falls sick and dies, just as cats and bears and fishes and butterflies do. But he has something more in his repertoire, too—he has laws and religions, theories and dogmas, because he lives not only through sense but through symbols. That is the special asset of his mind, which makes him the master of earth and all its progeny.

By the agency of symbols—marks, words, mental images, and icons of all sorts—he can hold his ideas for contemplation long after their original causes have passed away. Therefore, he can think of things that are not presented or even suggested by this actual environment. By associating symbols in his mind, he combines things and events that were never together in the real world. This gives him the power we call imagination. Further, he can symbolize only part of an idea and let the rest go out of consciousness; this gives him the faculty that has been his pride throughout the ages—the power of abstraction. The combined effect of these two powers is inestimable. They are the roots of his supreme talent, the gift of reason.

In the war of each against all which is the course of nature, man has an unfair advantage over his animal brethren; for he can see what is not yet there to be seen, know events that happened before his birth, and take possession of more than he actually eats; he can kill at a distance; and by rational design he can enslave other creatures to live and act for him instead of for themselves.

Yet this mastermind has strange aberrations. For in the whole animal kingdom there is no such unreason, no such folly and impracticality as man displays. He alone is hounded by imaginary fears, beset by ghosts and devils, frightened by mere images of things. No other creature wastes time in unprofitable ritual or builds nests for dead specimens of its race. Animals are always realists. They have intelligence in varying degrees—chickens are stupid, elephants are said to be very clever—but, bright or foolish, animals react only to reality. They may be fooled by appearance, by pictures or reflections, but once they know them as such, they promptly lose interest. Distance and darkness and silence are not fearful to them, filled with voices or forms, or invisible presences. Sheep in the pasture do not seem to fear phantom sheep beyond the fence, mice don't look for mouse goblins in the clock, birds do not worship a divine thunderbird.

But oddly enough, men do. They think of all these things and guard against them, worshiping animals and monsters even before they conceive of divinities in their own image. Men are essentially unrealistic. With all their extraordinary intelligence, they alone go in for patently impractical actions—magic and exorcism and holocausts—rites that have no connection with common-sense methods of self-preservation, such as a highly intelligent animal might use. In fact, the rites and sacrifices by which primitive man claims to control nature are sometimes fatal to the performers. Indian puberty rites are almost always intensely painful, and African natives have sometimes died during initiations into honorary societies.

We usually assume that very primitive tribes of men are closer to animal estate than highly civilized races; but in respect of practical attitudes, this is not true. The more primitive man's mind, the more fantastic it seems to be; only with high intellectual discipline do we gradually approach the realistic outlook of intelligent animals.

Yet this human mind, so beclouded by phantoms and superstitions, is probably the only mind on earth that can reach out to an awareness of things beyond its practical environment and can also conceive of such notions as truth, beauty, justice, majesty, space and time and creation.

There is another paradox in man's relationship with other creatures: namely, that those very qualities he calls animalian— "brutal," "bestial," "inhuman"—are peculiarly his own. No other animal is so deliberately cruel as man. No other creature intentionally imprisons its own kind, or invents special instruments of torture such as racks and thumbscrews for the sole purpose of punishment. No other animal keeps its own brethren in slavery; so far as we know, the lower animals do not commit anything like the acts of pure sadism that figure rather largely in our newspapers. There is no torment, spite, or cruelty for its own sake among beasts, as there is among men. A cat plays with its prey, but does not conquer and torture smaller cats. But man, who knows good and evil, is cruel for cruelty's sake, he who has a moral law is more brutal than the brutes, who have none; he alone inflicts suffering on his fellows with malice aforethought.

If man's mind is really a higher form of the animal mind, his morality a specialized form of herd instinct, then where in the course of evolution did he lose the realism of a clever animal and fall prey to subjective fears? And why should he take pleasure in torturing helpless members of his own race?

The answer is, I think, that man's mind is *not* a direct evolution from the beast's mind, but is a unique variant and therefore has had a meteoric and startling career very different from any other animal history. The trait that sets human mentality apart from every other is its preoccupation with symbols, with images and names that *mean* things, rather than with things themselves. This trait may have been a mere sport of nature once upon a time. Certain creatures do develop tricks and interests that seem biologically unimportant. Pack rats, for instance, and some birds of the crow family take a capricious pleasure in bright objects and carry away such things for which they have, presumably, no earthly use. Perhaps man's tendency to see certain forms as *images,* to hear certain sounds not only as signals but as expressive tones, and to be excited by sunset colors or starlight, was originally just a peculiar sensitivity in a rather highly developed brain. But whatever its cause, the ultimate destiny of this trait was momentous; for all human activity is based on the appreciation and use of symbols. Language, religion, mathematics, all learning, all science and superstition, even right and wrong, are products of symbolic expression rather than direct experience. Our commonest words, such as "house" and "red" and "walking," are symbols; the pyramids of Egypt and the mysterious circles of Stonehenge are symbols; so are dominions and empires and astronomical universes. We live in a mind-made world, where the things of prime importance are images or words that embody ideas and feelings and attitudes.

The animal mind is like a telephone exchange; it receives stimuli from outside through the sense organs and sends out appropriate responses through the nerves that govern muscles, glands, and other parts of the body. The organism is constantly interacting with its surroundings, receiving messages and acting on the new state of affairs that the messages signify.

But the human mind is not a simple transmitter like a telephone exchange. It is more like a great projector; for instead of merely mediating between an event in the outer world and a creature's responsive action, it transforms or, if you will, distorts the event into an image to be looked at, retained, and contemplated. For the images of things that we remember are not exact and faithful transcriptions even of our actual sense impressions. They are made as much by what we think as by what we see. It is a well-known fact that if you ask several people the size of the moon's disk as they look at it, their estimates will vary from the area of a dime to that of a barrel top. Like a magic lantern, the mind projects its ideas of things on the screen of what we call "memory"; but like all projections, these ideas are transformations of actual things. They are, in fact, *symbols* of reality, not pieces of it.

A symbol is not the same thing as a sign; that is a fact that psychologists and philosophers often overlook. All intelligent animals use signs; so do we. To them as well as to us sounds and smells and motions are signs of food, danger, the presence of other beings, or of rain or storm. Furthermore, some animals not only attend to signs but produce them for the benefit of others. Dogs bark at the door to be let in; rabbits thump to call each other; the cooing of doves and the growl of a wolf defending his kill are unequivocal signs of feelings and intentions to be reckoned with by other creatures.

We use signs just as animals do, though with considerably more elaboration. We stop at red lights and go on green; we answer calls and bells, watch the sky for coming storms, read trouble or promise or anger in each other's eyes. That is animal intelligence raised to the human level. Those of us who are dog lovers can probably all tell wonderful stories of how high our dogs have sometimes risen in the scale of clever sign interpretation and sign using.

A sign is anything that announces the existence or the imminence of some event, the presence of a thing or a person, or a change in a state of affairs. There are signs of the weather, signs of danger, signs of future good or evil, signs of what the past has been. In every case a sign is closely bound up with something to be noted or expected in experience. It is always a part of the situation to which it refers, though the reference may be remote in space and time. In so far as we are led to note or expect the signified event we are making correct use of a sign. This is the essence of rational behavior, which animals show in varying degrees. It is entirely realistic, being closely bound up with the actual objective course of history—learned by experience, and cashed in or voided by further experience.

If man had kept to the straight and narrow path of sign using, he would be like the other animals, though perhaps a little brighter. He would not talk, but grunt and gesticulate and point. He would make his wishes known, give warnings, perhaps develop a social system like that of bees and ants, with such a wonderful efficiency of communal enterprise that all men would have plenty to eat, warm apartments—all exactly alike and perfectly convenient—to live in, and everybody could and would sit in the sun or by the fire, as the climate demanded, not talking but just basking, with every want satisfied, most of his life. The young would romp and make love, the old would sleep, the middle-aged would do the routine work almost unconsciously and eat a great deal. But that would be the life of a social, superintelligent, purely sign-using animal.

To us who are human, it does not sound very glorious. We want to go places and do things, own all sorts of gadgets that we do not absolutely need, and when we sit down to take it easy we want to talk. Rights and property, social position, special talents and virtues, and above all our ideas, are what we live for. We have gone off on a tangent that takes us far away from the mere biological cycle that animal generations accomplish; and that is because we can use not only signs but symbols.

A symbol differs from a sign in that it does not announce the presence of the object, the being, condition, or whatnot, which is its meaning, but merely *brings this thing to mind.* It is not a mere "substitute sign" to which we react as though it were the object itself. The fact is that our reaction to hearing a person's name is quite different from our reaction to the person himself. There are certain rare cases where a symbol stands directly for its meaning: in religious experience, for instance, the Host is not only a symbol but a Presence. But symbols in the ordinary sense are not mystic. They are the same sort of thing that ordinary signs are; only they do not call our attention to something necessarily present or to be physically dealt with—they call up merely a conception of the thing they "mean."

The difference between a sign and a symbol is, in brief, that a sign causes us to think or act *in face of* the thing signified, whereas a symbol causes us to think *about* the thing symbolized. Therein lies the great importance of symbolism for human life, its power to make this life so different from any other animal biography that generations of men have found it incredible to suppose that they were of purely zoological origin. A sign is always embedded in reality, in a present that emerges from the actual past and stretches to the future; but a symbol may be divorced from reality altogether. It may refer to what is *not* the case, to a mere idea, a figment, a dream. It serves, therefore, to liberate thought from the immediate stimuli of a physically present world; and that liberation marks the essential difference between human and nonhuman mentality. Animals think, but they think *of* and *at* things; men think primarily *about* things. Words, pictures, and memory images are symbols that may be combined and varied in a thousand ways. The result is a symbolic structure whose meaning is a complex of all their respective meanings, and this kaleidoscope of *ideas* is the typical product of the human brain that we call the "stream of thought."

The process of transforming all direct experience into imagery or into that supreme mode of symbolic expression, language, has so completely taken possession of the human mind that it is not only a special talent but a dominant, organic need. All our sense impressions leave their traces in our memory not only as signs disposing our practical reactions in the future but also as symbols, images representing our *ideas* of things; and the tendency to manipulate ideas, to combine and abstract, mix and extend them by playing with symbols, is man's outstanding characteristic. It seems to be what his brain most naturally and spontaneously does. Therefore his primitive mental function is not judging reality, but *dreaming his desires.*

Dreaming is apparently a basic function of human brains, for it is free and unexhausting like our metabolism, heartbeat, and breath. It is easier to dream than not to dream, as it is easier to breathe than to refrain from breathing. The symbolic character of dreams is fairly well established. Symbol mongering, on this ineffectual, uncritical level, seems to be instinctive, the fulfillment of an elementary need rather than the purposeful exercise of a high and difficult talent.

The special power of man's mind rests on the evolution of this special activity, not on any transcendently high development of animal intelligence. We are not immeasurably higher than other animals; we are different. We have a biological need and with it a biological gift that they do not share.

Because man has not only the ability but the constant need of *conceiving* what has happened to him, what surrounds him, what is demanded of him—in short, of symbolizing nature, himself, and his hopes and fears—he has a constant and crying need of *expression.* What he cannot express, he cannot conceive; what he cannot conceive is chaos, and fills him with terror.

If we bear in mind this all-important craving for expression we get a new picture of man's behavior; for from this trait spring his powers and his weaknesses. The process of symbolic transformation that all our experiences undergo is nothing more nor less than the process of *conception,* which underlies the human faculties of abstraction and imagination.

When we are faced with a strange or difficult situation, we cannot react directly, as other creatures do, with flight, aggression, or any such simple instinctive pattern. Our whole reaction depends on how we manage to conceive the situation—whether we cast it in a definite dramatic form, whether we see it as a disaster, a challenge, a fulfillment of doom, or a fiat of the Divine Will. In words or dreamlike images, in artistic or religious or even in cynical form, we must *construe* the events of life. There is great virtue in the figure of speech, "I can *make* nothing of it," to express a failure to understand something. Thought and memory are processes of *making* the thought content and the memory image; the pattern of our ideas is given by the symbols through which we express them. And in the course of manipulating those symbols we inevitably distort the original experience, as we abstract certain features of it, embroider and reinforce those features with other ideas, until the conception we project on the screen of memory is quite different from anything in our real history.

Conception is a necessary and elementary process; what we do with our conceptions is another story. That is the entire history of human culture—of intelligence and morality, folly and superstition, ritual, language, and the arts—all the phenomena that set man apart from, and above, the rest of the animal kingdom. As the religious mind has to make all human history a drama of sin and salvation in order to define its own moral attitudes, so a scientist wrestles with the mere presentation of "the facts" before he can reason about them. The process of *envisaging* facts, values, hopes, and fears underlies our whole behavior pattern; and this process is reflected in the evolution of an extraordinary phenomenon found always, and only, in human societies—the phenomenon of language.

Language is the highest and most amazing achievement of the symbolistic human mind. The power it bestows is almost inestimable, for without it anything properly called "thought" is impossible. The birth of language is the dawn of humanity. The line between man and beast—between the highest ape and the lowest savage—is the language line. Whether the primitive Neanderthal man was anthropoid or human depends less on his cranial capacity, his upright posture, or even his use of tools and fire, than on one issue we shall probably never be able to settle— whether or not he spoke.

In all physical traits and practical responses, such as skills and visual judgments, we can find a certain continuity between animal and human mentality. Sign using is an ever evolving, ever improving function throughout the whole animal kingdom, from the lowly worm that shrinks into his hole at the sound of an approaching foot, to the dog obeying his master's command, and even to the learned scientist who watches the movements of an index needle.

This continuity of the sign-using talent has led psychologists to the belief that language is evolved from the vocal expressions, grunts and coos and cries, whereby animals vent their feelings or signal their fellows; that man has elaborated this sort of communion to the point where it makes a perfect exchange of ideas possible.

I do not believe that this doctrine of the origin of language is correct. The essence of language is symbolic, not signific; we use it first and most vitally to formulate and hold ideas in our own minds. Conception, not social control, is its first and foremost benefit.

Watch a young child that is just learning to speak play with a toy; he says the name of the object, e.g.: "Horsey! horsey! horsey!" over and over again, looks at the object, moves it, always saying the name to himself or to the world at large. It is quite a time before he talks to anyone in particular; he talks first of all to himself. This is his way of forming and fixing the *conception* of the object in his mind, and around this conception all his knowledge of it grows. *Names* are the essence of language; for the *name* is what abstracts the conception of the horse from the horse itself, and lets the mere idea recur at the speaking of the name. This permits the conception gathered from one horse experience to be exemplified again by another instance of a horse, so that the notion embodied in the name is a general notion.

To this end, the baby uses a word long before he *asks for* the object; when he wants his horsey he is likely to cry and fret, because he is reacting to an actual environment, not forming ideas. He uses the animal language of *signs* for his wants; talking is still a purely symbolic process—its practical value has not really impressed him yet.

Language need not be vocal; it may be purely visual, like written language, or even tactual, like the deaf-mute system of speech; but it *must be denotative*. The sounds, intended or unintended, whereby animals communicate do not constitute a language, because they are signs, not names. They never fall into an organic pattern, a meaningful syntax of even the most rudimentary sort, as all language seems to do with a sort of driving necessity. That is because signs refer to actual situations, in which things have obvious relations to each other that require only to be noted; but symbols refer to ideas, which are not physically there for inspection, so their connections and features have to be represented. This gives all true language a natural tendency toward growth and development, which seems almost like a life of its own. Languages are not invented; they grow with our need for expression.

In contrast, animal "speech" never has a structure. It is merely an emotional response. Apes may greet their ration of yams with a shout of "Nga!" But they do not say "Nga" between meals. If they could *talk about* their yams instead of just saluting them, they would be the most primitive men instead of the most anthropoid of beasts. They would have ideas, and tell each other things true or false, rational or irrational; they would make plans and invent laws and sing their own praises, as men do.

The history of speech is the history of our human descent. Yet the habit of transforming reality into symbols, of contemplating and combining and distorting symbols, goes beyond the confines of language. All *images* are symbols, which make us think about the things they mean.

This is the source of man's great interest in "graven images," and in *mere appearances* like the face of the moon or the human profiles he sees in rocks and trees. There is no limit to the meanings he can read into natural phenomena. As long as this power is undisciplined, the sheer enjoyment of finding meanings in everything, the elaboration of concepts without any regard to truth and usefulness, seems to run riot; superstition and ritual in their pristine strength go through what some anthropologists have called a "vegetative" stage, when dreamlike symbols, gods and ghouls and rites, multiply like the overgrown masses of life in a jungle. From this welter of symbolic forms emerge the images that finally govern a civilization; the great symbols of religion, society, and selfhood.

What does an image "mean"? Anything it is thought to resemble. It is only because we can abstract quite unobvious forms from the actual appearance of things that we see line drawings in two dimensions as images of colored, three-dimensional objects, find the likeness of a dipper in a constellation of seven stars, or see a face on a pansy. Any circle may represent the sun or moon; an upright monolith may be a man.

Wherever we can fancy a similarity we tend to see something represented. The first thing we do, upon seeing a new shape, is to assimilate it to our own idea of something that it resembles, something that is known and important to us. Our most elementary concepts are of our own actions, and the limbs or organs that perform them; other things are named by comparison with them. The opening of a cave is its mouth, the divisions of a river its arms. Language, and with it all articulate thought, grows by this process of unconscious metaphor. Every new idea urgently demands a word; if we lack a name for it, we call it after the first namable thing seen to bear even a remote analogy to it. Thus all the subtle and variegated vocabulary of a living language grows up from a few roots of very general application; words as various in meanings as "gentle" and "ingenious" and "general" spring from the one root "ge" meaning "to give life."

Yet there are conceptions that language is constitutionally unfit to express. The reason for this limitation of our verbal powers is a subject for logicians and need not concern us here. The point of interest to us is that, just as rational, discursive thought is bound up with language, so the life of feeling, of direct personal and social consciousness, the emotional stability of man and his sense of orientation in the world are bound up with images directly given to his senses: fire and water, noise and silence, high mountains and deep caverns, the brief beauty of flowers, the persistent grin of a skull. There seem to be irresistible parallels between the expressive forms we find in nature and the forms of our inner life; thus the use of light to represent all things good, joyful, comforting, and of darkness to express all sorts of sorrow, despair, or horror, is so primitive as to be well-nigh unconscious.

A flame is a soul; a star is a hope; the silence of winter is death. All such images, which serve the purpose of metaphorical thinking, are *natural symbols.* They have not conventionally assigned meanings, like words, but recommend themselves even to a perfectly untutored mind, a child's or a savage's, because they are definitely articulated *forms,* and to see something expressed in such forms is a universal human talent. We do not have to learn to use natural symbols; it is one of our primitive activities.

The fact that sensuous forms of natural processes have a significance beyond themselves makes the range of our symbolism, and with it the horizon of our consciousness, much wider and deeper than language. This is the source of ritual, mythology, and art. Ritual is a symbolic rendering of certain emotional *attitudes,* which have become articulate and fixed by being constantly expressed. Mythology is man's image of his world, and of himself in the world. Art is the exposition of his own subjective history, the life of feeling, the human spirit in all its adventures.

Yet this power of envisagement, which natural symbolism bestows, is a dangerous one; for human beings can envisage things that do not exist, and create horrible worlds, insupportable duties, monstrous gods and ancestors. The mind that can see past and future, the poles and the antipodes, and guess at obscure mechanisms of nature, is ever in danger of seeing what is not there, imagining false and fantastic causes, and courting death instead of life. Because man can play with ideas, he is unrealistic; he is inclined to neglect the all-important interpretation of signs for a rapt contemplation of symbols.

Some twenty years ago, Ernst Cassirer set forth a theory of human mentality that goes far toward explaining the vagaries of savage religions and the ineradicable presence of superstition even in civilized societies: a symbol, he observed, is the embodiment of an idea; it is at once an abstract and a physical fact. Now its great emotive value lies in the concept it conveys; this inspires our reverent attitude, the attention and awe with which we view it. But man's untutored thought always tends to lose its way between the symbol and the fact. A skull represents death; but to a primitive mind the skull *is* death. To have it in the house is not unpleasant but dangerous. Even in civilized societies, symbolic objects—figures of saints, relics, crucifixes—are revered for their supposed efficacy. Their actual power is a power of *expression,* of embodying and thus revealing the greatest concepts humanity has reached; these concepts are the commanding forces that change our estate from a brute existence to the transcendent life of the spirit. But the symbol-loving mind of man reveres the meaning not *through* the articulating form but *in* the form so that the image appears to be the actual object of love and fear, supplication and praise.

Because of this constant identification of concepts with their expressions, our world is crowded with unreal beings. Some societies have actually realized that these beings do not belong to nature, and have postulated a so-called "other world" where they have their normal existence and from which they are said to descend, or arise, into our physical realm. For savages it is chiefly a nether world that sends up spooks; for more advanced cults it is from the heavens that supernatural beings, the embodiments of human ideas—of virtue, triumph, immortality—descend to the mundane realm. But from this source emanates also a terrible world government, with heavy commands and sanctions. Strange worship and terrible sacrifices may be the tithes exacted by the beings that embody our knowledge of nonanimalian human nature.

So the gift of symbolism, which is the gift of reason, is at the same time the seat of man's peculiar weakness—the danger of lunacy. Animals go mad with hydrophobia or head injuries, but purely mental aberrations are rare; beasts are not generally subject to insanity except through a confusion of signs, such as the experimentally produced "nervous breakdown" in rats. It is man who hears voices and sees ghosts in the dark, feels irrational compulsions and holds fixed ideas. All these phantasms are symbolic forms that have acquired a false factual status. It has been truly said that everybody has some streak of insanity; i.e., the threat of madness is the price of reason.

Because we can think of things potential as well as actual, we can be held in nonphysical bondage by laws and prohibitions and commands and by images of a governing power. This makes men tyrants over their own kind. Animals control each other's actions by immediate threats, growls and snarls and passes; but when the bully is roving elsewhere, his former domain is free of him. We control our inferiors by setting up symbols of our power, and the mere idea that words or images convey stands there to hold our fellows in subjection even when we cannot lay our hands on them. There is no flag over the country where a wolf is king; he is king where he happens to prowl, so long as he is there. But men, who can embody ideas and set them up to view, oppress each other by symbols of might.

The envisagements of good and evil, which make man a moral agent, make him also a conscript, a prisoner, and a slave. His constant problem is to escape the tyrannies he has created. Primitive societies are almost entirely tyrannical, symbol-bound, coercive organizations; civilized governments are so many conscious schemes to justify or else to disguise man's inevitable bondage to law and conscience.

Slowly, through ages and centuries, we have evolved a picture of the world we live in; we have made a drama of the earth's history and enhanced it with a backdrop of divinely ordered, star-filled space. And all this structure of infinity and eternity against which we watch the pageant of life and death, and all the moral melodrama itself, we have wrought by a gradual articulation of such vast ideas in symbols—symbols of good and evil, triumph and failure, birth and maturity and death. Long before the beginning of any known history, people saw in the heavenly bodies, in the changes of day and night or of the seasons, and in great beasts, symbolic forms to express those ultimate concepts that are the very frame of human existence. So gods, fates, the cohorts of good and evil were conceived. Their myths were the first formulations of cosmic ideas. Gradually the figures and traditions of religion emerged; ritual, the overt expression of our mental attitudes, became more and more intimately bound to definite and elaborate concepts of the creative and destructive powers that seem to control our lives.

Such beings and stories and rites are sacred because they are the great symbols by which the human mind orients itself in the world. To a creature that lives by reason, nothing is more terrible than what is formless and meaningless; one of our primary fears is fear of chaos. And it is the fight against chaos that has produced our most profound and indispensable images—the myths of light and darkness, of creation and passion, the symbols of the altar flame, the daystar, and the cross.

For thousands of years people lived by the symbols that nature presented to them. Close contact with earth and its seasons, intimate knowledge of stars and tides, made them feel the significance of natural phenomena and gave them a poetic, unquestioning sense of orientation. Generations of erudite and pious men elaborated the picture of the temporal and spiritual realms in which each individual was a pilgrim soul.

Then came the unprecedented change, the almost instantaneous leap of history from the immemorial tradition of the plow and the anvil to the new age of the machine, the factory, and the ticker tape. Often in no more than the length of a life-time the shift from handwork to mass production, and with it from poetry to science and from faith to nihilism, has taken place. The old nature symbols have become remote and have lost their meanings; in the clatter of gears and the confusion of gadgets that fill the new world, there will not be any obvious and rich and sacred meanings for centuries to come. All the accumulated creeds and rites of men are suddenly in the melting pot. There is no fixed community, no dynasty, no family inheritance—only the one huge world of men, vast millions of men, still looking on each other in hostile amazement.

A sane, intelligent animal should have invented, in the course of ten thousand years or more, some sure and obvious way of accommodating indefinite numbers of its own kind on the face of a fairly spacious earth. Modern civilization has achieved the highest triumphs of knowledge, skill, ingenuity, theory; yet all around its citadels, engulfing and demolishing them, rages the maddest war and confusion, inspired by symbols and slogans as riotous and irrational as anything the "vegetative" stage of savage phantasy could provide. How shall we reconcile this primitive nightmare excitement with the achievements of our high, rational, scientific culture?

The answer is, I think, that we are no longer in possession of a definite, established culture; we live in a period between an exhausted age—the European civilization of the white race—and an age still unborn, of which we can say nothing as yet. We do not know what races shall inherit the earth. We do not know what even the next few centuries may bring. But it is quite evident, I think, that we live in an age of transition, and that before many more generations have passed, mankind will make a new beginning and build itself a different world. Whether it will be a "brave, new world," or whether it will start all over with an unchronicled "state of nature" such as Thomas Hobbes described, wherein the individual's life is "nasty, brutish, and short," we simply cannot tell. All we know is that every tradition, every institution, every tribe is gradually becoming uprooted and upset, and we are waiting in a sort of theatrical darkness between the acts.

Because we are at a new beginning, our imaginations tend to a wild, "vegetative" overgrowth. The political upheavals of our time are marked, therefore, by a veritable devil dance of mystical ideologies, vaguely conceived, passionately declared, holding out fanatic hopes of mass redemption and mass beatitudes. Governments vie with each other in proclaiming social plans, social aims, social enterprises, and demanding bloody sacrifices in the name of social achievements.

New conceptions are always clothed in an extravagant meta-phorical form, for there is no language to express genuinely new ideas. And in their pristine strength they imbue the symbols that express them with their own mystery and power and holiness. It is impossible to disengage the welter of ideas embodied in a swastika, a secret sign, or a conjuring word from the physical presence of the symbol itself; hence the apparently nonsensical symbol worship and mysticism that go with new movements and visions. This identification of symbolic form and half-articulate meaning is the essence of all mythmaking. Of course the emotive value is incomprehensible to anyone who does not see such fig-ments as expressive forms. So an age of vigorous new conception and incomplete formulation always has a certain air of madness about it. But it is really a fecund and exciting period in the life of reason. Such is our present age. Its apparent unreason is a tremendous unbalance and headiness of the human spirit, a con-flict not only of selfish wills but of vast ideas in the metaphorical state of emergence.

The change from fixed community life and ancient local custom to the mass of unpedigreed human specimens that ac-tually constitutes the world in our industrial and commercial age has been too sudden for the mind of man to negotiate. Some tran-sitional form of life had to mediate between those extremes. And so the idol of nationality arose from the wreckage of tribal organi-zation. The concept of the national state is really the old tribe concept applied to millions of persons, unrelated and different creatures gathered under the banner of a government. Neither birth nor language nor even religion holds such masses together, but a mystic bond is postulated even where no actual bond of race, creed, or color may ever have existed.

At first glance it seems odd that the concept of nationality should reach its highest development just as all actual marks of national origins—language, dress, physiognomy, and religion—are becoming mixed and obliterated by our new mobility and cosmo-politan traffic. But it is just the loss of these things that inspires this hungry seeking for something like the old egocentric pattern in the vast and formless brotherhood of the whole earth. While mass production and universal communication clearly portend a culture of world citizenship, we cling desperately to our national-ism, a more and more attenuated version of the old clan civilization. We fight passionate and horrible wars for the symbols of our nations, we make a virtue of self-glorification and exclusiveness and invent strange anthropologies to keep us at least theoretically set apart from other men.

Nationalism is a transition between an old and a new human order. But even now we are not really fighting a war of nations; we are fighting a war of fictions, from which a new vision of the order of nature will someday emerge. The future, just now, lies wide open—open and dark, like interstellar space; but in that emptiness there is room for new gods, new cultures, mysterious now and nameless as an unborn child.

## SUGGESTIONS FOR DISCUSSION

• What, in Professor Langer's terms, makes Man (including you) the Prince of Creation? How, in her view, do "symbols," "meanings," "power of abstraction," "conception," "reason," "myth," and "language" make Man superior to animals? Can you restate, using either her terms or your own, her explanation of Man's unique position among the creatures of the Earth?

• On the one hand, Professor Langer sees security, strength, and reason in Man's ability to use language; on the other, she sees danger, weakness, and madness. Can you give concrete instances that exemplify these paradoxes?

• Explain why Professor Langer describes any national state (including the United States) as a man-made symbol. What exactly does the nation-state symbolize? Do you agree with her conclusion that national states have outlived their purpose, that they are "conceptions" that have been outmoded by world conditions during and after World War II? Is her conclusion valid today? If you agree with her, explain why. Do you agree with her call for a "culture of world citizenship"? If you disagree, can you find that point in her essay where your disagreement begins?

• The flag is the most obvious example of a visual symbol of nationalism. Professor Langer says there is "no flag over the country where a wolf is king; he is king where he happens to prowl, so long as he is there. But men, who can embody ideas and set them up to view, oppress each other by symbols of might." Is the American flag a visual symbol of might? Did the addition of "under God" to the pledge of allegiance mean the symbol is also of "right"? What *does* the American flag symbolize?

• Marshall McLuhan and his followers have suggested that a way to "escape the tyrannies" is to turn from the spoken and written word to the new "languages" of the twentieth century, particularly television. What do you see as the possibilities of film and television in directing us toward a culture of world citizenship? Why, since the development of television after World War II, hasn't world citizenship advanced?

# 2

## PEOPLE

Students, instructors, and even deans are fallible human beings, with egos as well as minds, with blind spots as well as intellectual vision, with hearts as well as wrist watches that signal the end of the fifty-minute academic "hour." This chapter is by them and about them, recording their humanity or lack of it as it emerges (or fails to emerge) in the teaching-learning situation.

Herbert Gold's essay explains why he left teaching after one year; Marion Dunham, a freshman student, retorts that his compromise is a cop-out. Lionel Trilling's classic short story, "Of This Time, Of That Place," touches on the near-panic a student's love engenders in a young professor; it also deals with poetry and nonconformity, compromise and security. Jerry Farber, a teacher, uses a student publication and a student's language to incite not riot, but change. Poems by Langston Hughes, Harold Witt, Theodore Roethke, and John Berryman, and poetic statements by Austin Warren comment on the fragile quality of human relationships, especially when problems of race, sex, ego, and authority enter the classroom.

# A Dog in Brooklyn,
# A Girl in Detroit:
# Life Among the Humanities

*Herbert Gold*

*Herbert Gold, born in 1924, has won many literary awards for his fiction.* Fathers *and* The Great American Jackpot *are two of his recent novels.*

What better career for a boy who seeks to unravel the meaning of our brief span on earth than that of philosopher? We all wonder darkly, in the forbidden hours of the night, punishing our parents and building a better world, with undefined terms. Soon, however, most of us learn to sleep soundly; or we take to pills or love-making; or we call ourselves insomniacs, not philosophers. A few attempt to define the terms.

There is no code number for the career of philosophy in school, the Army, or out beyond in real life. The man with a peculiar combination of melancholic, nostalgic, and reforming instincts stands at three possibilities early in his youth. He can choose to be a hero, an artist, or a philosopher. In olden times, war, say, or the need to clean out the old west, might make up his mind for him. The old west had been pretty well cleaned up by the time I reached a man's estate, and Gary Cooper could finish the job. Heroism was an untimely option. With much bureaucratic confusion I tried a bit of heroic war, got stuck in the machine, and returned to the hectic, Quonset campus of the G.I. Bill, burning to Know, Understand, and Convert. After a season of ferocious burrowing in books, I was ready to be a Teacher, which seemed a stern neighbor thing to Artist and Philosopher. I took on degrees, a Fulbright fellowship, a wife, a child, a head crammed with foolish questions and dogmatic answers despite the English school of linguistic analysis. I learned to smile, pardner, when I asked questions of philosophers trained at Oxford or Cambridge, but I asked them nonetheless. I signed petitions against McCarthy, wrote a novel, went on a treasure hunt, returned to my roots in the Middle West and stood rooted there, discussed the menace of the mass media, and had another child.

By stages not important here, I found myself teaching the Humanities at Wayne University in Detroit. I am now going to report a succession of classroom events which, retrospectively, seems to have determined my abandonment of formal dealing with this subject. The evidence does not, however, render any conclusion about education in the "Humanities" logically impregnable. It stands for a state of mind and is no substitute for formal argument. However, states of mind are important in this area of experience and meta-experience. However and however: it happens that most of the misty exaltation of the blessed vocation of the teacher issues from the offices of deans, editors, and college presidents. The encounter with classroom reality has caused many teachers, like Abelard meeting the relatives of Eloise, to lose their bearings. Nevertheless this is a memoir, not a campaign, about a specific life in and out of the Humanities. Though I am not a great loss to the History of Everything in Culture, my own eagerness to teach is a loss to me.

News item of a few years ago. A young girl and her date are walking along a street in Brooklyn, New York. The girl notices that they are being followed by an enormous Great Dane. The dog is behaving peculiarly, showing its teeth and making restless movements. A moment later, sure enough, the dog, apparently maddened, leaps slavering upon the girl, who is borne to earth beneath its weight. With only an instant's hesitation, the boy jumps on the dog. Its fangs sunk in one, then in the other, the dog causes the three of them to roll like beasts across the sidewalk.

A crowd gathers at a safe distance to watch. No one interferes. They display the becalmed curiosity of teevee viewers.

A few moments later a truck driver, attracted by the crowd,

pulls his vehicle over to the curb. This brave man is the only human being stirred personally enough to leave the role of passive spectator. Instantaneously analyzing the situation, he leaps into the struggle—*attacking and beating the boy.* He has naturally assumed that the dog must be protecting an innocent young lady from the unseemly actions of a juvenile delinquent.

I recounted this anecdote in the classroom in order to introduce a course which attempted a summary experience of Humanities 610 for a monumental nine credits. There were a number of points to be made about the passivity of the crowd ("don't get involved," "not my business") and the stereotypical reaction of the truck driver who had been raised to think of man's best friend as not another human being but a dog. In both cases, addicted to entertainment and clichés, the crowd and the trucker could not recognise what was actually happening before their eyes; they responded irrelevantly to the suffering of strangers; they were not a part of the main. This led us to a discussion of the notion of "community." In a closely-knit society, the people on the street would have known the couple involved and felt a responsibility towards them. In a large city, everyone is a stranger. (Great art can give a sense of the brotherhood of men. Religion used to do this, too.) "Any questions?" I asked, expecting the authority of religion to be defended.

An eager hand shot up. Another. Another. Meditative bodies sprawled in their chairs. "Are all New Yorkers like that?" "Well, what can you do if there's a mad dog and you're not expecting it?" "Where does it say in what great book how you got to act in Brooklyn?"

I took note of humor in order to project humorousness. I found myself composing my face in the look of thought which teevee panelists use in order to project thinking. I discovered a serious point to elaborate—several. I mentioned consciousness and relevance and the undefined moral suggestion implied by the labor which produces any work of art or mind. A girl named Clotilda Adams asked me: "Why don't people try to get along better in this world?"

Somewhat digressively, we then discussed the nature of heroism, comparing the behavior of the boy and the truck driver. Both took extraordinary risks; why? We broke for cigarettes in the autumn air outside. Then, for fifty minutes more, we raised these interesting questions, referring forward to Plato, Aristotle, St. Thomas, Dostoevsky, Tolstoy, William James, and De Gaulle; and then boy, dog, girl, truck driver and crowd were left with me and the crowned ghosts of history in the deserted room while my students went on to Phys Ed, Music Appreciation, Sosh, and their other concerns. Having been the chief speaker, both dramatist and analyst, I was exalted by the lofty ideas floated up into the air around me. I was a little let down to return to our real life in which dog-eat-dog is man's closest pal. Fact. Neither glory nor pleasure nor power, and certainly not wisdom, provided the goal of my students. Not even wealth was the aim of most of them. They sought to make out, to do all right, more prideful than amorous in love, more security-hungry than covetous in status. I saw my duty as a teacher: Through the Humanities, to awaken them to the dream of mastery over the facts of our lives. I saw my duty plain: Through the Humanities, to lead them toward the exaltation of knowledge and the calm of control. I had a whole year in which to fulfill this obligation. It was a two-semester course.

Before she left the room, Clotilda Adams said, "You didn't answer my question." Fact.

Outside the university enclave of glass and grass, brick and trees, Detroit was agonizing in its last big year with the big cars. Automation, dispersion of factories, and imported automobiles were eroding a precarious confidence. Fear was spreading; soon the landlords would offer to decorate apartments and suffer the pain. Detroit remembered the war years with nostalgia. Brave days, endless hours, a three-shift clock, insufficient housing, men sleeping in the all-night, triple-feature movies on Woodward and Grand River. Though the area around the Greyhound and Trailways stations was still clotted with the hopeful out of the hill country of the mid-south and the driven from the deep south— they strolled diagonally across the boulevards, entire families holding hands—some people suspected what was already on its way down the road: twenty per cent unemployment in Detroit.

The semester continued. We churned through the great books. One could classify my students in three general groups, intelligent, mediocre, and stupid, allowing for the confusions of three general factors—background, capacity, and interest. This was how we classified the Humanities, too: ancient, medieval, and modern. It made a lot of sense, and it made me itch, scratch, and tickle. Series of three form nice distinctions. According to Jung and other authorities, they have certain mythic significances. The course was for nine credits. All the arts were touched upon. We obeyed Protagoras; man, just man, was our study. When I cited him—"the proper study of man is Man"—Clotilda Adams stirred uneasily in her seat. "By which Protagoras no doubt meant woman, too," I assured her. She rested.

Now imagine the winter coming and enduring, with explosions of storm and exfoliations of gray slush, an engorged industrial sky overhead and sinus trouble all around. The air was full of acid and a purplish, spleeny winter mist. Most of Detroit, in Indian times before the first French trappers arrived, had been a swamp and below sea level. The swamp was still present, but invisible; city stretched out in all directions, crawling along the highways. Though Detroit was choked by a dense undergrowth of streets and buildings, irrigated only by super-highways, its work was done with frantic speed. The Rouge plant roared, deafened. The assembly lines clanked to the limit allowed by the UAW. The old Hudson factory lay empty, denuded, waiting to become a parking lot. Then the new models were being introduced! Buick! Pontiac! Dodge! Ford and Chevrolet! Ford impudently purchased a huge billboard faced towards the General Motors Building on Grand Boulevard. General Motors retaliated by offering free ginger ale to all comers, and a whole bottle of Vernor's to take home if you would only consent to test-drive the new Oldsmobile, the car with the . . . I've forgotten what it had that year. All over town the automobile companies were holding revival meetings; hieratic salesmen preached to the converted and the hangers-back alike; lines at the loan companies stretched through the revolving doors and out on to the winter pavements. But many in those lines were trying to get additional financing on their last year's cars. The new models were an indifferent success despite all the uproar of display and Detroit's patriotic attention to it. Searchlights sliced up the heavens while the city lay under flu.

Teachers at Wayne University soon learn not to tease the American Automobile. *Lèse* Chrysler was a moral offense, an attack on the livelihood and the sanctity of the American garage. Detroit was a town in which men looked at hub caps as men elsewhere have sometimes looked at ankles. The small foreign car found itself treated with a violent Halloween kidding-on-the-square, scratched, battered, and smeared (another Jungian series of three!). A passionate and sullen town, Detroit had no doubts about its proper business. All it doubted was everything else.

I often failed at inspiring my students to do the assigned reading. Many of them had part-time jobs in the automobile industry or its annexes. Even a Philosopher found it difficult to top the argument, "I couldn't read the book this week, I have to *work*," with its implied reproach for a scholar's leisure. But alas, many of these stricken proletarians drove freshly-minted automobiles. They worked in order to keep up the payments, racing like laboratory mice around the cage of depreciation. Certain faculty deep thinkers, addicted to broad understanding of the problems of others, argued that these students were so poor they *had* to buy new cars in order to restore their confidence. The finance companies seemed to hear their most creative expressions, not me. Deep in that long Detroit winter, I had the task of going from the pre-Socratic mystics all the way to Sartre, for nine credits. Like an audio-visual monkey, I leapt from movie projector to records to slides, with concurrent deep labor in book and tablet. We read *The Brothers Karamazov*, but knowing the movie did not give credit. We studied *The Waste Land,* and reading the footnotes did not suffice. We listened to Wanda Landowska play the harpsichord on records. We sat in the dark before a slide of Seurat's "La Grande Jatte" while I explained the importance of the measles of *pointillisme* to students who only wanted to see life clear and true, see it comfortably. Clotilda Adams said that this kind of painting hurt her eyes. She said that there was too much reading for one course—"piling it on. This isn't the only course we take." She said that she liked music, though. Moses only had to bring the Law down the mountain to the children of Israel; I had to bring it pleasingly.

We made exegeses. I flatly turned down the request of a dean that I take attendance. As a statesmanlike compromise, I tested regularly for content and understanding.

Then, on a certain morning, I handed back some quiz papers at the beginning of class. Out on the street, a main thoroughfare through town, it was snowing; this was one of those magical days of late winter snowfall—pale, cold, clean, and the entire city momentarily muffled by the silence of snow. The room hissed with steam heat; a smell of galoshes and mackinaws arose from the class. "Let us not discuss the test—let us rise above grades. Let us try to consider nihilism as a byproduct of the Romantic revival—" I had just begun my lecture when an odd clashing, lumping noise occurred on Cass Avenue. "Eliot's later work, including *The Four Quartets,* which we will not discuss here. . . ."

But I was interrupted by a deep sigh from the class. A product of nihilism and the romantic revival? No. It was that strange tragic sigh of horror and satisfaction. Out in the street, beyond the window against which I stood, a skidding truck had sideswiped a taxi. The truck driver had parked and gone into a drugstore. The cab was smashed like a cruller. From the door, the driver had emerged, stumbling drunkenly on the icy road, holding his head. There was blood on his head. There was blood on his hands. He clutched his temples. The lines of two-way traffic, moving very slowly in the snow and ice, carefully avoided hitting him. There were streaks of perforated and patterned snow, frothed up by tyres. He was like an island around which the sea of traffic undulated in slow waves; but he was an island that moved in the sea and held hands to head. He slid and stumbled back and forth, around and about his cab in the middle of the wide street. He was in confusion, in shock. Even at this distance I could see blood on the new-fallen snow. Drivers turned their heads upon him like angry Halloween masks, but did not get involved. Snow spit at his feet.

No one in the class moved. The large window through which we gazed was like a screen, with the volume turned down by habit, by snow, by a faulty tube. As the teacher, my authority took precedence. I ran out to lead the cab driver into the building. An elderly couple sat huddled in the car, staring at the smashed door, afraid to come out the other. They said they were unhurt.

I laid the man down on the floor. He was bleeding from the head and his face was a peculiar purplish color, with a stubble of beard like that of a dead man. There was a neat prick in his forehead where the union button in his cap had been driven into the skin. I sent a student to call for an ambulance. The cab driver's color was like that of the bruised industrial sky. "You be okay till the ambulance—?"

Foolish question. No alternative. No answer.

We waited. The class was restless. When they weren't listening to me, or talking to themselves, or smudging blue books in an exam, they did not know what to do in this room devoted to the specialized absorption of ideas. Silence. Scraping of feet, crisping of paper. We watched the slow-motion traffic on the street outside.

The cab driver moved once in a rush, turning over face down against the floor, with such force that I thought he might break his nose. Then slowly, painfully, as if in a dream, he turned back and lay staring at the ceiling. His woollen lumberjacket soaked up the blood trickling from one ear; the blood travelled up separated cilia of wool which drew it in with a will of their own. There was a swaying, osmotic movement like love-making in the eager little wisps of wool. An astounded ring of Humanities 610 students watched, some still holding their returned quiz papers. One girl in particular, Clotilda Adams, watched him and me with her eyes brilliant, wet, and bulging, and her fist crumpling the paper. I tried by imagining it to force the ambulance through the chilled and snowfallen city. I saw it weaving around the injured who strutted with shock over ice and drift, its single red Cyclop's eye turning, the orderlies hunched over on benches, chewing gum and cursing the driver. The ambulance did not arrive. Clotilda Adams' eye had a thick, impenetrable sheen over it. She watched from the cab driver to me as if we were in some way linked. When would the authorities get there? When the medics? There must have been many accidents in town, and heart attacks, and fires with cases of smoke inhalation.

Before the ambulance arrived, the police were there. They came strolling into the classroom with their legs apart, as if they remembered ancestors who rode the plains. Their mouths were heavy in thought. They had noses like salamis, red and mottled with fat. They were angry at the weather, at the school, at the crowd, at me, and especially at the prostrate man at our feet. He gave them a means to the creative expression of pique. (Everyone needs an outlet.)

Now Clotilda Adams took a step backward, and I recall thinking this odd. She had been treading hard near the pool of blood about the cab driver, but when the cops strolled up, she drifted toward the outer edge of the group of students, with a sly look of caution in her downcast, sideways-cast eyes. Her hand still crisped at the returned exam paper. This sly, lid-fallen look did not do her justice. She was a hard little girl of the sort often thought to be passionate—skinny but well-breasted, a high hard rump with a narrow curve, a nervous mouth.

The two policemen stood over the body of the cab driver. They stared at him in the classic pose—one cop with a hand resting lightly on the butt of his gun and the other on his butt, the younger cop with lips so pouted that his breath made a snuffling sound in his nose. They both had head colds. Their Ford was pulled up on the snow-covered lawn outside, with raw muddled marks of tread in the soft dirt. When the snow melted, there would be wounded streaks in the grass. The cab driver closed his eyes under the finicking, distasteful examination. At last one spoke: "See your driver's license."

The cab driver made a clumsy gesture towards his pocket. The cop bent and went into the pocket. He flipped open the wallet, glanced briefly at the photographs and cash, glanced at me, and then began lip-reading the license.

The cab driver was in a state of shock. There was a mixture of thin and thick blood on his clothes and messing the floor. "This man is badly hurt," I said. "Can't we get him to the hospital first?"

"This is only your *driver* license," the cop said slowly, having carefully read through Color of Hair: *Brn,* Color of Eyes: *Brn,* and checked each item with a stare at the man on the floor. "Let me see your chauffeur license."

"He's badly hurt," I said. "Get an ambulance."

"Teach'," said the older cop, "you know your business? We know ours."

"It's on the way," said the other. "Didn't you call it yourself?"

"No, one of the students. . . ." I said.

He grinned with his great victory. "So—don't you trust your pupils neither?"

Shame. I felt shame at this ridicule of my authority in the classroom. A professor is not a judge, a priest, or a sea captain; he does not have the right to perform marriages on the high seas of audio-visual aids and close reasoning. But he is more than an intercom between student and fact; he can be a stranger to love for his students, but not to a passion for his subject; he is a student himself; his pride is lively. The role partakes of a certain heft and control. There is power to make decisions, power to abstain, power to bewilder, promote, hold back, adjust, and give mercy; power, an investment of pride, a risk of shame.

Clotilda Adams, still clutching her exam, stared at me with loathing. She watched me bested by the police. She barely glanced, and only contemptuously, at the man bleeding from the head on the floor. She moved slightly forward again in order to participate fully in an action which apparently had some important meaning for her. She had lost her fear of the police when she saw how we all stood with them. The limits were established.

The police were going through the cab driver's pockets. They took out a folding pocketknife and cast significant looks at it and at each other. It had a marbled plastic hilt, like a resort souvenir. It was attached to a key ring.

"Hey!" one said to the half-conscious man. "What's this knife for?"

"Where'd you get them keys?" the other demanded, prodding the cabbie with his toe.

"A *skeleton* key. These cab companies," one of the cops decided to explain to Clotilda Adams, who was standing nearby, "they get the dregs. Hillbillies, you know?"

I said nothing, found nothing to say. I now think of Lord Acton's famous law, which is accepted as true the way it was uttered. The opposite is also true—the commoner's way: Having no power corrupts; having absolutely no power corrupts absolutely.

The bleeding seemed to have stopped. The cab driver sat up, looking no better, with his bluish, greenish, drained head hanging between his knees. His legs were crumpled stiffly. He propped himself on his hands. The police shot questions at him. He mumbled, mumbled, explained, explained.

"How long you been in Detroit? How come you come out of the mountains?"

"Why you pick up this fare?"

"What makes you think Cass is a one-way street?"

Mumbling and mumbling, explaining and explaining, the

cab driver tried to satisfy them. He also said: "Hurt. Maybe you get me to the hospital, huh? Hurt real bad."

"Maybe," said one of the cops, "maybe we take you to the station house first. That boy you hit says reckless driving. I think personally you'd flunk the drunk test—what you think, Teach'?"

I sent one of the students to call for an ambulance again. In the infinitesimal pause between my suggestion and his action, an attentive reluctant expectant caesura, I put a dime in his hand for the call. One of the cops gave me that long look described by silent movie critics as the slow burn. "They drive careful," he finally said. "It's snowing. They got all that expensive equipment."

The snow had started again outside the window. The skid-marks on the lawn were covered. Though the sky was low and gray, the white sifting down gave a peaceful village glow to this industrial Detroit. Little gusts barely rattled the windows. With the class, the cops, and the driver, we were living deep within a snowy paper weight. I felt myself moving very slowly, swimming within thick glass, like the loosened plastic figure in a paper weight. The snow came down in large torn flakes, all over the buildings of Wayne University, grass, trees, and the pale radiance of a network of slow-motion super-highways beyond. Across the street a modern building—glass and aluminum strips—lay unfinished in this weather. Six months ago there had been a student boarding house on that spot, filled with the artists and the beat, the guitar-wielders and the modern dancers, with a tradition going all the way back to the Korean war. Now there were wheelbarrows full of frozen cement; there were intentions to build a Japanese garden, with Japanese proportions and imported goldfish.

My student returned from the telephone. He had reached a hospital.

The cab driver was fading away. Rootlets of shock hooded his eyes: the lid was closing shut. A cop asked him another question—what the button on his cap stood for—it was a union button—and then the man just went reclining on his elbow, he slipped slowly down, he lay in the little swamp of crusted blood on the floor. You know what happens when milk is boiled? The crust broke like the crust of boiled milk when a spoon goes into coffee. The cop stood with a delicate, disgusted grimace on his face. What a business to be in, he seemed to be thinking. In approximately ten years, at age forty-two, he could retire and sit comfortable in an undershirt, with a non-returnable can of beer, before the color teevee. He could relax. He could *start* to relax. But in the meantime—nag, nag, nag. Drunk cabbies, goddam hillbillies. The reckless driver on the floor seemed to sleep. His lips moved. He was alive.

Then a puffing intern rushed into the room. I had not heard the ambulance. The policeman gave room and the intern kneeled. He undid his bag. The orderlies glanced at the floor and went back out for their stretcher.

I stood on one side of the body, the kneeling intern with his necklace of stethoscope, and the two meditative cops. On the other side was the group of students, and at their head, like a leader filled with wrath, risen in time of crisis, stood Clotilda Adams, still clutching her exam paper. There were tears in her eyes. She was in a fury. She had been thinking all this time, and now her thinking had issue: *rage*. Over the body she handed me a paper, crying out, "I don't think I deserved a *D* on that quiz. I answered all the questions. I can't get my credit for Philo of Ed without I get a *B* off you."

I must have looked at her with pure stupidity on my face. There is a Haitian proverb: Stupidity won't kill you, but it'll make you sweat a lot. She took the opportunity to make me sweat, took my silence for guilt, took my openmouthed gaze for weakness. She said: "If I was a white girl, you'd grade me easier."

Guilt, a hundred years, a thousand years of it; pity for the disaster of ignorance and fear, pity for ambition rising out of ignorance; adoration of desire; trancelike response to passion—passion which justifies itself because passionate. . . . I looked at her with mixed feelings. I could not simply put her down. In order to *put down,* your own mind must be made up, put down. She had beauty and dignity, stretched tall and wrathful, with teeth for biting and eyes for striking dead.

"But I know my rights," she said, "*mister*. My mother told me about your kind—lent my father money on his car and then hounded him out of town. He's been gone since fifty-three. But you can't keep us down forever, no sir, you can't always keep us down—"

She was talking and I was yelling. She was talking and yelling about injustice and I, under clamps, under ice, was yelling in a whisper about the sick man. She was blaming me for all her troubles, all the troubles she had seen, and I was blaming her for not seeing what lay before her, and we were making an appointment to meet in my office and discuss this thing more calmly, Miss Adams. Okay. All right. Later.

The police, the doctor, the orderlies, and the injured cab driver were gone. The police car out front was gone and the snow was covering its traces. The janitor came in and swept up the blood-stains with green disinfectant powder. The frightened couple in the cab were released. They all disappeared silently into the great city, into the routine of disaster and recovery of a great city. I dismissed the class until tomorrow.

The next day I tried to explain to Miss Adams what I meant about her failing to respond adequately to the facts of our life together. Her mouth quivered. Yesterday rage; today a threat of tears. What did I mean she wasn't *adequate?* What did I know about adequate anyhow? Nothing. Just a word. Agreed, Miss Adams. I was trying to say that there were two questions at issue between us—her exam grade and her choice of occasion to dispute it. I would like to discuss each matter separately. I tried to explain why putting the two events together had disturbed me. I tried to explain the notions of empirical evidence and metaphor. Finally I urged her to have her exam looked at by the head of the department, but she refused because she knew in advance that he would support me. "White is Right," she said.

"Do you want to drop out of the class?"

"No. I'll stay," she said with a sudden patient, weary acceptance of her fate. "I'll do what I can."

"I'll do what I can too," I said.

She smiled hopefully at me. She was tuckered out by the continual alert for combat everywhere. She was willing to forgive and go easy. When she left my office, this smile, shy, pretty, and conventional, tried to tell me that she could be generous—a friend.

We had come to Thomas Hobbes and John Locke in our tour through time and the river of humanities. I pointed out that the English philosophers were noted for clarity and eloquence of style. I answered this question: The French? Isn't French noted for clarity? Yes, they too, but they were more abstract. On the whole. In general.

The class took notes on the truths we unfolded together. Spring came and the snow melted. There was that brief Detroit flowering of the new season—jasmine and hollyhocks—which, something like it, must have captivated the Frenchman Antoine de la Mothe Cadillac when he paused on the straits of Detroit in 1701. University gardeners planted grass seed where the patrol car had parked on the lawn. The new models, all except the Cadillac, were going at mean discounts.

"The 'Humanities,'" wrote Clotilda Adams in her final essay, "are a necessary additive to any teacher's development worth her 'salt' in the perilous times of today. The West and the 'Free World' must stand up to the war of ideas against the 'Iron' Curtain." This was in answer to a question about Beethoven, Goethe, and German romanticism. She did not pass the course, but she was nevertheless admitted on probation to the student teacher program because of the teacher shortage and the great need to educate our children in these perilous times. Of today.

Humanities 610 provided ballast for the ship of culture as it pitched and reeled in the heavy seas of real life; I lashed myself to the mast, but after hearing the siren song of grand course outlines, I cut myself free and leaned over the rail with the inside of my lip showing.

It would be oversimplifying to say that I left off teaching Humanities merely because of an experience. Such an argument is fit to be published under the title "I was a Teen-Age Humanities Professor." I also left for fitter jobs, more money, a different life. Still, what I remember of the formal study of Truth and Beauty, for advanced credit in education, is a great confusion of generalities, committees, conferences, audio-visual importunities, and poor contact. "Contact!" cried the desperate deans and chairmen, like radio operators in ancient war movies. And much, much discussion of how to get through to the students. How to get through? Miss Adams and Mr. Gold, cab driver and Thomas Hobbes, policemen and the faceless student who paused an instant for a dime for the telephone—we all have to discover how relevant we are to each other. Or do we *have* to? No, we can merely perish, shot down like mad dogs or diminished into time with no more than a glimpse of the light.

Words fade; our experience does not touch; we make do with babble and time-serving. We need to learn the meaning of words, the meaning of the reality those words refer to; we must clasp reality close. We cannot flirt forever, brown-nosing or brow-beating. We must act and build out of our own spirits. How? How? We continually need new politics, new cities, new marriages and families, new ways of work and leisure. We also need the fine old ways. For me, the primitive appeal to pleasure and pain of writing stories is a possible action, is the way in and out again, as teaching was not. As a teacher, I caught my students too late and only at the top of their heads, at the raw point of pride and ambition, and I had not enough love and pressure as a teacher to open the way through their intentions to the common human-ity which remains locked within. As a writer, I could hope to hit them in their bodies and needs, where lusts and ideals are murkily nurtured together, calling to the prime fears and joys directly, rising with them from the truths of innocence into the truths of experience.

The peculiar combination of ignorance and jadedness built into most institutions is a desperate parody of personal innocence, personal experience. Nevertheless, education, which means a drawing out—even formal education, a formal drawing out—is a variety of experience, and experience is the only evidence we have. After evidence comes our thinking upon it. Do the scientists, secreting their honey in distant hives, hear the barking of the black dog which follows them? Will the politicians accept the lead of life, or will they insist on a grade of *B* in Power and Domina-tion over a doomed race? We need to give proper answers to the proper questions.

Particular life is still the best map to truth. When we search our hearts and strip our pretenses, we all know this. Particular life—we know only what we *know*. Therefore the policemen stay with me: I have learned to despise most authority. The cab driver remains in his sick bleeding: pity for the fallen and helpless. And I think of Clotilda Adams in her power and weakness; like the cops, she has an authority of stupidity; like the victim of an acci-dent, she is fallen and helpless. But some place, since we persist in our cold joke against the ideal of democracy, the cops still have the right to push people around, Clotilda is leading children in the Pledge of Allegiance. We must find a way to teach better and to learn.

# The Talker

*Mona Van Duyn*

One person present steps on his pedal of speech
and, like a faulty drinking fountain, it spurts
all over the room in facts and puns and jokes,
on books, on people, on politics, on sports,

on everything. Two or three others, gathered
to chat, must bear his unending monologue
between their impatient heads like a giant buzz
of a giant fly, or magnanimous bullfrog

croaking for all the frogs in the world. Amid
the screech of traffic or in a hubbub crowd
he climbs the decibels toward some glorious view.
I think he only loves himself out loud.

## SUGGESTIONS FOR DISCUSSION

• Gold's personal-experience essay exposes the perhaps irreconcilable separation between the Humanities as they are taught in the classroom and human behavior in the real world. Gold assumed, when he entered teaching, that one outcome of education in the Humanities would be humanitarian behavior. If you were to enroll in a Humanities class, would you expect such an outcome? Is there any other reason for teaching the courses generally covered in the Humanities?

• One instance of "man's inhumanity to man" offered by Gold to his class is from the world of fact as reported by a newspaper. Gold analyzes the passivity of the crowd ("They display the becalmed curiosity of teevee viewers") as due to an addiction "to entertainment and clichés." Can television be blamed for the failure of people to get involved in others' suffering? Is this casual theory of human behavior any more or any less valid than the apparently opposite view that people who witness violence on television are more prone to acting in violent ways themselves?

• If TV and/or great humanistic books cannot teach people to treat each other humanely, what can? Can model behavior? Does Gold seem to subscribe to the "model-behavior" theory when he writes about his disappointment with his students when reality entered the classroom?

• Clotilda's timing is inappropriate in Gold's terms; can you justify it in her terms? Is there anything in Gold's writing about himself that suggests that Clotilda might have been right in accusing him: "If I was a white girl, you'd grade me easier"?

• Gold blames Clotilda "for not seeing what lay before her." What would have happened if Gold, instead of making an appointment to see her in his office later and discuss things more calmly, had replied to Clotilda's accusation: "Yes, I might have graded you differently. And if the guy lying there were black, you might regard his suffering differently."

• Do you think that Gold's decision to quit teaching was based on a realistic appraisal of the experiences he describes? Do you think he made the right decision? Given the same experiences, would you have made the same decision?

# Theme for English B

*Langston Hughes*

*Langston Hughes (1902–67), black American poet, began writing poetry in high school and had his first pieces published in the school paper. What it means to be black is a central theme in most of his poetry, which has won many awards and has been widely translated and read abroad. He also wrote a number of plays (including Mulatto) and songs. This poem obviously is related to the stories by Gold and Trilling in this section.*

The instructor said,

>Go home and write
>a page tonight.
>And let that page come out of you—
>Then, it will be true.

I wonder if it's that simple?
I am twenty-two, colored, born in Winston-Salem.
I went to school there, then Durham, then here
to this college on the hill above Harlem.
I am the only colored student in my class.
The steps from the hill lead down into Harlem,
through a park, then I cross St. Nicholas,
Eighth Avenue, Seventh, and I come to the Y,
the Harlem Branch Y, where I take the elevator
up to my room, sit down, and write this page:

It's not easy to know what is true for you or me
at twenty-two, my age. But I guess I'm what

I feel and see and hear, Harlem, I hear you:
hear you, hear me—we two—you, me, talk on this page.
(I hear New York, too.) Me—who?

Well, I like to eat, sleep, drink, and be in love.
I like to work, read, learn, and understand life.
I like a pipe for a Christmas present,
or records—Bessie, bop, or Bach.
I guess being colored doesn't make me *not* like
the same things other folks like who are other races.
So will my page be colored that I write?
Being me, it will not be white.
But it will be
a part of you, instructor.
You are white—
yet a part of me, as I am a part of you.
That's American.
Sometimes perhaps you don't want to be a part of me.
Nor do I often want to be a part of you.
But we are, that's true!
As I learn from you,
I guess you learn from me—
although you're older—and white—
and somewhat more free.

This is my page for English B.

# Truth, Beauty and Sour Grapes, or: Is Gold Getting Rich Telling Us What Rotten Shape Society Is In?

*Marion Dunham*

*One freshman composition student had a passionate reaction to Gold's essay. Her paper suggests, in strong language, that Gold does not, and in fact cannot, practice what he preaches. Is the student's reaction to Gold justified? Does her lack of sympathy leave her open to the same kind of criticism that she dishes out to Gold?*

Herbert Gold's essay, "A Dog in Brooklyn, A Girl in Detroit" enraged me. I want to call him a phony and tear him apart. I want to expose his real motivation. I want to kick him in the gut for trying to do a guilt trip on me while he collects prestige and fat residuals. But that sounds too hostile, too aggressive.

The man can write. He accomplishes what he sets out to do. He hits in the body, in the needs, "where lusts and ideals are murkily nurtured together." He sounds pretty cynical. Maybe he's just not a good teacher. Sour grapes. I wonder about his background, his credentials, his personality. He says of himself: "I had not enough love or pressure as a teacher to open the way through their intentions to the common humanity which remains locked within." He sounds like an ivory-tower type who can't reconcile Truth and Beauty to reality. He gives himself away: "Having been the chief speaker, both dramatist and analyst, I was exalted by the lofty ideas floated up into the air around me. I was a little let down to return to our real life in which dog-eat-dog is man's closest pal." He's probably just another malcontent getting rich and famous by telling us what rotten shape society is in.

But his sensitivity makes me squirm. Maybe he was right in making a big thing about the dog incident. We are thick-skinned strangers to one another. How many times have I felt chagrined yet angered that we pass one another on narrow sidewalks, glancing away, refusing even to acknowledge each other's existence. I've wanted to cry out: Hey! We're made of the same stuff. I bet I can understand some of your feelings. . . . Bitch! And how many more times have I ignored a passing "someone" who was alive enough to greet me? I've wanted to turn back and yell, Wait! Let's try that over—maybe we could begin to change the world. We didn't make it this way. . . . You look sad. . . . Maybe. . . . Jerk! . . . Who cares!

Yet Herbert Gold copped out! He saw his duty plain. He had a whole year to fulfill his obligation. It was a two-semester course! Fact.

Is the man noble or just clever? There's not enough to go on. He tells the story but I wonder how accurate he is. The evidence "stands for a state of mind." A totally negative state of mind—to my way of thinking. I wonder if Herbert Gold says Hi to a stranger passing him on the street.

And, despite his keen, penetrating observations, isn't his an uncomfortably aloof sensitivity? Perhaps that's why I squirmed. Am I right in picking up the quality of condescension on his part? Was there ever any warmth in his feelings? He only tells his side—and very effectively cuts down everyone else he talks about.

I wouldn't be surprised to learn that he walked into that classroom with a big, ugly chip on his shoulder wanting only to dominate and control. It seems to me he was down on that whole period in his life. He speaks of community, involvement, responsibility towards each other. But he also speaks contemptuously of "bodies sprawled in their chairs." He cavalierly categorizes "intelligent, mediocre, and stupid" students. He brings in historic reference to the "swamp" of Detroit and despises the "stricken proletarians . . . racing like laboratory mice around the cage of depreciation." He oozes a generalization concerning loathing, but masks it in glib sarcasm: "Deep in that long Detroit winter, I had the task of going from the pre-Socratic mystics all the way to Sartre, for nine credits. Like an audio-visual monkey, I leapt from movie projector to records to slides. . . ." Nowhere in this essay could I detect any hint of even a budding rapport with his class or an attempt at establishing one. His very manner of speaking to them was a put-down: "Let us not discuss this test—let us rise above grades. Let us try to consider. . . ."

But the cab driver incident best reveals his own alienation and his egocentric thirst for power. Throughout that entire episode he was keenly aware—not of any particularly human feelings, but of the role he played and the power struggle in which he engaged with authority and responsibility, the police and his students. He said: "As the teacher, my authority took precedence. I ran out to lead the cab driver into the building." How kind. But how much better to have been able to say: "As a man, my compassion took precedence." After a feeble attempt at inane conversation, he was as uninvolved as those he condemned with subtle but caustic invective. He stepped outside himself, detached, schizophrenic, aware of the minute details of cilia of the wool in swaying, osmotic, love-making movement. But worse, he was inordinately concerned with face. And since "everyone needs an outlet," he seized the opportunity to mull on his fateful commentaries. Was he feeling any sympathy or even genuine concern for that injured cab driver while he coldly watched Clotilda Adams, attributing to her "sly" looks and calling her "a hard little girl of the *sort* . . ."? And doesn't he betray the fact that his hang-up with authority started before the "cops" with "noses like salamis" and "hand on butt" ever walked into that room?

I'm afraid that what really happened in that room was something that Gold had coming to him. I think he was threatened by the authority the police represented because his own classroom authority was so tenuous. He probably feared reprisal for the hatred he felt for his students.

He tried to take control by using the wounded man as a shield. Concern for his welfare should have been paramount. Insensitive, pig cops! When he was bested by the police, losing face in front of Clotilda Adams, he sputtered that he'd been shamed, his authority ridiculed. He protested that he was a "professor"— he couldn't be expected to handle every situation, but he was something important, "more than an intercom." He tried to defend himself, a professor "can be a stranger to love for his students, but not to a passion for his subject. . . ." And he digresses about "lively pride," the "role" partaking of "a certain heft and control" and "power."

Clotilda Adams was pretty perceptive for all her less favorable qualities. She knifed Gold in his pride, that vulnerable point which he had inadvertently exposed. He lined up physically on the side of authority—"on the side of the body" with the intern and the police. His students were on the other side. All he saw was "a leader filled with wrath." I wonder if she took his silence for guilt, his open-mouthed gaze for weakness, or if these weren't his own unconscious admissions. And oh, how noble, Mr. Gold, how superior of you to feel pity. Mr. Gold, pity is a "don't involve me" attitude. It lets you feel you've more than done your duty—you've been sensitive to another human being. Aware but not involved. It's too bad that nasty Clotilda Adams put two separate events together and it "disturbed" you. Shit on your notions of "empirical evidence and metaphor." You deserved to have your shabby Professor of Humanities Halloween-mask ripped off.

But even that wasn't enough to expose your common humanity. You had failed as a human being and as a teacher, so you copped out. Clotilda Adams didn't. She said she'd do what she could. She tried to tell you that she could be generous—a friend. And you locked yourself away even tighter, despising her power and weakness. Her power by virtue of her very existence to make you see your responsibility and your failure; the weakness of her need for your help and her submission to your power. You, with your elitist contemptuousness, persist in the cold joke against the ideal of democracy.

In the *Great Dialogues,* Plato gives a parable of education and ignorance as a description of man's nature. He concludes that the ignorant are not fit to be leaders of society and neither are those who spend their entire life in education. He says, "The first have no simple object in life," nothing to aim for, while "the second will never do anything if they can help it, believing they have already found mansions abroad in the Island of the Blest." I see Clotilda Adams and Herbert Gold in this parable. Plato goes on to say that it is only just to command just men to go back to the prisoners of ignorance, "to share their troubles and their honors whether they are worth having or not . . ." because only education and educated men can lead wisely. He says education "is more than a game; the turning round of a soul from a day which is like night to a true day—this is the ascent into real being, which we shall say is true philosophy."

# Of This Time, Of That Place

*Lionel Trilling*

*Lionel Trilling (1905–     ), teacher and literary critic, has spent his entire professional life in the academic world, for the most part at Columbia University. He was younger than the hero of the following story when he started teaching college English, and the story testifies to his intimate knowledge of the scene, at least from the instructor's point of view.*

It was a fine September day. By noon it would be summer again, but now it was true autumn with a touch of chill in the air. As Joseph Howe stood on the porch of the house in which he lodged, ready to leave for his first class of the year, he thought with pleasure of the long indoor days that were coming. It was a moment when he could feel glad of his profession.

On the lawn the peach tree was still in fruit and young Hilda Aiken was taking a picture of it. She held the camera tight against her chest. She wanted the sun behind her, but she did not want her own long morning shadow in the foreground. She raised the camera, but that did not help, and she lowered it, but that made things worse. She twisted her body to the left, then to the right. In the end she had to step out of the direct line of the sun. At last she snapped the shutter and wound the film with intense care.

Howe, watching her from the porch, waited for her to finish and called good morning. She turned, startled, and almost sullenly lowered her glance. In the year Howe had lived at the Aikens', Hilda had accepted him as one of her family, but since his absence of the summer she had grown shy. Then suddenly she lifted her head and smiled at him, and the humorous smile confirmed his pleasure in the day. She picked up her bookbag and set off for school.

The handsome houses on the streets to the college were not yet fully awake, but they looked very friendly. Howe went by the Bradby house where he would be a guest this evening at the first dinner party of the year. When he had gone the length of the picket fence, the whitest in town, he turned back. Along the path there was a fine row of asters and he went through the gate and picked one for his buttonhole. The Bradbys would be pleased if they happened to see him invading their lawn and the knowledge of this made him even more comfortable.

He reached the campus as the hour was striking. The students were hurrying to their classes. He himself was in no hurry. He stopped at his dim cubicle of an office and lit a cigarette. The prospect of facing his class had suddenly presented itself to him and his hands were cold; the lawful seizure of power he was about to make seemed momentous. Waiting did not help. He put out his cigarette, picked up a pad of theme paper, and went to his classroom.

As he entered, the rattle of voices ceased, and the twenty-odd freshmen settled themselves and looked at him appraisingly. Their faces seemed gross, his heart sank at their massed impassivity, but he spoke briskly.

'My name is Howe,' he said, and turned and wrote it on the blackboard. The carelessness of the scrawl confirmed his authority. He went on, 'My office is 412 Slemp Hall, and my office-hours are Monday, Wednesday and Friday from eleven-thirty to twelve-thirty.'

He wrote, 'M., W., F., 11:30–12:30.' He said, 'I'll be very glad to see any of you at that time. Or if you can't come then, you can arrange with me for some other time.'

He turned again to the blackboard and spoke over his shoulder. 'The text for the course is Jarman's *Modern Plays,* revised edition. The Co-op has it in stock.' He wrote the name, underlined 'revised edition' and waited for it to be taken down in the new notebooks.

When the bent heads were raised again he began his speech of prospectus. 'It is hard to explain—' he said, and paused as they composed themselves. 'It is hard to explain what a course like this is intended to do. We are going to try to learn something about modern literature and something about prose composition.'

As he spoke, his hands warmed and he was able to look directly at the class. Last year on the first day the faces had seemed just as cloddish, but as the term wore on they became gradually alive and quite likable. It did not seem possible that the same thing could happen again.

'I shall not lecture in this course,' he continued. 'Our work will be carried on by discussion and we will try to learn by an exchange of opinion. But you will soon recognize that my opinion is worth more than anyone else's here.'

He remained grave as he said it, but two boys understood and laughed. The rest took permission from them and laughed too. All Howe's private ironies protested the vulgarity of the joke, but the laughter made him feel benign and powerful.

When the little speech was finished, Howe picked up the pad of paper he had brought. He announced that they would write an extemporaneous theme. Its subject was traditional, 'Who I am and why I came to Dwight College.' By now the class was more at ease and it gave a ritualistic groan of protest. Then there was a stir as fountain pens were brought out and the writing-arms of the chairs were cleared, and the paper was passed about. At last, all the heads bent to work, and the room became still.

Howe sat idly at his desk. The sun shone through the tall clumsy windows. The cool of the morning was already passing. There was a scent of autumn and of varnish and the stillness of the room was deep and oddly touching. Now and then a student's head was raised and scratched in the old, elaborate students' pantomime that calls the teacher to witness honest intellectual effort.

Suddenly a tall boy stood within the frame of the open door. 'Is this,' he said, and thrust a large nose into a college catalogue, 'is this the meeting place of English 1A? The section instructed by Dr. Joseph Howe?'

He stood on the very sill of the door, as if refusing to enter until he was perfectly sure of all his rights. The class looked up from work, found him absurd and gave a low mocking cheer.

The teacher and the new student, with equal pointedness, ignored the disturbance. Howe nodded to the boy, who pushed his head forward and then jerked it back in a wide elaborate arc to clear his brow of a heavy lock of hair. He advanced into the room and halted before Howe, almost at attention. In a loud, clear voice he announced, 'I am Tertan, Ferdinand R., reporting at the direction of Head of Department Vincent.'

The heraldic formality of this statement brought forth another cheer. Howe looked at the class with a sternness he could not really feel, for there was indeed something ridiculous about this boy. Under his displeased regard the rows of heads dropped to work again. Then he touched Tertan's elbow, led him up to the desk and stood so as to shield their conversation from the class.

'We are writing an extemporaneous theme,' he said. 'The subject is, "Who I am and why I came to Dwight College." '

He stripped a few sheets from the pad and offered them to the boy. Tertan hesitated and then took the paper, but he held it only tentatively. As if with the effort of making something clear, he gulped, and a slow smile fixed itself on his face. It was at once knowing and shy.

'Professor,' he said, 'to be perfectly fair to my classmates'—he made a large gesture over the room—'and to you'—he inclined his head to Howe—'this would not be for me an extemporaneous subject.'

Howe tried to understand. 'You mean you've already thought about it—you've heard we always give the same subject? That doesn't matter.'

Again the boy ducked his head and gulped. It was the gesture of one who wishes to make a difficult explanation with perfect candor. 'Sir,' he said, and made the distinction with great care, 'the topic I did not expect, but I have given much ratiocination to the subject.'

Howe smiled and said, 'I don't think that's an unfair advantage. Just go ahead and write.'

Tertan narrowed his eyes and glanced sidewise at Howe. His strange mouth smiled. Then in quizzical acceptance, he ducked his head, threw back the heavy, dank lock, dropped into a seat with a great loose noise and began to write rapidly.

The room fell silent again and Howe resumed his idleness. When the bell rang, the students who had groaned when the task had been set now groaned again because they had not finished.

Howe took up the papers, and held the class while he made the first assignment. When he dismissed it, Tertan bore down on him, his slack mouth held ready for speech.

'Some professors,' he said, 'are pedants. They are Dryasdusts. However, some professors are free souls and creative spirits. Kant, Hegel and Nietzsche were all professors.' With this pronouncement he paused. 'It is my opinion,' he continued, 'that you occupy the second category.'

Howe looked at the boy in surprise and said with good-natured irony, 'With Kant, Hegel and Nietzsche?'

Not only Tertan's hand and head but his whole awkward body waved away the stupidity. 'It is the kind and not the quantity of the kind,' he said sternly.

Rebuked, Howe said as simply and seriously as he could, 'It would be nice to think so.' He added, 'Of course I am not a professor.'

This was clearly a disappointment but Tertan met it. 'In the French sense,' he said with composure. 'Generically, a teacher.'

Suddenly he bowed. It was such a bow, Howe fancied, as a stage-director might teach an actor playing a medieval student who takes leave of Abelard—stiff, solemn, with elbows close to the body and feet together. Then, quite as suddenly, he turned and left.

A queer fish, and as soon as Howe reached his office, he sifted through the batch of themes and drew out Tertan's. The boy had filled many sheets with his unformed headlong scrawl. 'Who am I?' he had begun. 'Here, in a mundane, not to say commercialized academe, is asked the question which from time long immemorably out of mind has accreted doubts and thoughts in the psyche of man to pester him as a nuisance. Whether in St. Augustine (or Austin as sometimes called) or Miss Bashkirtsieff or Frederic Amiel or Empedocles, or in less lights of the intellect than these, this posed question has been ineluctable.'

Howe took out his pencil. He circled 'academe' and wrote 'vocab.' in the margin. He underlined 'time long immemorably out of mind' and wrote 'Diction!' But this seemed inadequate for what was wrong. He put down his pencil and read ahead to discover the principle of error in the theme. 'Today as ever, in spite of gloomy prophets of the dismal science (economics) the question is uninvalidated. Out of the starry depths of heaven hurtles this spear of query demanding to be caught on the shield of the mind ere it pierces the skull and the limbs be unstrung.'

Baffled but quite caught, Howe read on. 'Materialism, by which is meant the philosophic concept and not the moral idea, provides no aegis against the question which lies beyond the tangible (metaphysics). Existence without alloy is the question presented. Environment and heredity relegated aside, the rags and old clothes of practical life discarded, the name and the instrumentality of livelihood do not, as the prophets of the dismal science insist on in this connection, give solution to the interrogation which not from the professor merely but veritably from the cosmos is given. I think, therefore I am (cogito etc.) but who am I? Tertan I am, but what is Tertan? Of this time, of that place, of some parentage, what does it matter?'

Existence without alloy: the phrase established itself. Howe put aside Tertan's paper and at random picked up another. 'I am Arthur J. Casebeer, Jr.,' he read. 'My father is Arthur J. Casebeer and my grandfather was Arthur J. Casebeer before him. My mother is Nina Wimble Casebeer. Both of them are college graduates and my father is in insurance. I was born in St. Louis eighteen years ago and we still make our residence there.'

Arthur J. Casebeer, who knew who he was, was less interesting than Tertan, but more coherent. Howe picked up Tertan's paper again. It was clear that none of the routine marginal comments, no 'sent. str.' or 'punct.' or 'vocab.' could cope with this torrential rhetoric. He read ahead, contenting himself with underscoring the errors against the time when he should have the necessary 'conference' with Tertan.

It was a busy and official day of cards and sheets, arrangements and small decisions, and it gave Howe pleasure. Even when it was time to attend the first of the weekly Convocations he felt the charm of the beginning of things when intention is still innocent and uncorrupted by effort. He sat among the young instructors on the platform, and joined in their humorous complaints at having to assist at the ceremony, but actually he got a clear satisfaction from the ritual of prayer, and prosy speech, and even from wearing his academic gown. And when the Convocation was over the pleasure continued as he crossed the campus, exchanging greetings with men he had not seen since the spring. They were people who did not yet, and perhaps never would, mean much to him, but in a year they had grown amiably to be part of his life. They were his fellow-townsmen.

The day had cooled again at sunset, and there was a bright chill in the September twilight. Howe carried his voluminous gown over his arm, he swung his doctoral hood by its purple neckpiece, and on his head he wore his mortarboard with its heavy gold tassel bobbing just over his eye. These were the weighty and absurd symbols of his new profession and they pleased him. At twenty-six Joseph Howe had discovered that he was neither so well off nor so bohemian as he had once thought. A small income, adequate when supplemented by a sizable cash legacy, was genteel poverty when the cash was all spent. And the literary life—the room at the Lafayette, or the small apartment without a lease, the long summers on the Cape, the long after-noons and the social evenings—began to weary him. His writing filled his mornings, and should perhaps have filled his life, yet it did not. To the amusement of his friends, and with a certain sense that he was betraying his own freedom, he had used the last of his legacy for a year at Harvard. The small but respectable reputation of his two volumes of verse had proved useful—he continued at Harvard on a fellowship and when he emerged as Doctor Howe he received an excellent appointment, with pros-pects, at Dwight.

He had his moments of fear when all that had ever been said of the dangers of the academic life had occurred to him. But after a year in which he had tested every possibility of corruption and seduction he was ready to rest easy. His third volume of verse, most of it written in his first years of teaching, was not only ampler but, he thought, better than its predecessors.

There was a clear hour before the Bradby dinner party, and Howe looked forward to it. But he was not to enjoy it, for lying with his mail on the hall table was a copy of this quarter's issue of *Life and Letters,* to which his landlord subscribed. Its severe cover announced that its editor, Frederic Woolley, had this month contributed an essay called "Two Poets," and Howe, picking it up, curious to see who the two poets might be, felt his own name start out at him with cabalistic power—Joseph Howe. As he con-tinued to turn the pages his hand trembled.

Standing in the dark hall, holding the neat little magazine, Howe knew that his literary contempt for Frederic Woolley meant nothing, for he suddenly understood how he respected Woolley in the way of the world. He knew this by the trembling of his hand. And of the little world as well as the great, for although the literary groups of New York might dismiss Woolley, his name carried high authority in the academic world. At Dwight it was even a revered name, for it had been here at the college that Frederic Woolley had made the distinguished scholarly career from which he had gone on to literary journalism. In middle life he had been induced to take the editorship of *Life and Letters,* a literary monthly not widely read but heavily endowed, and in its pages he had carried on the defense of what he sometimes called the older values. He was not without wit, he had great knowledge and considerable taste, and even in the full movement of the 'new' literature he had won a certain respect for his refusal to accept it. In France, even in England, he would have been connected with a more robust tradition of conservatism, but America gave him an audience not much better than genteel. It was known in the college that to the subsidy of *Life and Letters* the Bradbys contributed a great part.

As Howe read, he saw that he was involved in nothing less than an event. When the Fifth Series of *Studies in Order and Value* came to be collected, this latest of Frederic Woolley's essays would not be merely another step in the old direction. Clearly and unmistakably, it was a turning point. All his literary life Woolley had been concerned with the relation of literature to morality, religion, and the private and delicate pieties, and he had been unalterably opposed to all that he had called 'inhuman humanitarianism.' But here, suddenly, dramatically late, he had made an about-face, turning to the public life and to the humanitarian politics he had so long despised. This was the kind of incident the histories of literature make much of. Frederic Woolley was opening for himself a new career and winning a kind of new youth. He contrasted the two poets, Thomas Wormser, who was admirable, Joseph Howe, who was almost dangerous. He spoke of the 'precious subjectivism' of Howe's verse. 'In times like ours,' he wrote, 'with millions facing penury and want, one feels that the qualities of the *tour d'ivoire* are well-nigh inhuman, nearly insulting. The *tour d'ivoire* becomes the *tour d'ivresse,* and it is not self-intoxicated poets that our people need.' The essay said more: 'The problem is one of meaning. I am not ignorant that the creed of the esoteric poets declares that a poem does not and should not *mean* anything, that it *is* something. But poetry is what the poet makes it, and if he is a true poet he makes what his society needs. And what is needed now is the tradition in which Mr. Wormser writes, the true tradition of poetry. The Howes do no harm, but they do no good when positive good is demanded of all responsible men. Or do the Howes indeed do no harm? Perhaps Plato would have said they do, that in some ways theirs is the Phrygian music that turns men's minds from the struggle. Certainly it is true that Thomas Wormser writes in the lucid Dorian mode which sends men into battle with evil.'

It was easy to understand why Woolley had chosen to praise Thomas Wormser. The long, lilting lines of *Corn Under Willows* hymned, as Woolley put it, the struggle for wheat in the Iowa fields, and expressed the real lives of real people. But why out of the dozen more notable examples he had chosen Howe's little volume as the example of 'precious subjectivism' was hard to guess. In a way it was funny, this multiplication of himself into 'the Howes.' And yet this becoming the multiform political symbol by whose creation Frederic Woolley gave the sign of a sudden new life, this use of him as a sacrifice whose blood was necessary for the rites of rejuvenation, made him feel oddly unclean.

Nor could Howe get rid of a certain practical resentment. As a poet he had a special and respectable place in the college life. But it might be another thing to be marked as the poet of a wilful and selfish obscurity.

As he walked to the Bradbys', Howe was a little tense and defensive. It seemed to him that all the world knew of the 'attack' and agreed with it. And, indeed, the Bradbys had read the essay but Professor Bradby, a kind and pretentious man, said, 'I see my old friend knocked you about a bit, my boy,' and his wife Eugenia looked at Howe with her childlike blue eyes and said, 'I shall *scold* Frederic for the untrue things he wrote about you. You aren't the least obscure.' They beamed at him. In their genial snobbery they seemed to feel that he had distinguished himself. He was the leader of Howeism. He enjoyed the dinner party as much as he had thought he would.

And in the following days, as he was more preoccupied with his duties, the incident was forgotten. His classes had ceased to be mere groups. Student after student detached himself from the mass and required or claimed a place in Howe's awareness. Of them all it was Tertan who first and most violently signaled his separate existence. A week after classes had begun Howe saw his silhouette on the frosted glass of his office door. It was motionless for a long time, perhaps stopped by the problem of whether or not to knock before entering. Howe called, 'Come in!' and Tertan entered with his shambling stride.

He stood beside the desk, silent and at attention. When Howe asked him to sit down, he responded with a gesture of head and hand, as if to say that such amenities were beside the point. Nevertheless, he did take the chair. He put his ragged, crammed briefcase between his legs. His face, which Howe now observed fully for the first time, was confusing, for it was made up of florid curves, the nose arched in the bone and voluted in the nostril, the mouth loose and soft and rather moist. Yet the face was so thin and narrow as to seem the very type of asceticism. Lashes of unusual length veiled the eyes and, indeed, it seemed as if there were a veil over the whole countenance. Before the words actually came, the face screwed itself into an attitude of preparation for them.

'You can confer with me now?' Tertan said.

'Yes, I'd be glad to. There are several things in your two themes I want to talk to you about.' Howe reached for the packet of themes on his desk and sought for Tertan's. But the boy was waving them away.

'These are done perforce,' he said. 'Under the pressure of your requirement. They are not significant; mere duties.' Again his great hand flapped vaguely to dismiss his themes. He leaned forward and gazed at his teacher.

'You are,' he said, 'a man of letters? You are a poet?' It was more declaration than question.

'I should like to think so,' Howe said.

At first Tertan accepted the answer with a show of appreciation, as though the understatement made a secret between himself and Howe. Then he chose to misunderstand. With his shrewd and disconcerting control of expression, he presented to Howe a puzzled grimace. 'What does that mean?' he said.

Howe retracted the irony. 'Yes. I am a poet.' It sounded strange to say.

'That,' Tertan said, 'is a wonder.' He corrected himself with his ducking head. 'I mean that is wonderful.'

Suddenly, he dived at the miserable briefcase between his legs, put it on his knees, and began to fumble with the catch, all intent on the difficulty it presented. Howe noted that his suit was worn thin, his shirt almost unclean. He became aware, even, of a vague and musty odor of garments worn too long in unaired rooms. Tertan conquered the lock and began to concentrate upon a search into the interior. At last he held in his hand what he was after, a torn and crumpled copy of *Life and Letters*.

'I learned it from here,' he said, holding it out.

Howe looked at him sharply, his hackles a little up. But the boy's face was not only perfectly innocent, it even shone with a conscious admiration. Apparently nothing of the import of the essay had touched him except the wonderful fact that his teacher was a 'man of letters.' Yet this seemed too stupid, and Howe, to test it, said, 'The man who wrote that doesn't think it's wonderful.'

Tertan made a moist hissing sound as he cleared his mouth of saliva. His head, oddly loose on his neck, wove a pattern of contempt in the air. 'A critic,' he said, 'who admits *prima facie* that he does not understand.' Then he said grandly, 'It is the inevitable fate.'

It was absurd, yet Howe was not only aware of the absurdity but of a tension suddenly and wonderfully relaxed. Now that the 'attack' was on the table between himself and this strange boy, and subject to the boy's funny and absolutely certain contempt, the hidden force of his feeling was revealed to him in the very moment that it vanished. All unsuspected, there had been a film over the world, a transparent but discoloring haze of danger. But he had no time to stop over the brightened aspect of things. Tertan was going on. 'I also am a man of letters. Putative.'

'You have written a good deal?' Howe meant to be no more than polite, and he was surprised at the tenderness he heard in his words.

Solemnly the boy nodded, threw back the dank lock, and sucked in a deep, anticipatory breath. 'First, a work of homiletics, which is a defense of the principles of religious optimism against the pessimism of Schopenhauer and the humanism of Nietzsche.'

'Humanism? Why do you call it humanism?'

'It is my nomenclature for making a deity of man,' Tertan

replied negligently. "Then three fictional works, novels. And numerous essays in science, combating materialism. Is it your duty to read these if I bring them to you?'

Howe answered simply, 'No, it isn't exactly my duty, but I shall be happy to read them.'

Tertan stood up and remained silent. He rested his bag on the chair. With a certain compunction—for it did not seem entirely proper that, of two men of letters, one should have the right to blue-pencil the other, to grade him or to question the quality of his 'sentence structure'—Howe reached for Tertan's papers. But before he could take them up, the boy suddenly made his bow-to-Abelard, the stiff inclination of the body with the hands seeming to emerge from the scholar's gown. Then he was gone.

But after his departure something was still left of him. The timbre of his curious sentences, the downright finality of so quaint a phrase as 'It is the inevitable fate' still rang in the air. Howe gave the warmth of his feeling to the new visitor who stood at the door announcing himself with a genteel clearing of the throat.

'Doctor Howe, I believe?' the student said. A large hand advanced into the room and grasped Howe's hand. 'Blackburn, sir, Theodore Blackburn, vice-president of the Student Council. A great pleasure, sir.'

Out of a pair of ruddy cheeks a pair of small eyes twinkled good-naturedly. The large face, the large body were not so much fat as beefy and suggested something 'typical'—monk, politician, or innkeeper.

Blackburn took the seat beside Howe's desk. 'I may have seemed to introduce myself in my public capacity, sir,' he said. 'But it is really as an individual that I came to see you. That is to say, as one of your students to be.'

He spoke with an English intonation and he went on, 'I was once an English major, sir.'

For a moment Howe was startled, for the roast-beef look of the boy and the manner of his speech gave a second's credibility to one sense of his statement. Then the collegiate meaning of the phrase asserted itself, but some perversity made Howe say what was not really in good taste even with so forward a student, 'Indeed? What regiment?'

Blackburn stared and then gave a little pouf-pouf of laughter. He waved the misapprehension away. '*Very* good, sir. It certainly is an ambiguous term.' He chuckled in appreciation of Howe's joke, then cleared his throat to put it aside. 'I look forward to taking your course in the romantic poets, sir,' he said earnestly. 'To me the romantic poets are the very crown of English literature.'

Howe made a dry sound, and the boy, catching some meaning in it, said, 'Little as I know them, of course. But even Shakespeare who is so dear to us of the Anglo-Saxon tradition is in a sense but the preparation for Shelley, Keats and Byron. And Wadsworth.'

Almost sorry for him, Howe dropped his eyes. With some embarrassment, for the boy was not actually his student, he said softly, 'Wordsworth.'

'Sir?'

'Wordsworth, not Wadsworth. You said Wadsworth.'

'Did I, sir?' Gravely he shook his head to rebuke himself for the error. 'Wordsworth, of course—slip of the tongue.' Then, quite in command again, he went on, 'I have a favor to ask of you, Doctor Howe. You see, I began my college course as an English major,'—he smiled—'as I said.'

'Yes?'

'But after my first year I shifted. I shifted to the social sciences. Sociology and government—I find them stimulating and very *real*.' He paused, out of respect for reality. 'But now I find that perhaps I have neglected the other side.'

'The other side?' Howe said.

'Imagination, fancy, culture. A well-rounded man.' He trailed off as if there were perfect understanding between them. 'And so, sir, I have decided to end my senior year with your course in the romantic poets.'

His voice was filled with an indulgence which Howe ignored as he said flatly and gravely, 'But that course isn't given until the spring term.'

'Yes, sir, and that is where the favor comes in. Would you let me take your romantic prose course? I can't take it for credit, sir, my program is full, but just for background it seems to me that I ought to take it. I do hope,' he concluded in a manly way, 'that you will consent.'

'Well, it's no great favor, Mr. Blackburn. You can come if

you wish, though there's not much point in it if you don't do the reading.'

The bell rang for the hour and Howe got up.

'May I begin with this class, sir?' Blackburn's smile was candid and boyish.

Howe nodded carelessly and together, silently, they walked to the classroom down the hall. When they reached the door Howe stood back to let his student enter, but Blackburn moved adroitly behind him and grasped him by the arm to urge him over the threshold. They entered together with Blackburn's hand firmly on Howe's biceps, the student inducing the teacher into his own room. Howe felt a surge of temper rise in him and almost violently he disengaged his arm and walked to the desk, while Blackburn found a seat in the front row and smiled at him.

## II

The question was, At whose door must the tragedy be laid?

All night the snow had fallen heavily and only now was abating in sparse little flurries. The windows were valanced high with white. It was very quiet; something of the quiet of the world had reached the class, and Howe found that everyone was glad to talk or listen. In the room there was a comfortable sense of pleasure in being human.

Casebeer believed that the blame for the tragedy rested with heredity. Picking up the book he read, 'The sins of the fathers are visited on their children.' This opinion was received with general favor. Nevertheless, Johnson ventured to say that the fault was all Pastor Manders' because the Pastor had made Mrs. Alving go back to her husband and was always hiding the truth. To this Hibbard objected with logic enough, 'Well then, it was really all her husband's fault. He *did* all the bad things.' De Witt, his face bright with an impatient idea, said that the fault was all society's. 'By society I don't mean upper-crust society,' he said. He looked around a little defiantly, taking in any members of the class who might be members of upper-crust society. 'Not in that sense. I mean the social unit.'

Howe nodded and said, 'Yes, of course.'

'If the society of the time had progressed far enough in science,' De Witt went on, 'then there would be no problem for Mr.

Ibsen to write about. Captain Alving plays around a little, gives way to perfectly natural biological urges, and he gets a social disease, a venereal disease. If the disease is cured, no problem. Invent salvarsan and the disease is cured. The problem of heredity disappears and li'l Oswald just doesn't get paresis. No paresis, no problem—no problem, no play.'

This was carrying the ark into battle, and the class looked at De Witt with respectful curiosity. It was his usual way and on the whole they were sympathetic with his struggle to prove to Howe that science was better than literature. Still, there was something in his reckless manner that alienated them a little.

'Or take birth-control, for instance,' De Witt went on. 'If Mrs. Alving had some knowledge of contraception, she wouldn't have had to have li'l Oswald at all. No li'l Oswald, no play.'

The class was suddenly quieter. In the back row Stettenhover swung his great football shoulders in a righteous sulking gesture, first to the right, then to the left. He puckered his mouth ostentatiously. Intellect was always ending up by talking dirty.

Tertan's hand went up, and Howe said, 'Mr. Tertan.' The boy shambled to his feet and began his long characteristic gulp. Howe made a motion with his fingers, as small as possible, and Tertan ducked his head and smiled in apology. He sat down. The class laughed. With more than half the term gone, Tertan had not been able to remember that one did not rise to speak. He seemed unable to carry on the life of the intellect without this mark of respect for it. To Howe the boy's habit of rising seemed to accord with the formal shabbiness of his dress. He never wore the casual sweaters and jackets of his classmates. Into the free and comfortable air of the college classroom he brought the stuffy sordid strictness of some crowded, metropolitan high school.

'Speaking from one sense,' Tertan began slowly, 'there is no blame ascribable. From the sense of determinism, who can say where the blame lies? The preordained is the preordained and it cannot be said without rebellion against the universe, a palpable absurdity.'

In the back row Stettenhover slumped suddenly in his seat, his heels held out before him, making a loud, dry, disgusted sound. His body sank until his neck rested on the back of his chair. He folded his hands across his belly and looked significantly out of the window, exasperated not only with Tertan, but with Howe, with the class, with the whole system designed to encourage this kind of thing. There was a certain insolence in the movement and Howe flushed. As Tertan continued to speak, Howe stalked casually toward the window and placed himself in the line of Stettenhover's vision. He stared at the great fellow, who pretended not to see him. There was so much power in the big body, so much contempt in the Greek-athlete face under the crisp Greek-athlete curls, that Howe felt almost physical fear. But at last Stettenhover admitted him to focus and under his disapproving gaze sat up with slow indifference. His eyebrows raised high in resignation, he began to examine his hands. Howe relaxed and turned his attention back to Tertan.

'Flux of existence,' Tertan was saying, 'produces all things, so that judgment wavers. Beyond the phenomena, what? But phenomena are adumbrated and to them we are limited.'

Howe saw it for a moment as perhaps it existed in the boy's mind—the world of shadows which are cast by a great light upon a hidden reality as in the old myth of the Cave. But the little brush with Stettenhover had tired him, and he said irritably, 'But come to the point, Mr. Tertan.'

He said it so sharply that some of the class looked at him curiously. For three months he had gently carried Tertan through his verbosities, to the vaguely respectful surprise of the other students, who seemed to conceive that there existed between this strange classmate and their teacher some special understanding from which they were content to be excluded. Tertan looked at him mildly, and at once came brilliantly to the point. 'This is the summation of the play,' he said and took up his book and read, ' "Your poor father never found any outlet for the overmastering joy of life that was in him. And I brought no holiday into his home, either. Everything seemed to turn upon duty and I am afraid I made your poor father's home unbearable to him, Oswald." Spoken by Mrs. Alving.'

Yes that was surely the 'summation' of the play and Tertan had hit it, as he hit, deviously and eventually, the literary point of almost everything, But now, as always, he was wrapping it away from sight. 'For most mortals,' he said, 'there are only joys of biological urgings, gross and crass, such as the sensuous Captain Alving. For certain few there are the transmutations beyond these to a contemplation of the utter whole.'

Oh, the boy was mad. And suddenly the word, used in hyperbole, intended almost for the expression of exasperated admiration, became literal. Now that the word was used, it became simply apparent to Howe that Tertan was mad.

It was a monstrous word and stood like a bestial thing in the room. Yet it so completely comprehended everything that had puzzled Howe, it so arranged and explained what for three months had been perplexing him that almost at once its horror became domesticated. With this word Howe was able to understand why he had never been able to communicate to Tertan the value of a single criticism or correction of his wild, verbose themes. Their conferences had been frequent and long but had done nothing to reduce to order the splendid confusion of the boy's ideas. Yet, impossible though its expression was, Tertan's incandescent mind could always strike for a moment into some dark corner of thought.

And now it was suddenly apparent that it was not a faulty rhetoric that Howe had to contend with. With his new knowledge he looked at Tertan's face and wondered how he could have so long deceived himself. Tertan was still talking, and the class had lapsed into a kind of patient unconsciousness, a coma of respect for words which, for all that most of them knew, might be profound. Almost with a suffusion of shame, Howe believed that in some dim way the class had long ago had some intimation of Tertan's madness. He reached out as decisively as he could to seize the thread of Tertan's discourse before it should be entangled further.

'Mr. Tertan says that the blame must be put upon whoever kills the joy of living in another. We have been assuming that Captain Alving was a wholly bad man, but what if we assume that he became bad only because Mrs. Alving, when they were first married, acted toward him in the prudish way she says she did?'

It was a ticklish idea to advance to freshmen and perhaps not profitable. Not all of them were following.

'That would put the blame on Mrs. Alving herself, whom most of you admire. And she herself seems to think so.' He glanced at his watch. The hour was nearly over. 'What do you think, Mr. De Witt?'

De Witt rose to the idea; he wanted to know if society

couldn't be blamed for educating Mrs. Alving's temperament in the wrong way. Casebeer was puzzled, Stettenhover continued to look at his hands until the bell rang.

Tertan, his brows louring in thought, was making as always for a private word. Howe gathered his books and papers to leave quickly. At this moment of his discovery and with the knowledge still raw, he could not engage himself with Tertan. Tertan sucked in his breath to prepare for speech and Howe made ready for the pain and confusion. But at that moment Casebeer detached himself from the group with which he had been conferring and which he seemed to represent. His constituency remained at a tactful distance. The mission involved the time of an assigned essay. Casebeer's presentation of the plea—it was based on the freshmen's heavy duties at the fraternities during Carnival Week —cut across Tertan's preparations for speech. 'And so some of us fellows thought,' Casebeer concluded with heavy solemnity, 'that we could do a better job, give our minds to it more, if we had more time.'

Tertan regarded Casebeer with mingled curiosity and revulsion. Howe not only said that he would postpone the assignment but went on to talk about the Carnival, and even drew the waiting constituency into the conversation. He was conscious of Tertan's stern and astonished stare, then of his sudden departure.

Now that the fact was clear, Howe knew that he must act on it. His course was simple enough. He must lay the case before the Dean. Yet he hesitated. His feeling for Tertan must now, certainly, be in some way invalidated. Yet could he, because of a word, hurry to assign to official and reasonable solicitude what had been, until this moment, so various and warm? He could at least delay and, by moving slowly, lend a poor grace to the necessary, ugly act of making his report.

It was with some notion of keeping the matter in his own hands that he went to the Dean's office to look up Tertan's records. In the outer office the Dean's secretary greeted him brightly, and at his request brought him the manila folder with the small identifying photograph pasted in the corner. She laughed. 'He was looking for the birdie in the wrong place,' she said.

Howe leaned over her shoulder to look at the picture. It was as bad as all the Dean's-office photographs were, but it differed from all that Howe had ever seen. Tertan, instead of looking into the camera, as no doubt he had been bidden, had, at the moment of exposure, turned his eyes upward. His mouth, as though conscious of the trick played on the photographer, had the sly superior look that Howe knew.

The secretary was fascinated by the picture. 'What a funny boy,' she said. 'He looks like Tartuffe!'

And so he did, with the absurd piety of the eyes and the conscious slyness of the mouth and the whole face bloated by the bad lens.

'Is he *like* that?' the secretary said.

'Like Tartuffe? No.'

From the photograph there was little enough comfort to be had. The records themselves gave no clue to madness, though they suggested sadness enough. Howe read of a father, Stanislaus Tertan, born in Budapest and trained in engineering in Berlin, once employed by the Hercules Chemical Corporation—this was one of the factories that dominated the south end of the town—but now without employment. He read of a mother Erminie (Youngfellow) Tertan, born in Manchester, educated at a Normal School at Leeds, now housewife by profession. The family lived on Greenbriar Street which Howe knew as a row of once elegant homes near what was now the factory district. The old mansion had long ago been divided into small and primitive apartments. Of Ferdinand himself there was little to learn. He lived with his parents, had attended a Detroit high school and had transferred to the local school in his last year. His rating for intelligence, as expressed in numbers, was high, his scholastic record was remarkable, he held a college scholarship for his tuition.

Howe laid the folder on the secretary's desk. 'Did you find what you wanted to know?' she asked.

The phrases from Tertan's momentous first theme came back to him. 'Tertan I am, but what is Tertan? Of this time, of that place, of some parentage, what does it matter?'

'No, I didn't find it,' he said.

Now that he had consulted the sad, half-meaningless record he knew all the more firmly that he must not give the matter out of his own hands. He must not release Tertan to authority. Not that he anticipated from the Dean anything but the greatest kindness for Tertan. The Dean would have the experience and skill which he himself could not have. One way or another the

Dean could answer the question, 'What is Tertan?' Yet this was precisely what he feared. He alone could keep alive—not forever but for a somehow important time—the question, 'What is Tertan?' He alone could keep it still a question. Some sure instinct told him that he must not surrender the question to a clean official desk in a clear official light to be dealt with, settled and closed.

He heard himself saying, 'Is the Dean busy at the moment? I'd like to see him.'

His request came thus unbidden, even forbidden, and it was one of the surprising and startling incidents of his life. Later when he reviewed the events, so disconnected in themselves, or so merely odd, of the story that unfolded for him that year, it was over this moment, on its face the least notable, that he paused longest. It was frequently to be with fear and never without a certainty of its meaning in his own knowledge of himself that he would recall this simple, routine request, and the feeling of shame and freedom it gave him as he sent everything down the official chute. In the end, of course, no matter what he did to 'protect' Tertan, he would have had to make the same request and lay the matter on the Dean's clean desk. But it would always be a land-mark of his life that, at the very moment when he was rejecting the official way, he had been, without will or intention, so gladly drawn to it.

After the storm's last delicate flurry, the sun had come out. Reflected by the new snow, it filled the office with a golden light which was almost musical in the way it made all the common-place objects of efficiency shine with a sudden sad and noble sig-nificance. And the light, now that he noticed it, made the ut-terance of his perverse and unwanted request even more mo-mentous.

The secretary consulted the engagement pad. 'He'll be free any minute. Don't you want to wait in the parlor?'

She threw open the door of the large and pleasant room in which the Dean held his Committee meetings, and in which his visitors waited. It was designed with a homely elegance on the masculine side of the eighteenth-century manner. There was a small coal fire in the grate and the handsome mahogany table was strewn with books and magazines. The large windows gave on the snowy lawn, and there was such a fine width of window that the white casements and walls seemed at this moment but a continuation of the snow; the snow but an extension of casement and walls. The outdoors seemed taken in and made safe, the indoors seemed luxuriously freshened and expanded.

Howe sat down by the fire and lighted a cigarette. The room had its intended effect upon him. He felt comfortable and relaxed, yet nicely organized, some young diplomatic agent of the eighteenth century, the newly fledged Swift carrying out Sir William Temple's business. The rawness of Tertan's case quite vanished. He crossed his legs and reached for a magazine.

It was that famous issue of *Life and Letters* that his idle hand had found and his blood raced as he sifted through it, and the shape of his own name, Joseph Howe, sprang out at him, still cabalistic in its power. He tossed the magazine back on the table as the door of the Dean's office opened and the Dean ushered out Theodore Blackburn.

'Ah, Joseph!' the Dean said.

Blackburn said, 'Good morning, Doctor.' Howe winced at the title and caught the flicker of amusement over the Dean's face. The Dean stood with his hand high on the door-jamb and Blackburn, still in the doorway, remained standing almost under the long arm.

Howe nodded briefly to Blackburn, snubbing his eager deference. 'Can you give me a few minutes?' he said to the Dean.

'All the time you want. Come in.' Before the two men could enter the office, Blackburn claimed their attention with a long full 'er.' As they turned to him, Blackburn said, 'Can *you* give *me* a few minutes, Doctor Howe?' His eyes sparkled at the little audacity he had committed, the slightly impudent play with hierarchy. Of the three of them Blackburn kept himself the lowest, but he reminded Howe of his subaltern relation to the Dean.

'I mean, of course,' Blackburn went on easily, 'when you've finished with the Dean.'

'I'll be in my office shortly,' Howe said, turned his back on the ready 'Thank you, sir,' and followed the Dean into the inner room.

'Energetic boy,' said the Dean. 'A bit beyond himself but very energetic. Sit down.'

The Dean lighted a cigarette, leaned back in his chair, sat easy and silent for a moment, giving Howe no signal to go ahead with business. He was a young Dean, not much beyond forty, a tall handsome man with sad, ambitious eyes. He had been a Rhodes scholar. His friends looked for great things from him, and it was generally said that he had notions of education which he was not yet ready to try to put into practice.

His relaxed silence was meant as a compliment to Howe. He smiled and said, 'What's the business, Joseph?'

'Do you know Tertan—Ferdinand Tertan, a freshman?'

The Dean's cigarette was in his mouth and his hands were clasped behind his head. He did not seem to search his memory for the name. He said, 'What about him?'

Clearly the Dean knew something, and he was waiting for Howe to tell him more. Howe moved only tentatively. Now that he was doing what he had resolved not to do, he felt more guilty at having been so long deceived by Tertan and more need to be loyal to his error.

'He's a strange fellow,' he ventured. He said stubbornly, 'In a strange way he's very brilliant.' He concluded, 'But very strange.'

The springs of the Dean's swivel chair creaked as he came out of his sprawl and leaned forward to Howe. 'Do you mean he's so strange that it's something you could give a name to?'

Howe looked at him stupidly. 'What do you mean?' he said.

'What's his trouble?' the Dean said more neutrally.

'He's very brilliant, in a way. I looked him up and he has a top intelligence rating. But somehow, and it's hard to explain just how, what he says is always on the edge of sense and doesn't quite make it.'

The Dean looked at him and Howe flushed up. The Dean had surely read Woolley on the subject of 'the Howes' and the *tour d'ivresse*. Was that quick glance ironical?

The Dean picked up some papers from his desk, and Howe could see that they were in Tertan's impatient scrawl. Perhaps the little gleam in the Dean's glance had come only from putting facts together.

'He sent me this yesterday,' the Dean said. 'After an interview I had with him. I haven't been able to do more than glance at it. When you said what you did, I realized there was something wrong.'

Twisting his mouth, the Dean looked over the letter. 'You seem to be involved,' he said without looking up. 'By the way, what did you give him at mid-term?'

Flushing, setting his shoulders, Howe said firmly, 'I gave him A-minus.'

The Dean chuckled. 'Might be a good idea if some of our nicer boys went crazy—just a little.' He said, 'Well,' to conclude the matter and handed the papers to Howe. 'See if this is the same thing you've been finding. Then we can go into the matter again.'

Before the fire in the parlor, in the chair that Howe had been occupying, sat Blackburn. He sprang to his feet as Howe entered.

'I said my office, Mr. Blackburn.' Howe's voice was sharp. Then he was almost sorry for the rebuke, so clearly and naively did Blackburn seem to relish his stay in the parlor, close to authority.

'I'm in a bit of a hurry, sir,' he said, 'and I did want to be sure to speak to you, sir.'

He was really absurd, yet fifteen years from now he would have grown up to himself, to the assurance and mature beefiness. In banks, in consular offices, in brokerage firms, on the bench, more seriously affable, a little sterner, he would make use of his ability to be administered by his job. It was almost reassuring. Now he was exercising his too-great skill on Howe. 'I owe you an apology, sir,' he said.

Howe knew that he did, but he showed surprise.

'I mean, Doctor, after your having been so kind about letting me attend your class, I stopped coming.' He smiled in deprecation. 'Extracurricular activities take up so much of my time. I'm afraid I undertook more than I could perform.'

Howe had noticed the absence and had been a little irritated by it after Blackburn's elaborate plea. It was an absence that might be interpreted as a comment on the teacher. But there was only one way for him to answer. 'You've no need to apologize,' he said. 'It's wholly your affair.'

Blackburn beamed. 'I'm so glad you feel that way about it, sir. I was worried you might think I had stayed away because I was influenced by—' he stopped and lowered his eyes.

Astonished, Howe said, 'Influenced by what?'

'Well, by—' Blackburn hesitated and for answer pointed to the table on which lay the copy of *Life and Letters*. Without looking at it, he knew where to direct his hand. 'By the unfavorable publicity, sir.' He hurried on. 'And that brings me to another point, sir. I am secretary of Quill and Scroll, sir, the student literary society, and I wonder if you would address us. You could read your own poetry, sir, and defend your own point of view. It would be very interesting.'

It was truly amazing. Howe looked long and cruelly into Blackburn's face, trying to catch the secret of the mind that could have conceived this way of manipulating him, this way so daring and inept—but not entirely inept—with its malice so without malignity. The face did not yield its secret. Howe smiled broadly and said, 'Of course I don't think you were influenced by the unfavorable publicity.'

'I'm still going to take—regularly, for credit—your romantic poets course next term,' Blackburn said.

'Don't worry, my dear fellow, don't worry about it.'

Howe started to leave and Blackburn stopped him with, 'But about Quill, sir?'

'Suppose we wait until next term? I'll be less busy then.'

And Blackburn said, 'Very good, sir, and thank you.'

In his office the little encounter seemed less funny to Howe, was even in some indeterminate way disturbing. He made an effort to put it from his mind by turning to what was sure to disturb him more, the Tertan letter read in the new interpretation. He found what he had always found, the same florid leaps beyond fact and meaning, the same headlong certainty. But as his eye passed over the familiar scrawl it caught his own name, and for the second time that hour he felt the race of his blood.

'The Paraclete,' Tertan had written to the Dean, 'from a Greek word meaning to stand in place of, but going beyond the primitive idea to mean traditionally the helper, the one who comforts and assists, cannot without fundamental loss be jettisoned. Even if taken no longer in the supernatural sense, the concept remains deeply in the human consciousness inevitably. Humanitarianism is no reply, for not every man stands in the place of every other man for this other comrade's comfort. But certain are chosen out of the human race to be the consoler of some other. Of these, for example, is Joseph Barker Howe, Ph.D. Of intellects not the first yet of true intellect and lambent instructions, given to that which is intuitive and irrational, not to what is logical in the strict word, what is judged by him is of the heart and not the head. Here is one chosen, in that he chooses himself to stand in the place of another for comfort and consolation. To him more than another I give my gratitude, with all respect to our Dean who reads this, a noble man, but merely dedicated, not consecrated. But not in the aspect of the Paraclete only is Dr. Joseph Barker Howe established, for he must be the Paraclete to another aspect of himself, that which is driven and persecuted by the lack of understanding in the world at large, so that he in himself embodies the full history of man's tribulations and, overflowing upon others, notably the present writer, is the ultimate end.'

This was love. There was no escape from it. Try as Howe might to remember that Tertan was mad and all his emotions invalidated, he could not destroy the effect upon him of his student's stern, affectionate regard. He had betrayed not only a power of mind but a power of love. And, however firmly he held before his attention the fact of Tertan's madness, he could do nothing to banish the physical sensation of gratitude he felt. He had never thought of himself as 'driven and persecuted' and he did not now. But still he could not make meaningless his sensation of gratitude. The pitiable Tertan sternly pitied him, and comfort came from Tertan's never-to-be-comforted mind.

### III

In an academic community, even an efficient one, official matters move slowly. The term drew to a close with no action in the case of Tertan, and Joseph Howe had to confront a curious problem. How should he grade his strange student, Tertan?

Tertan's final examination had been no different from all his other writing, and what did one 'give' such a student? De Witt must have his A, that was clear. Johnson would get a B. With Casebeer it was a question of a B-minus or a C-plus, and Stettenhover, who had been crammed by the team tutor to fill half a blue-book with his thin feminine scrawl, would have his C-minus which he would accept with mingled indifference and resentment. But with Tertan it was not so easy.

The boy was still in the college process and his name could not be omitted from the grade sheet. Yet what should a mind under suspicion of madness be graded? Until the medical verdict was given, it was for Howe to continue as Tertan's teacher and to keep his judgment pedagogical. Impossible to give him an F: he had not failed. B was for Johnson's stolid mediocrity. He could not be put on the edge of passing with Stettenhover, for he exactly did not pass. In energy and richness of intellect he was perhaps even De Witt's superior, and Howe toyed grimly with the notion of giving him an A, but that would lower the value of the A De Witt had won with his beautiful and clear, if still arrogant, mind. There was a notation which the Registrar recognized—Inc., for Incomplete, and in the horrible comedy of the situation, Howe considered that. But really only a mark of M for Mad would serve.

In his perplexity, Howe sought the Dean, but the Dean was out of town. In the end, he decided to maintain the A-minus he had given Tertan at mid-term. After all, there had been no falling away from that quality. He entered it on the grade sheet with something like bravado.

Academic time moves quickly. A college year is not really a year, lacking as it does three months. And it is endlessly divided into units which, at their beginning, appear larger than they are —terms, half-terms, months, weeks. And the ultimate unit, the hour, is not really an hour, lacking as it does ten minutes. And so the new term advanced rapidly, and one day the fields about the town were all brown, cleared of even the few thin patches of snow which had lingered so long.

Howe, as he lectured on the romantic poets, became conscious of Blackburn emanating wrath. Blackburn did it well, did it with enormous dignity. He did not stir in his seat, he kept his eyes fixed on Howe in perfect attention, but he abstained from using his notebook, there was no mistaking what he proposed to himself as an attitude. His elbow on the writing-wing of the chair, his chin on the curled fingers of his hand, he was the embodiment of intellectual indignation. He was thinking his own thoughts, would give no public offense, yet would claim his due, was not to be intimidated. Howe knew that he would present himself at the end of the hour.

Blackburn entered the office without invitation. He did not smile; there was no cajolery about him. Without invitation he sat down beside Howe's desk. He did not speak until he had taken the blue-book from his pocket. He said, 'What does this mean, sir?'

It was a sound and conservative student tactic. Said in the usual way it meant, 'How could you have so misunderstood me?' or 'What does this mean for my future in the course?' But there were none of the humbler tones in Blackburn's way of saying it.

Howe made the established reply, 'I think that's for you to tell me.'

Blackburn continued icy. 'I'm sure I can't, sir.'

There was a silence between them. Both dropped their eyes to the blue-book on the desk. On its cover Howe had penciled: 'F. This is very poor work.'

Howe picked up the blue-book. There was always the possibility of injustice. The teacher may be bored by the mass of papers and not wholly attentive. A phrase, even the student's handwriting, may irritate him unreasonably. 'Well,' said Howe, 'let's go through it.'

He opened the first page. 'Now here: you write, "In *The Ancient Mariner,* Coleridge lives in and transports us to a honey-sweet world where all is rich and strange, a world of charm to which we can escape from the humdrum existence of our daily lives, the world of romance. Here, in this warm and honey-sweet land of charming dreams we can relax and enjoy ourselves." '

Howe lowered the paper and waited with a neutral look for Blackburn to speak. Blackburn returned the look boldly, did not speak, sat stolid and lofty. At last Howe said, speaking gently, 'Did you mean that, or were you just at a loss for something to say?'

'You imply that I was just "bluffing"?' The quotation marks hung palpable in the air about the word.

'I'd like to know. I'd prefer believing that you were bluffing to believing that you really thought this.'

Blackburn's eyebrows went up. From the height of a great and firm-based idea he looked at his teacher. He clasped the crags for a moment and then pounced, craftily, suavely. 'Do you mean, Doctor Howe, that there aren't two opinions possible?'

It was superbly done in its air of putting all of Howe's intellectual life into the balance. Howe remained patient and simple. 'Yes, many opinions are possible, but not this one. Whatever anyone believes of *The Ancient Mariner,* no one can in reason believe that it represents a—a honey-sweet world in which we can relax.'

'But that is what I *feel,* sir.'

This was well-done, too. Howe said, 'Look, Mr. Blackburn.

Do you really relax with hunger and thirst, the heat and the sea-serpents, the dead men with staring eyes, Life in Death and the skeletons? Come now, Mr. Blackburn.'

Blackburn made no answer, and Howe pressed forward. 'Now, you say of Wordsworth, "Of peasant stock himself, he ·turned from the effete life of the salons and found in the peasant the hope of a flaming revolution which would sweep away all the old ideas. This is the subject of his best poems." '

Beaming at his teacher with youthful eagerness, Blackburn said, 'Yes, sir, a rebel, a bringer of light to suffering mankind. I see him as a kind of Prothemeus.'

'A kind of what?'

'Prothemeus, sir.'

'Think, Mr. Blackburn. We were talking about him only today and I mentioned his name a dozen times. You don't mean Prothemeus. You mean—' Howe waited, but there was no response.

'You mean Prometheus.'

Blackburn gave no assent, and Howe took the reins. 'You've done a bad job here, Mr. Blackburn, about as bad as could be done.' He saw Blackburn stiffen and his genial face harden again. 'It shows either a lack of preparation or a complete lack of understanding.' He saw Blackburn's face begin to go to pieces and he stopped.

'Oh, sir,' Blackburn burst out, 'I've never had a mark like this before, never anything below a B, never. A thing like this has never happened to me before.'

It must be true, it was a statement too easily verified. Could it be that other instructors accepted such flaunting nonsense? Howe wanted to end the interview. 'I'll set it down to lack of preparation,' he said. 'I know you're busy. That's not an excuse, but it's an explanation. Now, suppose you really prepare, and then take another quiz in two weeks. We'll forget this one and count the other.'

Blackburn squirmed with pleasure and gratitude. 'Thank you, sir. You're really very kind, very kind.'

Howe rose to conclude the visit. 'All right, then—in two weeks.'

It was that day that the Dean imparted to Howe the conclusion of the case of Tertan. It was simple and a little anti-climactic. A physician had been called in, and had said the word, given the name.

'A classic case, he called it,' the Dean said. 'Not a doubt in the world,' he said. His eyes were full of miserable pity, and he clutched at a word. 'A classic case, a classic case.' To his aid and to Howe's there came the Parthenon and the form of the Greek drama, the Aristotelian logic, Racine and the Well-Tempered Clavichord, the blueness of the Aegean and its clear sky. Classic— that is to say, without a doubt, perfect in its way, a veritable model, and, as the Dean had been told, sure to take a perfectly predictable and inevitable course to a foreknown conclusion.

It was not only pity that stood in the Dean's eyes. For a moment there was fear too. 'Terrible,' he said, 'it is simply terrible.'

Then he went on briskly. 'Naturally, we've told the boy nothing. And, naturally, we won't. His tuition's paid by his scholarship, and we'll continue him on the rolls until the end of the year. That will be kindest. After that the matter will be out of our control. We'll see, of course, that he gets into the proper hands. I'm told there will be no change, he'll go on like this, be as good as this, for four to six months. And so we'll just go along as usual.'

So Tertan continued to sit in Section 5 of English 1A, to his classmates still a figure of curiously dignified fun, symbol to most of them of the respectable but absurd intellectual life. But to his teacher he was now very different. He had not changed—he was still the greyhound casting for the scent of ideas, and Howe could see that he was still the same Tertan, but he could not feel it. What he felt as he looked at the boy sitting in his accustomed place was the hard blank of a fact. The fact itself was formidable and depressing. But what Howe was chiefly aware of was that he had permitted the metamorphosis of Tertan from person to fact.

As much as possible he avoided seeing Tertan's upraised hand and eager eye. But the fact did not know of its mere factuality, it continued its existence as if it were Tertan, hand up and eye questioning, and one day it appeared in Howe's office with a document.

'Even the spirit who lives egregiously, above the herd, must have its relations with the fellowman,' Tertan declared. He laid the document on Howe's desk. It was headed 'Quill and Scroll Society of Dwight College. Application for Membership.'

'In most ways these are crass minds,' Tertan said, touching the paper. 'Yet as a whole, bound together in their common love of letters, they transcend their intellectual lacks since it is not a paradox that the whole is greater than the sum of its parts.'

'When are the elections?' Howe asked.

'They take place tomorrow.'

'I certainly hope you will be successful.'

'Thank you. Would you wish to implement that hope?' A rather dirty finger pointed to the bottom of the sheet. 'A faculty recommender is necessary,' Tertan said stiffly, and waited.

'And you wish me to recommend you?'

'It would be an honor.'

'You may use my name.'

Tertan's finger pointed again. 'It must be a written sponsorship, signed by the sponsor.' There was a large blank space on the form under the heading, 'Opinion of Faculty Sponsor.'

This was almost another thing and Howe hesitated. Yet there was nothing else to do and he took out his fountain pen. He wrote, 'Mr. Ferdinand Tertan is marked by his intense devotion to letters and by his exceptional love of all things of the mind.' To this he signed his name, which looked bold and assertive on the white page. It disturbed him, the strange affirming power of a name. With a businesslike air, Tertan whipped up the paper, folding it with decision, and put it into his pocket. He bowed and took his departure, leaving Howe with the sense of having done something oddly momentous.

And so much now seemed odd and momentous to Howe that should not have seemed so. It was odd and momentous, he felt, when he sat with Blackburn's second quiz before him, and wrote in an excessively firm hand the grade of C-minus. The paper was a clear, an indisputable failure. He was carefully and consciously committing a cowardice. Blackburn had told the truth when he had pleaded his past record. Howe had consulted it in the Dean's office. It showed no grade lower than a B-minus. A canvass of some of Blackburn's previous instructors had brought vague attestations to the adequate powers of a student imperfectly remembered, and sometimes surprise that his abilities could be questioned at all.

As he wrote the grade, Howe told himself that his cowardice sprang from an unwillingness to have more dealings with a student he disliked. He knew it was simpler than that. He knew he feared Blackburn; that was the absurd truth. And cowardice did not solve the matter after all. Blackburn, flushed with a first success, attacked at once. The minimal passing grade had not assuaged his feelings and he sat at Howe's desk and again the bluebook lay between them. Blackburn said nothing. With an enormous impudence, he was waiting for Howe to speak and explain himself.

At last Howe said sharply and rudely, 'Well?' His throat was tense and the blood was hammering in his head. His mouth was tight with anger at himself for his disturbance.

Blackburn's glance was almost baleful. 'This is impossible, sir.'

'But there it is,' Howe answered.

'Sir?' Blackburn had not caught the meaning but his tone was still haughty.

Impatiently Howe said, "There it is, plain as day. Are you here to complain again?'

'Indeed I am, sir.' There was surprise in Blackburn's voice that Howe should ask the question.

'I shouldn't complain if I were you. You did a thoroughly bad job on your first quiz. This one is a little, only a very little, better.' This was not true. If anything, it was worse.

'That might be a matter of opinion, sir.'

'It is a matter of opinion. Of my opinion.'

'Another opinion might be different, sir.'

'You really believe that?' Howe said.

'Yes.' The omission of the 'sir' was monumental.

'Whose, for example?'

'The Dean's, for example.' Then the fleshy jaw came forward a little. 'Or a certain literary critic's, for example.'

It was colossal and almost too much for Blackburn himself to handle. The solidity of his face almost crumpled under it. But he withstood his own audacity and went on. 'And the Dean's opinion might be guided by the knowledge that the person who gave me this mark is the man whom a famous critic, the most eminent judge of literature in this country, called a drunken man. The Dean might think twice about whether such a man is fit to teach Dwight students.'

Howe said in quiet admonition, 'Blackburn, you're mad,' meaning no more than to check the boy's extravagance.

But Blackburn paid no heed. He had another shot in the locker. 'And the Dean might be guided by the information, of which I have evidence, documentary evidence,'—he slapped his breast pocket twice—'that this same person personally recommended to the college literary society, the oldest in the country, that he personally recommended a student who is crazy, who threw the meeting into an uproar—a psychiatric case. The Dean might take that into account.'

Howe was never to learn the details of that 'uproar.' He had always to content himself with the dim but passionate picture which at that moment sprang into his mind, of Tertan standing on some abstract height and madly denouncing the multitude of Quill and Scroll who howled him down.

He sat quiet a moment and looked at Blackburn. The ferocity had entirely gone from the student's face. He sat regarding his teacher almost benevolently. He had played a good card and now, scarcely at all unfriendly, he was waiting to see the effect. Howe took up the blue-book and negligently sifted through it. He read a page, closed the book, struck out the C-minus and wrote an F.

'Now you may take the paper to the Dean,' he said. 'You may tell him that after reconsidering it, I lowered the grade.'

The gasp was audible. 'Oh, sir!' Blackburn cried. 'Please!' His face was agonized. 'It means my graduation, my livelihood, my future. Don't do this to me.'

'It's done already.'

Blackburn stood up. 'I spoke rashly, sir, hastily. I had no intention, no real intention, of seeing the Dean. It rests with you —entirely, entirely. I *hope* you will restore the first mark.'

'Take the matter to the Dean or not, just as you choose. The grade is what you deserve and it stands.'

Blackburn's head dropped. 'And will I be failed at mid-term, sir?'

'Of course.'

From deep out of Blackburn's great chest rose a cry of anguish. 'Oh, sir, if you want me to go down on my knees to you, I will, I will.'

Howe looked at him in amazement.

'I will, I will. On my knees, sir. This mustn't, mustn't happen.'

He spoke so literally, meaning so very truly that his knees and exactly his knees were involved and seeming to think that he was offering something of tangible value to his teacher, that Howe, whose head had become icy clear in the nonsensical drama, thought, 'The boy is mad,' and began to speculate fantastically whether something in himself attracted or developed aberration. He could see himself standing absurdly before the Dean and saying, 'I've found another. This time it's the vice-president of the Council, the manager of the debating team and secretary of Quill and Scroll.'

One more such discovery, he thought, and he himself would be discovered! And there, suddenly, Blackburn was on his knees with a thump, his huge thighs straining his trousers, his hand outstretched in a great gesture of supplication.

With a cry, Howe shoved back his swivel chair and it rolled away on its casters half across the little room. Blackburn knelt for a moment to nothing at all, then got to his feet.

Howe rose abruptly. He said, 'Blackburn, you will stop acting like an idiot. Dust your knees off, take your paper and get out. You've behaved like a fool and a malicious person. You have half a term to do a decent job. Keep your silly mouth shut and try to do it. Now get out.'

Blackburn's head was low. He raised it and there was a pious light in his eyes. 'Will you shake hands, sir?' he said. He thrust out his hand.

'I will not,' Howe said.

Head and hand sank together. Blackburn picked up his blue-book and walked to the door. He turned and said, 'Thank you, sir.' His back, as he departed, was heavy with tragedy and stateliness.

## IV

After years of bad luck with the weather, the College had a perfect day for Commencement. It was wonderfully bright, the air so transparent, the wind so brisk that no one could resist talking about it.

As Howe set out for the campus he heard Hilda calling from

the back yard. She called, 'Professor, professor,' and came running to him.

Howe said, 'What's this "professor" business?'

'Mother told me,' Hilda said. 'You've been promoted. And I want to take your picture.'

'Next year,' said Howe. 'I won't be a professor until next year. And you know better than to call anybody "professor." '

'It was just in fun,' Hilda said. She seemed disappointed.

'But you can take my picture if you want. I won't look much different next year.' Still, it was frightening. It might mean that he was to stay in this town all his life.

Hilda brightened. 'Can I take it in this?' she said, and touched the gown he carried over his arm.

Howe laughed. 'Yes, you can take it in this.'

'I'll get my things and meet you in front of Otis,' Hilda said. 'I have the background all picked out.'

On the campus the Commencement crowd was already large. It stood about in eager, nervous little family groups. As he crossed, Howe was greeted by a student, capped and gowned, glad of the chance to make an event for his parents by introducing one of his teachers. It was while Howe stood there chatting that he saw Tertan.

He had never seen anyone quite so alone, as though a circle had been woven about him to separate him from the gay crowd on the campus. Not that Tertan was not gay, he was the gayest of all. Three weeks had passed since Howe had last seen him, the weeks of examination, the lazy week before Commencement, and this was now a different Tertan. On his head he wore a panama hat, broad-brimmed and fine, of the shape associated with South American planters. He wore a suit of raw silk, luxurious, but yellowed with age and much too tight, and he sported a whangee cane. He walked sedately, the hat tilted at a devastating angle, the stick coming up and down in time to his measured tread. He had, Howe guessed, outfitted himself to greet the day in the clothes of that ruined father whose existence was on record in the Dean's office. Gravely and arrogantly he surveyed the scene—in it, his whole bearing seemed to say, but not of it. With his haughty step, with his flashing eye, Tertan was coming nearer. Howe did not wish to be seen. He shifted his position slightly. When he looked again, Tertan was not in sight.

The chapel clock struck the quarter hour. Howe detached himself from his chat and hurried to Otis Hall at the far end of the campus. Hilda had not yet come. He went up into the high portico and, using the glass of the door for a mirror, put on his gown, adjusted the hood on his shoulders and set the mortarboard on his head. When he came down the steps, Hilda had arrived.

Nothing could have told him more forcibly that a year had passed than the development of Hilda's photographic possessions from the box camera of the previous fall. By a strap about her neck was hung a leather case, so thick and strong, so carefully stitched and so molded to its contents that it could only hold a costly camera. The appearance was deceptive, Howe knew, for he had been present at the Aikens' pre-Christmas conference about its purchase. It was only a fairly good domestic camera. Still, it looked very impressive. Hilda carried another leather case from which she drew a collapsible tripod. Decisively she extended each of its gleaming legs and set it up on the path. She removed the camera from its case and fixed it to the tripod. In its compact efficiency the camera almost had a life of its own, but Hilda treated it with easy familiarity, looked into its eye, glanced casually at its gauges. Then from a pocket she took still another leather case and drew from it a small instrument through which she looked first at Howe, who began to feel inanimate and lost, and then at the sky. She made some adjustment on the instrument, then some adjustment on the camera. She swept the scene with her eye, found a spot and pointed the camera in its direction. She walked to the spot, stood on it and beckoned to Howe. With each new leather case, with each new instrument, and with each new adjustment she had grown in ease and now she said, 'Joe, will you stand here?'

Obediently Howe stood where he was bidden. She had yet another instrument. She took out a tape-measure on a mechanical spool. Kneeling down before Howe, she put the little metal ring of the tape under the tip of his shoe. At her request, Howe pressed it with his toe. When she had measured her distance, she nodded to Howe who released the tape. At a touch, it sprang back into the spool. 'You have to be careful if you're going to get what you want,' Hilda said. 'I don't believe in all this snap-snap-snapping,' she remarked loftily. Howe nodded in agreement, although he was beginning to think Hilda's care excessive.

Now at last the moment had come. Hilda squinted into the camera, moved the tripod slightly. She stood to the side, holding the plunger of the shutter-cable. 'Ready,' she said. 'Will you relax, Joseph, please?' Howe realized that he was standing frozen. Hilda stood poised and precise as a setter, one hand holding the little cable, the other extended with curled dainty fingers like a dancer's, as if expressing to her subject the precarious delicacy of the moment. She pressed the plunger and there was the click. At once she stirred to action, got behind the camera, turned a new exposure. 'Thank you,' she said. 'Would you stand under that tree and let me do a character study with light and shade?'

The childish absurdity of the remark restored Howe's ease. He went to the little tree. The pattern the leaves made on his gown was what Hilda was after. He had just taken a satisfactory position when he heard in the unmistakable voice, 'Ah, Doctor! Having your picture taken?'

Howe gave up the pose and turned to Blackburn who stood on the walk, his hands behind his back, a little too large for his bachelor's gown. Annoyed that Blackburn should see him posing for a character study in light and shade, Howe said irritably, 'Yes, having my picture taken.'

Blackburn beamed at Hilda. 'And the little photographer?' he said. Hilda fixed her eyes on the ground and stood closer to her brilliant and aggressive camera. Blackburn, teetering on his heels, his hands behind his back, wholly prelatical and benignly patient, was not abashed at the silence. At last Howe said, 'If you'll excuse us, Mr. Blackburn, we'll go on with the picture.'

'Go right ahead, sir. I'm running along.' But he only came closer. 'Doctor Howe,' he said fervently, 'I want to tell you how glad I am that I was able to satisfy your standards at last.'

Howe was surprised at the hard, insulting brightness of his own voice, and even Hilda looked up curiously as he said, 'Nothing you have ever done has satisfied me, and nothing you could ever do would satisfy me, Blackburn.'

With a glance at Hilda, Blackburn made a gesture as if to hush Howe—as though all his former bold malice had taken for granted a kind of understanding between himself and his teacher, a secret which must not be betrayed to a third person. 'I only meant, sir,' he said, 'that I was able to pass your course after all.'

Howe said, 'You didn't pass my course. I passed you out of

my course. I passed you without even reading your paper. I wanted to be sure the college would be rid of you. And when all the grades were in and I did read your paper, I saw I was right not to have read it first.'

Blackburn presented a stricken face. 'It was very bad, sir?'

But Howe had turned away. The paper had been fantastic. The paper had been, if he wished to see it so, mad. It was at this moment that the Dean came up behind Howe and caught his arm. 'Hello, Joseph,' he said. 'We'd better be getting along, it's almost late.'

He was not a familiar man, but when he saw Blackburn, who approached to greet him, he took Blackburn's arm, too. 'Hello, Theodore,' he said. Leaning forward on Howe's arm and on Blackburn's, he said, 'Hello, Hilda dear.' Hilda replied quietly, 'Hello, Uncle George.'

Still clinging to their arms, still linking Howe and Blackburn, the Dean said, 'Another year gone, Joe, and we've turned out another crop. After you've been here a few years, you'll find it reasonably upsetting—you wonder how there can be so many graduating classes while you stay the same. But of course you don't stay the same.' Then he said, 'Well,' sharply, to dismiss the thought. He pulled Blackburn's arm and swung him around to Howe. 'Have you heard about Teddy Blackburn?' he asked. 'He has a job already, before graduation—the first man of his class to be placed.' Expectant of congratulations, Blackburn beamed at Howe. Howe remained silent.

'Isn't that good?' the Dean said. Still Howe did not answer and the Dean, puzzled and put out, turned to Hilda. 'That's a very fine-looking camera, Hilda.' She touched it with affectionate pride.

'Instruments of precision,' said a voice. 'Instruments of precision.' Of the three with joined arms, Howe was the nearest to Tertan, whose gaze took in all the scene except the smile and the nod which Howe gave him. The boy leaned on his cane. The broad-brimmed hat, canting jauntily over his eye, confused the image of his face that Howe had established, suppressed the rigid lines of the ascetic and brought out the baroque curves. It made an effect of perverse majesty.

'Instruments of precision,' said Tertan for the last time, addressing no one, making a casual comment to the universe. And it occurred to Howe that Tertan might not be referring to Hilda's equipment. The sense of the thrice-woven circle of the boy's loneliness smote him fiercely. Tertan stood in majestic jauntiness, superior to all the scene, but his isolation made Howe ache with a pity of which Tertan was more the cause than the object, so general and indiscriminate was it.

Whether in his sorrow he made some unintended movement toward Tertan which the Dean checked, or whether the suddenly tightened grip on his arm was the Dean's own sorrow and fear, he did not know. Tertan watched them in the incurious way people watch a photograph being taken, and suddenly the thought that, to the boy, it must seem that the three were posing for a picture together made Howe detach himself almost rudely from the Dean's grasp.

'I promised Hilda another picture,' he announced—needlessly, for Tertan was no longer there, he had vanished in the last sudden flux of visitors who, now that the band had struck up, were rushing nervously to find seats.

'You'd better hurry,' the Dean said. 'I'll go along, it's getting late for me.' He departed and Blackburn walked stately by his side.

Howe again took his position under the little tree which cast its shadow over his face and gown. 'Just hurry, Hilda, won't you?' he said. Hilda held the cable at arm's length, her other arm crooked and her fingers crisped. She rose on her toes and said 'Ready,' and pressed the release. 'Thank you,' she said gravely and began to dismantle her camera as he hurried off to join the procession.

---

# Leslie Aumaire

*Harold Witt*

Few in my school understood Leslie Aumaire,
who plucked and penciled his eyebrows and dyed his hair
and dared the difference it takes to be a dancer—

in that night dark of my school not many cared
for any attempt at art if we didn't have to
and wouldn't go near the edge where his feet veered.

We booed him offstage that time he came dancing on
with a painted face, in a tight ridiculous costume,
after which I don't think he ever came back—
for us Swan Lake was someplace on the moon
and Leslie, if not a fairy, at least a freak—
who else would whirl with girls all afternoon

When bullshouldered helmeted heroes cleated the field?
I never found out what happened to Leslie Aumaire—
snickered from school, he may have left for the city
and danced into crime or into the limelight there—
but few of us stopped to remember, and less to pity
a boy who practiced what we could only desire.

---

*SUGGESTIONS FOR DISCUSSION*

• Point of view in any piece of writing involves more than the author's decision to use the first person *I* or *we* or the third-person, *he*, *she*, or *they*; it also involves the author's attitude toward his subject and toward his readers. In "Of This Time, Of That Place," Trilling relates the story in the third person. But is he objective? Is he closer to, more sensitive to, the instructor Howe than to the students? Does this point of view prejudice you against the students? That is, are you allowed to see Tertan and Blackburn as they really are, or only as Howe sees them? Does the author's attention to Howe prejudice you against the instructor, rather than the students?

• Would you judge Howe to be a good teacher? Examine his behavior in the classroom, in his conferences with students, in his assignments and discussions, in his grading. Would you want to take Freshman Composition with him? Or would you rather take it with Gold?

• What about his behavior as a new teacher who wants to make the academic life his career? Is he overcautious about doing the "right thing" in reporting a student's erratic behavior to the proper authority, the dean? Is his interest in helping Tertan, or in protecting himself from possible criticism?

• Does the fact that Tertan is later said to be really mentally ill justify Howe's "betrayal" to himself? To you?

• To what extent do Tertan and Blackburn represent the conflict of values, of goals, of desires operating inside Howe? To what extent does Howe's "betrayal" of Tertan represent a betrayal of himself? What could the instructor Howe or the college have offered Tertan that they did not? (What, in fact, does Howe try to do for Tertan?) Does the fact that the dean tells Howe that Tertan is officially mad let Howe off the hook? Does the author create sympathy for Howe by making his judgment correct, although Howe himself cannot get rid of his feelings of guilt and confusion?

• In *Waiting for the End,* literary critic Leslie A. Fiedler tells us that the fictional student Ferdinand R. Tertan, "the victim of his own language and imagination," was based on the real person of Allen Ginsberg, a leading poet-rebel of the "Beat" generation who has survived to become a *guru* for the "Hip" generation. Fiedler's discussion of Ginsberg partially explains why this anthology contains little fiction dealing with the college experience written by students from the student point of view: little of it exists. (Another explanation is the fact that students are urged to maintain a distance from the immediate when they try to write fiction; student literary magazines attest to this.)

Ginsberg, once a student of Trilling's, has never written about his college years in any detail. Says Fiedler:

> Such self-conscious devotees of un-reason, to whom the phrase "to flip," i.e., to go out of one's head, represents a supreme achievement, do not ordinarily write about classroom experience, for they are likely to be well out of it, and immune to nostalgia, before they have begun to define themselves. It is their teachers, therefore, loved for having, with whatever doubts, protected the right of others to "flip," but despised for not having dared cross that frontier themselves, for having preferred academic security to insanity, who must write the record as best they can.

Although Ginsberg frequently reads his poetry on college campuses, Fiedler suggests that his relationship to college is a "mockery and evasion," and quotes from Ginsberg's *Howl:*

> who passed through the universities with radiant cool eyes
> hallucinating Arkansas and Blake-light tragedy among
> the scholars of war,

> Who were expelled from the academies for crazy & pub-
> lishing obscene odes on the windows of the skull

• Trilling's story suggests that colleges often fail the brightest and most original thinkers among their students, and establish conditions whereby the well-adjusted or well-rounded Blackburns can acquire the background for successful careers. Is this as it should be? Should college instructors devote a disproportionate amount of time and energy to the brightest students, the potential poets? Would the mediocre students get shortchanged if they did so?

# The Student As Nigger

*Jerry Farber*

*Jerry Farber wrote this article for the campus paper at California State College at Los Angeles. It has had wide circulation since its first publication on April 4, 1967. He is presently on the English faculty of Cal State at San Diego. The young teacher now has published a book titled, like this essay,* The Student As Nigger.

Students are niggers. When you get that straight, our schools begin to make sense. It's more important, though, to understand why they're niggers. If we follow that question seriously enough, it will lead us past the zone of academic bullshit, where dedicated teachers pass their knowledge on to a new generation, and into the nitty-gritty of human needs and hang-ups. And from there we can go on to consider whether it might ever be possible for students to come up from slavery.

First let's see what's happening now. Let's look at the role students play in what we like to call education.

At Cal State, L.A. where I teach, the students have separate and unequal dining facilities. If I take them into the faculty dining room, my colleagues get uncomfortable, as though there were a bad smell. If I eat in the student cafeteria, I become known as the educational equivalent of a niggerlover. In at least one building there are even restrooms which students may not use. At Cal State, also, there is an unwritten law barring student-faculty love-making. Fortunately, this anti-miscegenation law, like its Southern counterpart, is not 100 per cent effective.

Students at Cal State are politically disenfranchised. They are in an academic Lowndes County. Most of them can vote in national elections—their average age is about 26—but they have no voice in the decisions which affect their academic lives. The students are, it is true, allowed to have a toy government of their own. It is a government run for the most part by Uncle Toms and concerned principally with trivia. The faculty and administrators decide what courses will be offered; the students get to choose their own Homecoming Queen. Occasionally, when student leaders get uppity and rebellious, they're either ignored, put off with trivial concessions, or maneuvered expertly out of position.

A student at Cal State is expected to know his place. He calls a faculty member "Sir" or "Doctor" or "Professor"—and he smiles and shuffles some as he stands outside the professor's office waiting for permission to enter. The faculty tell him what courses to take (in my department, English, even electives have to be approved by a faculty member); they tell him what to read, what to write, and, frequently, where to set the margins on his typewriter. They tell him what's true and what isn't. Some teachers insist that they encourage dissent but they're almost always jiving and every student knows it. Tell the man what he wants to hear or he'll fail your ass out of the course.

When a teacher says "jump" students jump. I know of one professor who refused to take up class time for exams and required students to show up for tests at 6:30 in the morning. And they did, by God! Another, at exam time, provides answer cards to be filled out—each one enclosed in a paper bag with a hole cut in the top to see through. Students stick their writing hands in the bags while taking the test. The teacher isn't a provo; I wish he were. He does it to prevent cheating. Another colleague once caught a student reading during one of his lectures and threw her book against the wall. Still another lectures his students into a stupor and then screams at them in a rage when they fall asleep.

Just last week, during the first meeting of a class, one girl got up to leave after about ten minutes had gone by. The teacher rushed over, grabbed her by the arm, saying "This class is NOT dismissed!" and led her back to her seat. On the same day another teacher began by informing his class that he does not like beards, mustaches, long hair on boys, or capri pants on girls, and will not tolerate any of that in his class. The class, incidentally, consisted mostly of high school teachers.

Even more discouraging than this Auschwitz approach to

education is the fact that the students take it. They haven't gone through twelve years of public school for nothing. They've learned one thing and perhaps only one thing during those twelve years. They've forgotten their algebra. They're hopelessly vague about chemistry and physics. They've grown to fear and resent literature. They write like they've been lobotomized. But, Jesus, can they follow orders! Freshmen come up to me with an essay and ask if I want it folded and whether their name should be in the upper right hand corner. And I want to cry and kiss them and caress their poor tortured heads.

Students don't ask that orders make sense. They give up expecting things to make sense long before they leave elementary school. Things are true because the teacher says they're true. At a very early age we all learn to accept "two truths" as did certain medieval churchmen. Outside of class, things are true to your tongue, your fingers, your stomach, your heart. Inside class, things are true by reason of authority. And that's just fine because you don't care anyway. Miss Wiedemeyer tells you a noun is a person, place or thing. So let it be. You don't give a rat's ass; she doesn't give a rat's ass.

The important thing is to please her. Back in kindergarten, you found out that teachers only love children who stand in nice straight lines. And that's where it's been at ever since. Nothing changes except to get worse. School becomes more and more obviously a prison. Last year I spoke to a student assembly at Manual Arts High School and then couldn't get out of the goddamn school. I mean there was NO WAY OUT. Locked doors. High fences. One of the inmates was trying to make it over a fence when he saw me coming and froze in panic. For a moment, I expected sirens, a rattle of bullets, and him clawing the fence.

Then there's the infamous "code of dress." In some high schools, if your skirt looks too short, you have to kneel before the principal, in a brief allegory of fellatio. If the hem doesn't reach the floor, you go home to change while he, presumably, jacks off. Boys in high school can't be too sloppy and they can't even be too sharp. You'd think the school board would be delighted to see all the spades trooping to school in pointy shoes, suits, ties and stingy brims. Uh-uh. They're too visible.

What school amounts to, then, for white and black kids alike, is a 12-year course in how to be slaves. What else could explain what I see in a freshman class? They've got that slave mentality: obliging and ingratiating on the surface but hostile and resistant underneath.

As do black slaves, students vary in their awareness of what's going on. Some recognize their own put-on for what it is and even let their rebellion break through to the surface now and then. Others—including most of the "good students"—have been more deeply brainwashed. They swallow the bullshit with greedy mouths. They honest-to-God believe in grades, in busy work, in General Education requirements. They're pathetically eager to be pushed around. They're like those old grey-headed house niggers you can still find in the South who don't see what all the fuss is about because Mr. Charlie "treats us real good."

College entrance requirements tend to favor the Toms and screen out the rebels. Not entirely, of course. Some students at Cal State, L.A. are expert con artists who know perfectly well what's happening. They want the degree or the 2-S and spend their years on the old plantation alternately laughing and cursing as they play the game. If their egos are strong enough they cheat a lot. And, of course, even the Toms are angry down deep somewhere. But it comes out in passive rather than active aggression. They're unexplainably thick-witted and subject to frequent spells of laziness. They misread simple questions. They spend their nights mechanically outlining history chapters while meticulously failing to comprehend a word of what's in front of them.

The saddest cases among both black slaves and student slaves are the ones who have so thoroughly introjected their masters' values that their anger is all turned inward. At Cal State these are the kids for whom every low grade is torture, who stammer and shake when they speak to a professor, who go through an emotional crisis every time they're called upon during class. You can recognize them easily at finals time. Their faces are festooned with fresh pimples; their bowels boil audibly across the room. If there really is a Last Judgment, then the parents and teachers who created these wrecks are going to burn in hell.

So students are niggers. It's time to find out why, and to do this, we have to take a long look at Mr. Charlie.

The teachers I know best are college professors. Outside the classroom and taken as a group, their most striking characteristic is timidity. They're short on balls.

Just look at their working conditions. At a time when even migrant workers have begun to fight and win, college professors are still afraid to make more than a token effort to improve their pitiful economic status. In California State colleges the faculties are screwed regularly and vigorously by the Governor and Legislature and yet they still won't offer any solid resistance. They lie flat on their stomachs, with their pants down, mumbling catch phrases like "professional dignity" and "meaningful dialogue."

Professors were no different when I was an undergraduate at UCLA during the McCarthy era; it was like a cattle stampede as they rushed to cop out. And in more recent years, I found that my being arrested in sit-ins brought from my colleagues not so much approval or condemnation as open-mouthed astonishment. "You could lose your job!"

Now, of course, there's the Vietnamese war. It gets some opposition from a few teachers. Some support it. But a vast number of professors who know perfectly well what's happening, are copping out again. And in the high schools, you can forget it. Stillness reigns.

I'm not sure why teachers are so chickenshit. It could be that academic training itself forces a split between thought and action. It might also be that the tenured security of a teaching job attracts timid persons who are unsure of themselves and need weapons and the other external trappings of authority.

At any rate teachers ARE short of balls. And, as Judy Eisenstein has eloquently pointed out, the classroom offers an artificial and protected environment in which they can exercise their will to power. Your neighbors may drive a better car; gas station attendants may intimidate you; your wife may dominate you; the State Legislature may shit on you; but in the classroom, by God, students do what you say—or else. The grade is a hell of a weapon. It may not rest on your hip, potent and rigid like a cop's gun, but in the long run it's more powerful. At your personal whim—any time you choose—you can keep 35 students up for nights and have the pleasure of seeing them walk into the classroom pasty-faced and red eyed carrying a sheaf of typewritten pages, with title page, MLA footnotes and margins set at 15 and 91.

The general timidity which causes teachers to make niggers of their students usually includes a more specific fear—fear of the students themselves. After all, students are different, just like black people. You stand exposed in front of them, knowing that their interests, their values and their language are different from yours. To make matters worse, you may suspect that you yourself are not the most engaging of persons. What then can protect you from their ridicule and scorn? Respect for Authority. That's what. It's the policeman's gun again. The white bwana's pith helmet. So you flaunt that authority. You wither whispers with a murderous glance. You crush objectors with erudition and heavy irony. And, worst of all, you make your own attainments seem not accessible but awesomely remote. You conceal massive ignorance—and parade a slender learning.

The teacher's fear is mixed with an understandable need to be admired and to feel superior, a need which also makes him cling to his "White supremacy." Ideally, a teacher should minimize the distance between himself and his students. He should encourage them not to need him . . . eventually or even immediately. But this is rarely the case. Teachers make themselves high priests of arcane mysteries. They become masters of mumbo-jumbo. Even a more or less conscientious teacher may be torn between the need to give and the need to hold back, the desire to free his students and the desire to hold them in bondage to him. I can find no other explanation that accounts for the way my own subject, literature, is generally taught. Literature, which ought to be a source of joy, solace and enlightenment, often becomes in the classroom nothing more than a source of anxiety—at best an arena for expertise, a ledger book for the ego. Literature teachers, often afraid to join a real union, nonetheless may practice the worst kind of trade-unionism in the classroom; they do to literature what Beckmesser does to song in Wagner's "Meistersinger." The avowed purpose of English departments is to teach literature; too often their real function is to kill it.

Finally, there's the darkest reason of all for the master-slave approach to education. The less trained and the less socialized a person, the more he constitutes a sexual threat, and the more he will be subjugated by institutions such as penitentiaries and schools. Many of us are aware by now of the sexual neurosis which makes white man so fearful of integrated schools and neighborhoods and which makes the castration of Negroes a deeply entrenched Southern folkway. We should recognize a similar pattern in education. There is a kind of castration that goes on in schools. It begins, before school years, with parents' first encroachment on their children's free unashamed sexuality and continues right up to the day when they hand you your doctoral diploma with a bleeding, shriveled pair of testicles stapled to the parchment. It's not that sexuality has no place in the classroom. You'll find it there but only in certain perverted and vitiated forms.

How does sex show up in school? First of all, there's the sado-masochistic relationship between teachers and students. That's plenty sexual, although the price of enjoying it is to be unaware of what's happening. In walks the teacher in his Ivy League equivalent of a motorcycle jacket. In walks the teacher—a kind of intellectual rough trade—and flogs his students with grades, tests, sarcasm and snotty superiority until their very brains are bleeding. In Swinburne's England, the whipped school boy frequently grew up to be a flagellant. With us the perversion is intellectual but it's no less perverse.

Sex also shows up in the classroom as academic subject matter—sanitized and abstracted, thoroughly divorced from feeling. You get "sex education" now in both high school and college classes: everyone determined not to be embarrassed, to be very up to date, very contempo. These are the classes for which sex, as Feiffer puts it, "can be a beautiful thing if properly administered." And then, of course, there's still another depressing manifestation of sex in the classroom: the "off-color" teacher, who keeps his class awake with sniggering sexual allusions, obscene titters and academic innuendo. The sexuality he purveys, it must be admitted, is at least better than none at all.

What's missing, from kindergarten to graduate school, is honest recognition of what's actually happening—turned-on awareness of hairy goodies underneath the petti-pants, the chinos and the flannels. It's not that sex needs to be pushed in school; sex is push enough. But we should let it be, where it is and like it is. I don't insist that ladies in junior high lovingly caress their students' cocks (someday, maybe); however, it is reasonable to ask that the ladies don't, by example and stricture, teach their students to pretend that those cocks aren't there. As things stand now, students are psychically castrated and spayed—and for the very same reason that black men are castrated in Georgia: because they're a threat.

So you can add sexual repression to the list of causes, along with vanity, fear and will to power, that turn the teacher into Mr. Charlie. You might also want to keep in mind that he was a nigger once himself and has never really gotten over it. And there are more causes, some of which are better described in sociological than psychological terms. Work them out. It's not hard. But in the meantime what we've got on our hands is a whole lot of niggers. And what makes this particularly grim is that the student has less chance than the black man of getting out of his bag. Because the student doesn't even know he's in it. That, more or less, is what's happening in higher education. And the results are staggering.

For one thing damn little education takes place in the schools. How could it? You can't educate slaves; you can only train them. Or, to use an even uglier and more timely word, you can only program them.

I like to folk dance. Like other novices, I've gone to the Intersection or to the Museum and laid out good money in order to learn how to dance. No grades, no prerequisites, no separate dining rooms; they just turn you on to dancing. That's education. Now look at what happens in college. A friend of mine, Milt, recently finished a folk dance class. For his final exam, he had to learn things like this: "The Irish are known for their wit and imagination, qualities reflected in their dances, which include the jig, the reel and the hornpipe." And then the teacher graded him A, B, C, D, or F, while he danced in front of her. That's not education. That's not even training. That's an abomination on the face of the earth. It's especially ironic because Milt took that dance class trying to get out of the academic rut. He took crafts for the same reason. Great, right? Get your hands in some clay? Make something? Then the teacher announced that a 20-page term paper would be required—with footnotes.

At my school we even grade people on how they read poetry. That's like grading people on how they fuck. But we do it. In fact, God help me, I do it. I'm the Adolph Eichmann of English 323. Simon Legree on the poetry plantation. "Tote that iamb! Lift that spondee!" Even to discuss a good poem in that environment is potentially dangerous because the very classroom is contaminated. As hard as I may try to turn students on to poetry, I know that the desks, the tests, the IBM cards, their own attitudes toward school and my own residue of UCLA method are turning them off.

Another result of student slavery is equally serious. Students don't get emancipated when they graduate. As a matter of fact, we don't let them graduate until they've demonstrated their willingness—over 16 years—to remain slaves. And for important jobs, like teaching, we make them go through more years, just to make sure. What I'm getting at is that we're all more or less niggers and slaves, teachers and students alike. This is a fact you want to start with in trying to understand wider social phenomena, say, politics, in our country and in other countries.

Educational oppression is trickier to fight than racial oppression. If you're a black rebel, they can't exile you; they either have to intimidate you or kill you. But in high school or college, they can just bounce you out of the fold. And they do. Rebel students and renegade faculty members get smothered or shot down with devastating accuracy. In high school, it's usually the student who gets it; in college, it's more often the teacher. Others get tired of fighting and voluntarily leave the system. This may be a mistake, though. Dropping out of college for a rebel, is a little like going North, for a Negro. You can't really get away from it so you might as well stay and raise hell.

How do you raise hell? That's a whole other article. But just for a start, why not stay with the analogy? What have black people done? They have, first of all, faced the fact of their slavery. They've stopped kidding themselves about an eventual reward in the Great Watermelon Patch in the sky. They've organized; they've decided to get freedom now, and they've started taking it.

Students, like black people, have immense unused power. They could, theoretically, insist on participating in their own education. They could make academic freedom bilateral. They could teach their teachers to thrive on love and admiration, rather than fear and respect, and to lay down their weapons. Students could discover community. And they could learn to dance by dancing on the IBM cards. They could make coloring books out of the catalogs and they could put the grading system in a museum. They could raze one set of walls and let life come blowing into the classroom. They could raze another set of walls and let education flow out and flood the streets. They could turn the classroom into where it's at—a "field of action" as Peter Marin describes it. And, believe it or not, they could study eagerly and learn prodigiously for the best of all possible reasons—their own reasons.

They could. Theoretically. They have the power. But only in a very few places, like Berkeley, have they even begun to think about using it. For students as for black people, the hardest battle isn't with Mr. Charlie. It's what Mr. Charlie has done to your mind.

## SUGGESTIONS FOR DISCUSSION

• Do you consider yourself, as a student, a "nigger" or a slave to any or all of your teachers, or to the educational system in general? If not, can you define your status by using another analogy? Explain why you chose the simile or analogy you did.

• How much does Farber tell you about California State, L.A., which, to his way of thinking, classifies students as "niggers," slaves unwilling to protest their slavery? Are all of his specifics of equal value in making the analogy legitimate? For instance, does waiting for an instructor outside of his office make a student a "nigger"? Does having a teacher who doesn't give a "rat's ass" about his subject matter make the student a "nigger"? Do college entrance interviews that tend to screen out rebels make those students who are accepted "Uncle Tom"-type "niggers"?

• If the evidence does not justify the analogy, does the purpose? What is Farber's purpose? Where in the essay does it become clear?

• Apply Farber's analysis of student-teacher-administration relationships, and his analogy, to the Trilling story. Are the students at Dwight College "niggers"? Of the two students most fully developed as characters, Tertan and Blackburn, which best fits the Farber analogy? Explain. Is Howe a teacher "without balls"?

• Apply the analogy to the Gold essay and discuss.

• Apply the analogy, or parts of it, to students you have known. Have you observed students being brainwashed? How did this take place? Be specific.

• How do your fellow students react to rebel types or misfits? Have you ever been in a class in which a student refused to salute the flag? Or refused to cut his hair? Or challenged the teacher's scholarly opinions or his authority to conduct the class? What happened to this student? How did the rest of the class react to his rebellion? To the consequences of his rebellion?

• Would *you* rather be in a class of rebels or in one of "Uncle Toms"? Or are you unaffected by the behavior and attitudes of your fellow students?

# THREE
# SELECTIONS

*Austin Warren, distinguished critic, scholar, and teacher, once said, "According to ancient traditions, the great teacher does not write, he speaks. Truths are endangered when committed to writing. A book can't comment on its own context. The living voice is necessary to the written word, to comment on it and to restore it." Here are classroom words of Austin Warren as hoarded by his students and former students at the University of Michigan.*

*Following this brief selection are two poems which indicate the almost pathetic restrictions faced by teachers and students who want to establish a close relationship. The poet John Berryman reflects on his own student experience in "Down and Out." "Elegy for Jane" was written by the late Theodore Roethke about one of his students at the University of Washington.*

## There Is Nothing I Can't
## Use in My Teaching

*Austin Warren*

To see this class again! Each of you with your own instress of inscape, every one with his own pungent tang or savor! How individual you are!

I want, in a sense, to teach something which I have not yet learned.

174

The boundaries set to a course should be delicate and evasive.

Today we have no arranged program, but we shall all speak in tongues . . . not a rigid scheme on the blackboard . . . nothing skeletal but something incarnational . . . .

I know what "good teaching" is; I just don't believe in it. It is like Sir Walter Scott's novels—first, a chapter of historical background; next, a chapter of character description; then, a chapter of . . . .

This is a class in which students are free to interrupt. It is far ruder than anything except an American high school. We listen controversially and polemically. We have a Platonic symposium, with quickness of dialogue and dialectic. Two or three people talk rapidly at once. I may be one of them. Intense attack, with specific questions darted at you, may come from anybody.

You can't be prepared in advance. The answer is not in the back of the book. It comes not out of the teacher, not out of the General Library, nor the adjoining Undergraduate Library. An existential answer, it comes out of honest self-examination; not out of calculation, but out of experience.

An author should take his art seriously, but not himself. A writer has to be spiritually naked—that is why some people prefer to be scholars—to keep their clothes on. Leave happiness to the animals. If a poet gets too happy, his poetry won't be any good.

I for one do not intend to mellow in time, but to be metaphoric, idiotic, and silly till the end of my days.

The laughter which I love most of all is not satirical, not derisive, not stereotyped. Mozart, that child of joy, expressed it in *The Magic Flute*. It is like Alleluia. Alleluia is a lovely kind of cosmic laugh.

I have a fascination in digesting all of reality. Everything outer must become inner. Only everything is enough.

No two leaves are alike, no two cats are alike, no two human beings are alike, but we all overlap.

# Down & Back

*John Berryman*

It is supernal what a youth can take
& barely notice or be bothered by
which to an older man would spell ruin.
Over Atherton I almost lost not only my mind

but my physical well-being!
night on night till 4 till 5 a.m.
intertangled breathless, sweating, on a verge
six or seven nerve-destroying hours

Sometimes a foul dawn saw me totter home
Mental my torment too all that fierce time
she "loved" me; but she wouldn't quite sleep with me
although each instant brought a burning chance

she suddenly might! O yes: it hung in the air
her livingroom was thick with it like smoke
both of us smelt it
blood sludges from a martini

This was during vacation, then my God
she went back to Northampton
& only wrote once or twice a day
in that prize-winning penmanship

I went back to the world sore & chagrined
with a hanging head & no interest
in anything.
I think it was then I flunked my 18th Century

I wrote a strong exam, but since it was Mark
a personal friend, I had to add a note
saying of the 42 books in the bloody course
I'd only read 17.
                    He liked my candour
(he wrote) & had enjoyed the exam
but had no option except to give me F in the course—

costing my scholarship. The Dean was nice
but thought the College & I should part company
at least for a term, to give me "time to think"
& regroup my forces (if I'd any left).

A *jolt*. And almost worse, I had let Mark down.
I set about to fix the second thing.
I paged the whole century through for five monk's months
keeping an encyclopedic notebook.

I made among other things an abridgement of Locke's *Essay*
down to some hundred pages
preserving all his points & skeleton
but chopping away superfluous exposition.

Mark thought it ought to be published
but we found out there was one in print already.
Anyway he changed my grade retroactively & talked to the Dean.
My scholarship was restored, the Prodigal Son
welcomed with crimson joy.

# Elegy for Jane

*Theodore Roethke*

I remember the neckcurls, limp and damp as tendrils;
And her quick look, a sidelong pickerel smile;
And how, once startled into talk, the light syllables leaped for her,
And she balanced in the delight of her thought,
A wren, happy, tail into the wind,
Her song trembling the twigs and small branches.
The shade sang with her;
The leaves, their whispers turned to kissing;
And the mould sang in the bleached valleys under the rose.

Oh, when she was sad, she cast herself down into such a pure
     depth,
Even a father could not find her:
Scraping her cheek against straw;
Stirring the clearest water.

My sparrow, you are not here,
Waiting like a fern, making a spiney shadow.
The sides of wet stones cannot console me,
Nor the moss, wound with the last light.

If only I could nudge you from this sleep,
My maimed darling, my skittery pigeon.
Over this damp grave I speak the words of my love:
I, with no rights in this matter,
Neither father nor lover.

# 3

## INSTITUTIONS

Colleges and universities have been created to honor man's loftiest and perhaps most loving concept of himself: Man is an intelligent animal who wants to, and can, learn. This chapter questions the ideal of learning and tries to discover why our institutions of learning frequently turn into nightmarish, Moloch-like creations rather than realizations of a dream. The selections describe the "it-ness" of the educational institution, which has acquired a life and purpose of its own.

David Boroff's "Status-Seeking in Academe" explains how to describe the "life" of a college, particularly as it affects the student. "Life in the Yellow Submarine" is Barbara Solomon's description of her experience at a university on its way to the academic "big time." Burton Clark analyzes a "hidden" function of the junior college (and, by implication, other colleges): how to cool off students who "unrealistically" aspire to the college degree. James S. Kunen takes on the Biggees, symbols of what he sees as the corrupt relationship higher education has developed with the military-industrial complex.

Oh! Come let's sing Ohio's praise,
and songs to Alma Mater raise;
while our hearts rebounding thrill,
with joy which death alone can still.

Summer's heat or Winter's cold,
the seasons pass, the years will roll;
Time and change will surely show
how firm thy friendship O-hi-o.
　　　　　　　　—*Carmen Ohio,* Ohio State University Alma Mater

To say that the major institutions of the new society will be predominantly intellectual is to say, primarily, that the basic *innovative* features of the society will derive not from business as we know it today, principally the "product corporation," but from the research corporations, the industrial laboratories, the experimental stations, and the universities. The skeleton structure of that new society is already visible.
　　　　　　　　—DANIEL BELL, *The Reforming of General Education*

# Status-Seeking in Academe

*David Boroff*

*A college has an identity. The tradition and reputation; the campus buildings and their location, the students, teachers, deans, and clerks; the rules and procedures; the athletic, cultural, social, and publishing activities of the college; the degrees offered; the orientation to the community—all of these make up the identity (or identities) of a college. David Boroff, who spent many years observing and writing about campuses, suggests five criteria for determining, informally and in terms that relate to the student's experience, the identity of the college as a whole and, also in student terms, for appraising the "excellence" of that identity.*

I wonder if I might draw from my own techniques in appraising colleges to suggest some "informal" indices of institutional excellence. A few of these things may seem absurdly homely, mere domestic bric-a-brac of the college community, but they are far more important than one might think. I have witnessed a direct correlation between the intellectual vitality of a school and the bravura of its bulletin boards. Harvard, Swarthmore, St. John's in Maryland, and Bennington provided some of the most entertaining and revealing of bulletin board *graffiti*. (Bulletin boards, after all, are the latrine scribblings of the literate.) At the other end of the spectrum, at a school grievously afflicted with lower middle-class anxiety, all bulletin board notices have to be cleared with a prissy office of student activities determined to civilize the barbarians. What does one do—schedule a course in bulletin board writing? Hardly. The sense of play, the social passions, the sheer idiosyncratic energy that turn up on a bulletin board are an expression of a school's ethos.

The bookstore is another cultural index. I have observed some terrifying displays of philistinism and intellectual torpor in some bookstores. At a small college I had occasion to visit, the bookstore was a kind of general store in which books were tucked away behind Bermuda shorts and long woolen stockings. And there wasn't a single magazine above the level of *Life* and *Time*. And let me make a plea right now for the enormous educative value of magazines. . . .

The browsing room in the library is another sensitive area. Here again the self-image of the institution is reflected. In a newly converted state university in the Southwest, I visited a browsing room that didn't venture beyond *The Collected Works of Robert Louis Stevenson* that some good soul had donated, and back issues of *Good Housekeeping*. How seriously can one take this institution's protestations of academic virtue? . . .

. . . The vital schools have meeting places where students—and faculty—can repair for coffee and conversation. One shrewdly administered college in the South combines its snack bar with its paperback bookstore—a conspicuously happy marriage! The most justly celebrated hangout in academia is the University of Wisconsin's Rathskeller ("The Rat"), where beer has corrupted no one, and where political debates flourish at any hour, class lines criss-cross (freshman girls meet *real* graduate students), and professors sit in earnest conference with students over cups of coffee.

Another index of cultural health is the student newspaper. Here again the itch for respectability among administrators can prove the undoing of an independent student press. I am amazed and appalled at the curious myopia among some college administrators—as if some schoolboy japery in print had serious consequences! The best schools are those in which the student press is untrammeled, where, in fact, interference is simply unthinkable, the ultimate impiety. At Harvard, Wisconsin, Michigan, Swarthmore, the student newspaper is not only an organ of information but a soapbox, a circus, an arena for the whimsical and sportive. Administrators afflicted with status problems are prone to overreact to such tomfoolery, but it obviously has its place.

To be sure, one can't "organize" an effervescent bulletin board, a spirited hangout, or an irreverent student newspaper. One can only create a climate which enables these to flourish.

## SUGGESTIONS FOR DISCUSSION

• Appraise your own college's spirit, using Boroff's "informal" indices. Add other indices—perhaps the literary magazine, school catalogue, student dress (is there a dress code?), free speech platforms, political organizations, architecture, the events calendar. Is there a unified image? Several images?

• Before enrolling at your college, what image did you have of the school? How was that image formed? Has the image changed? If you had a choice of colleges, what influenced the choice? The image of the college? Money? Distance from home?

• Do you believe you have been typed or are being typed by the image of the school you are attending? Will this influence (positively or negatively) your ability to get what you want (job, mate, and so on) after you graduate?

• Boroff says the best schools are those where "the student press is untrammeled, where . . . interference is simply unthinkable." Is there a totally free press at your college? To what extent can a paper put out by a journalism class be free? Are at least two publications necessary?

# Life in the Yellow Submarine: Buffalo's SUNY

*Barbara Probst Solomon*

*Barbara Solomon offers the reader a chance to look at a new state university which had a specific identity it wanted to create. From the perspective of a teacher who commuted from New York City to the upstate New York campus, the author questions the kind of "life" inside and outside the university.*

*The article, written during the popularity of the Beatles' song and movie "Yellow Submarine," was published in the October 1968 issue of* Harper's *magazine.*

I used to think that Los Angeles—the place where when you are looking to buy a home you are told you are buying "prime dirt" and the houses are called "structures"—I used to think *that* was the American nightmare of the twenty-first century, but things have speeded up, and now New York State is rivaling California. We now have our multi-university system, our State University of New York (SUNY); and in the midst of the dying elms of the dying town of Buffalo we have our own LA gone wild not far from the choked defunct Erie Canal.

I planed into Buffalo last fall, on what amounts to one of those writer-in-residence sort of things, and spent a few days walking through the city. In certain parts of Buffalo one still hears the Polish of another century. On the east side of town, along East Ferry, are the scars of the summer riots, open American wounds of summers past and summers to come. Poles, Negroes, a thriving Mafia, a Peace Bridge to Canada, the Albright-Knox Art Gallery, four Frank Lloyd Wright houses, sprawling old Victorian homes with the smell of the East and the shape of the Midwest colliding together—this is the landscape of Buffalo. There are, to be sure, new suburbs built in classic American monotonous style, and it has its dying Main Street—with the usual steady stream of garages, Sears Roebuck, and milk-shake stands, and there are, too, the surprising parts of Buffalo, rather beautiful circles, parks, and homes that on a foggy day recall Paris and the Luxembourg Gardens, some of that air of faded comfort that one associates with Proust, and the Avenue Foch.

Walking through the west side of the old parts of Buffalo I suddenly remember that at the turn of the century Buffalo was a prosperous middle-class town; the ladies of Pittsburgh and Cleveland wrote to Buffalo for their patterns and silks, until, perhaps symbolically, all that seemed to end with a post-Victorian shot in the air. An anarchist rebuffed by Emma Goldman as being "unstable" shot McKinley at the Pan-American Exposition, and because of a doctor's reluctance to use a new X-ray machine McKinley died of gangrene. Buffalo, too, slowly died of gangrene. The turn-of-the-century wealthy middle class wished nothing to be changed, and no new industry has come into the town— though of the belt of dying Northeastern towns Buffalo is a little luckier than most in that it is one of the major seats of the Mafia in the U. S. In the summer of 1967 its citizens were surprised that they, like the rest of America, could have their riots. . . .

Off Main Street with its Sears Roebuck, its garages and highway interstices, its delicatessens and malted delights, is the State University of New York at Buffalo, part of the explosion which includes Harpur and Stony Brook, and into which the state is pouring the usual billions of dollars. At present, it sits on a postage stamp of a campus of old buildings which was six years ago the private University of Buffalo—a small second-rate university famed primarily for its law school, which, way back in the 'thirties, was the seedbed for better schools. Louis Howe and David Riesman were among those who came out of it.

Old pseudo-Gothic, new slabs of Germanic concrete, and pink and blue Army-type quonset huts crammed together is about what Buffalo looks like now, a crowded mishmash, while everybody breathlessly waits for the enormous new building which is to serve as "campus," a presumed architectural glory that will, I gather, cost billions and be the largest single building outside of Brasilia. In the meantime, the student population is expanding at a galloping pace: some are still locals, left over from the days when this was a trolley-car university; the majority are pouring upstate from greater New York City and environs: they jet into Buffalo and are part of the experiment known as mass education. Martin Meyerson, formerly of Berkeley, presides over the vast complex and what he has to deal with is nothing less than a microcosm of America *Now:* new young hippie faculty, expensive "star" faculty, deadwood old faculty, eager students, hippie students, sullen students, an alien, generally hostile town, and a bureaucratic mess.

## LIVING OFF ITS FUTURE

After one week in the quonset hut known as the English department I felt I was going completely crackers, and then, like Yossarian in *Catch 22,* I decided there was nothing else to do but go *with* it and hope for survival.

One result of this decision was that—someone having noticed that at one point in my life I had done some film criticism—in a moment of weakness I found myself being prevailed upon to teach a course on film. Within a week my identity went from writer to film critic to *film expert,* and everybody, in breathless enthusiasm, pounced upon me as if I were personally bringing the latest word from Goddard, Warhol, etc.

One week we are living through the usual tensions and storms over Dow Chemical and the CIA, and when one of the students comes into my office shrieking that he's had it, is about to blow everything up, I assume he means the CIA. "No," he cries, "the milk machine! It's a thief. Eating my dimes, eating my dimes." I sympathize. Somehow, I feel, this one has got right smack to the heart of the problem.

For Buffalo, a university without a true past, is at present a Blanche du Bois, living off its electronic fantasy future. Its basic timidity and uncertainty about its own image make it lack the courage to be at times conventional, and fearfully and provincially it is desperately grasping at the "new." Filthy rich, it is buying up scholars and, along with them, supersalesmen who have no idea what they are selling or who the "customer" is—and, in line with its futurity, it is of course buying equipment like mad. There is so much money floating around as to create total chaos. Events pile upon pseudo-events in shrieking hysteria. More poetry readings are held, more East Europeans invited, more movies shown on any given day than anyone can absorb. Buffalo, like all provincial towns, vacillates between the poles of thinking that everything is going on elsewhere and that everything is going on in Buffalo. As a result, in order to make up for lacks and simultaneously prove its lack of lacks, there are the poets, the East Europeans, and the movies—in a greater density per square inch than anything on Morningside Heights. The University suffers constantly from indigestion.

The equipment is bought in bulk. Somewhere there is a reactor that either no one can locate or no one knows how to use. In the basement of the classics department is a printing press grinding out ancient Byzantine. Though library facilities are appalling, one is told not to worry—within a year we will have a new dial-a-matic book system.

Daily there are dreams spun to relieve the dreariness of Main Street, Buffalo, and most of the dreams center around the wonders of the Pentagonesque new campus to come: a movie theater that will show films twenty-four hours a day, a complex of seven theaters for a drama school complete with prosceniums to fit each theatrical era, and, as one administrator groaned to me, in sober recognition that the best thing that could possibly happen to Buffalo is to get it to "hold still" for a moment, "Do you realize that when examined closely to scale the theater they have planned is only slightly larger than Lincoln Center?"

At the heart of this is the good old-fashioned American principle that the past does not exist—and a tendency to put all one's paper chips into ideas about the future and progress which are irrevocably bound to a notion of happiness and goodness that is our natural national birthright, like manifest destiny.

One faculty member breathlessly announced to me that studies have been made about academic children. (Statistics are floating around for just about everything.) "We are producing a race of mental giants." The children are better, the campuses are unique, the future is glorious; meanwhile the fog in Buffalo is awful, and one professor has just bolted. To Haifa!

I quickly realize that one of my main functions is to read

the torrent of messages that are ground out daily by the purple mimeographing machine bought by the English department. There are memos for grants, for feelings, sentiments, sporadic student underground pronunciamentos, and lots of memos about MONEY. For people who live in the future, present time has no meaning. One of the first memos that comes my way is an apology to new faculty suggesting that if one has been in the university for less than four weeks it would be better to wait until spring before applying for summer grants. At the end of the day I am exhausted by the financial opportunities offered to me.

Well, I quickly adjust to the rhythm that nobody knows what is going on and if nothing works, it doesn't matter, because Buffalo is a child of the future. My second adjustment is to paranoia. I've always been fond of paranoia as a life style, but paranoia on a grand scale, preferably in some major European capital with good restaurants to plot in. Of course, for paranoia to work, I've always believed you have to have a lot of spare time; with the new small teaching loads (average of two courses a week), the placing of sixty-five assorted geniuses, would-be geniuses, poets, writers (Lionel Abel, Robert Creeley, John Logan, Leslie Fiedler, John Barth among them), the scholars looking nervously at writers, writers feeling sullen among all those Ph.D. types, all crammed together in a cinder-block Stalag 17 office, additionally huddled together because the university has no connection with the town of Buffalo—and even more intensely huddled because the Life of the Mind is being carried on in brutal weather and with an ugliness of surroundings that took imagination to produce—one is often overwhelmed by the sheer weight of the paranoia. I figure Tuesdays to read the memos (statistics: fifty thousand words come through the mimeo every week—about the size of a nice Françoise Sagan novel), and Wednesdays I save for the paranoia. I am greeted in the morning by a young assistant professor, Howard Wolf; he looks at the corridors with their attempts at McLuhan, posters frantically placed on every wall to cover the cinder blocks, "*Veh is mir,*" he groans, "the leftist gabardine axis, basement of the mind." Freud, Jung, Maoism, existentialism, Marcuse, agrarian anarchism, you name it, we have it, Buffalo gray, Klein's basement of the mind.

Buffalo, like all instant universities, in order to combat a physical environment that is hell, acquires faculty quickly by offering high pay and low teaching loads. While it flounders searching for an image of itself on paper, in practice its own style takes form. Many of the young faculty come from California, bringing with them an idea of Western mobility, of Western enthusiasm for new ideas, and a casualness of dress and life style; cramping Westerners into Dostoevskian-cum-American physical conditions results in a high degree of nervous tension. There are no crannies here, neither the electric feeling of a large city, nor the trees and buildings of a country campus to absorb any cultural or emotional shocks, to buffer professors' eccentricities, and here among the cinder blocks, everybody's emotional problems hit you unprotected.

The placing of a jet strip at the Buffalo airport three years ago has also made Buffalo into a suburb of New York City. More and more of the students are coming from Queens, Brooklyn, and the Bronx; for them, Buffalo, forty-five minutes' flying time out of La Guardia, is merely an extension of the New York megalopolis. Sitting in the English department one day, I looked down the hall and realized that the jet professor is truly here. I myself live in New York City, my home, my children are there, and having lived all over when my husband was a floating academic, distances truly meant nothing either to me or to my children.

I often gave my children breakfast in New York, in the morning, saw them off to school, spent forty-five minutes on a jet to Buffalo, taught a few classes, and then came back home to New York not long after they got home from school. In looking down the hall it came to me (and I'm not talking about the $100,000-per-year elite, but ordinary associate professors) that one man commutes between Houston and Buffalo, another is on the New York-London circuit, another is on the Toronto-Buffalo-New York circuit, etc. In actual practice I see as many people from Buffalo in New York, at the end of a week, as I see in Buffalo during the week. Obviously the university is coming more and more to resemble the city, with all the problems of the city: it is inchoate, vast, confused, overly mobile, caught in a series of happenings and pseudo-events and visiting lectures. The students "watch events" with all the pitfalls of the anonymousness of the city; one professor found himself deeply shaken when he questioned a student about the problems of draft exile in Canada and realized that the student simply didn't know what he was referring to by way of place, family, home; the very words appearing to have lost their meaning.

The new professors are a cross between credit-card intellectuals, businessmen, and performing artists. One visualizes that within five, ten years, professors will be based wherever they choose to live and will essentially be delivering a series of lectures at a series of universities—which is more or less what is being done now. If the university resembles the city, emotionally it also resembles the Army. Allegiance is not to a specific post (a given school)—one is based at some post and transferred around within the total system (the university in America). The student is also on the move, and the problem of who might be where at a phone call already boggles the mind. The reality stands out clearer within the confines of a provincial university, and it is a frightening reality. The least discernible consideration, behind all the new academic window dressing, is the question of who is being taught what, and when.

Feeling a little discouraged, and often restless, I would have been glad to do more teaching than I was scheduled for—idle time in Buffalo is boring—but I quickly understood that to suggest such a thing would brand me a subversive in the system; they have graduate assistants for *that*. I once asked one of the university's vice presidents if any faculty ever, well, like did they ever discuss actual teaching, and he thought for a minute and said, well no, he couldn't remember any time offhand, occasionally students dropped by, but never faculty. At some point (he was showing me a great many graphs, and like those of every administrator I ever saw on the campus, all his graphs had to do with life ten years hence) I asked him how many students were on the campus.

"Do you mean real bodies or FTEs?"

"I mean *students*." I shuddered at the "real bodies," and I could not avoid imagining them stretched out, ready for a grave somewhere. "What's an FTE?"

"A full time equivalent," he rattled off. "You add up a number of credits, which is the equivalent to one real student—"

I shuddered again, told him I had a slow mind.

"We have *two sets of figures*," he explained, shoving yet another graph in front of my face, "one for real students."

"One for full time equivalents," I repeated after him, my eyes following the double graphs that look like a series of Mount

Everests in combat with one another. I gave up. As I was leaving, the vice president began to question me about, well, what exactly seemed to be going on around the place.

There are all types of paranoia. The form that that of the administrators takes—and the only thing I remember about my conversations with any of them, which I presume weren't very interesting—is the conviction that someone "down there," the reverse of the faculty's "someone up there," actually knows what's going on. That someone probably being a computer.

Administrators, I rapidly found, weren't worth talking to, as they seemed primarily to be armed with statistics pulled together for the purpose of implying that a youngster had to give some evidence of genius in his high-school average in order to get in to Buffalo. But once, downstairs in Hays Hall, as I waited for the snow to let up so I could leave, I talked with two students, one of whom said she liked it here but she had worked harder at the University of Miami, it had been a more serious place. Then what, I mentally asked of a graph, has intervened since high school?

Later in New York an architect friend of mine explained the whole thing to me. He's out at Stony Brook, a fellow university in the state system located in the far reaches of Long Island. He told me, "I, Barbara, am designing multi-interdisciplinary units for your full time equivalents. Capiche?" Buffalo believes in the rebirth of the humanities. . . .

## NIGHTMARES AND SOLUTIONS

Buffalo's basic problem is that it is a rapidly growing Goliath of an institution dealing with students who, despite the fancy statistics, arrive at the university as mixed-bag products of the bad American secondary schools from which they spring. Rather than concerning itself with this as a genuine educational problem —that is, how to give these students a general corpus of knowledge in which they are sadly lacking—the university has chosen to cover the basic mess with a quick and thick coat of fashionable instant gloss. Most of the professors have too much professional ego at stake to come to terms with the type of students they should be educating; and since the faster route to establishing the prestige of a university is via the graduate school and the Ph.D., the undergraduates, who should be the most important part of the process, get the short end of the stick. They are taught by the graduate assistants. Meanwhile there is no adequate advisory system for the students, and no very structured program. The present facilities are intolerable, and the present crop of students, like a generation of guinea pigs, are quite unmistakably being sacrificed to some fantasy of Buffalo's future greatness. One expects a new university to have problems; what is disturbing about Buffalo—and many other state institutions—is the sense one gets of the fraudulent, of the abrogation of faculty responsibility to the student, which the student in turn reflects in a lack of responsibility toward his own work.

Many of the young faculty don't seem to be in the least aware that the idea of the "new" is old-fashioned American nativism, or that all their talk about "free expression" is in fact a pretty stale inheritance from the 1930s (progressive education *in extremis*), that it was tried and proved a dismal failure, and that true intellectual freedom is hardly identical with chaos.

I watched the students one day when a visiting European novelist soberly contradicted a faculty member who referred to his work as "experimental." He replied that talk of the experimental is always nonsense, that everything he wrote was real, and came out of his experiences with a nightmare world. He told the students that nothing existed except reality, one had no "choice" in the matter, and proceeded to give them a solemn lecture on twentieth-century history. I felt their response, their eagerness and thirst for some sort of genuine encounter with true knowledge, their own fatigue at the word game which made up most of their instruction. Most of all, I felt their ability to perceive the truth when it is being told them. This is something they rarely get from their own faculty, especially those members of it who appear to have spent their own young adult lives on the Ph.D. track. Certainly the degree craze of American universities is one of the most anti-intellectual inventions ever conceived of. Between the Ph.D. requirement and the problem of tenure, the university in America is being reduced to a Bell Telephone psychology.

What then about Martin Meyerson, president of this whole complex? As former acting chancellor of Berkeley he has been burned once. As an urban planner, his dream is for the open campus—the university related to the town—a hard feat to accomplish in a sullen city which intensely dislikes the university and whose newspapers often heckle it for the wrong reasons.

Perhaps the most sophisticated and intelligent man on the campus and perhaps its most valuable asset—a shy man who does not come across well in public and is much more at ease in private conversation—Meyerson is faced with almost insurmountable problems. He is quite aware of the problems he has inherited— a new faculty, which veers spastically in a thousand directions at once, too many students, and these added to the worst kind of traditional, hidebound, rigid faculty inherited from the past regime. The combination is explosive. Then, too, there is Albany, one minute handing the university too much money for the wrong reasons, the next minute cutting the budget, also for the wrong reasons, creating more chaos of another kind as programs started cannot be finished: treating the university, in the way of state legislatures, as an angry parent treats a child, now I will be nice to you, now I will punish you.

Toward the end of the second term I am beginning to get nightmares about the whole thing. In the middle of one of those graying Buffalo nights, I sit up in bed, dreaming of solutions. The only group I had seen actually make something *work* on the campus were the Maoists—at least there was bright-eyed organizational discipline in their teach-in. Everything went off on schedule. Certainly there was good in Buffalo—the sense at least of life going on in the place, if at times a bit mad, it was better than no life at all. I thought of the children playing with balloons in a psychedelic tent with strobe lights and music, while nearby the old heated Marxist-Leninist rhetoric of the 'thirties was blanketing the teach-in, and there was something oddly moving and wistful about this American university, this "Buffalo Is a Winter Carnival" ambience that one didn't want to see altogether disappear—and something quite moving in Martin Meyerson's dream of a free and open campus. Still, something had to be done to make the whole thing work, so that geniuses, poets, students, and faculty could all go about their business in peace. Now the Maoists, they definitely had discipline—down to the last man, they would make far better administrators than the ones we had now. Meyerson, for a sort of gentle sobriety, a mediator . . . and to give the place a touch of intellectual elegance. But, for someone to do a crash job on the chaos . . . McNamara. Two weeks with him clearing up the yellow submarine, Pentagon style, and everything would be shipshape. He could lead the Maoists, and together they could attack. Mao and Mac, Mac and Mao, I went to sleep happily.

---

# University Examinations in Egypt

*D. J. Enright*

The air is thick with nerves and smoke: pens tremble in sweating
    hands:
Domestic police flit in and out, with smelling salts and aspirin:
And servants, grave-faced but dirty, pace the aisles,
With coffee, Players and Coca-Cola.

Was it like this in my day, at my place? Memory boggles
Between the aggressive fly and curious ant—but did I really
Pause in my painful flight to light a cigarette or swallow drugs?

The nervous eye, patrolling these hot unhappy victims,
Flinches at the symptoms of a year's hard teaching—
'Falstaff indulged in drinking and sexcess', and then,
'Doolittle was a dusty man' and 'Dr. Jonson edited the Yellow
    Book.'

Culture and aspirin: the urgent diploma, the straining brain—all
    in the evening fall
To tric-trac in the cafe, to Hollywood in the picture-house:
Behind, like tourist posters, the glamour of laws and committees,
Wars for freedom, cheap textbooks, national aspirations—

And, further still and very faint, the foreign ghost of happy
    Shakespeare,
Keats who really loved things, Akhenaton who adored the Sun,
And Goethe who never thought of Thought.

---

A University is a community of free men and women devoted to the preservation, increase, and application of knowledge. The University of Mississippi is dedicated to the service of Mississippi and the nation through the threefold functions of research, teaching, and public service.

The University is a community of teachers and students bound together by a common love for learning and by their cooperative efforts to preserve and increase our intellectual heritage. Good learning increases, minds are creative, and knowledge is turned to useful purposes when men and women are free to question and seek for answers, free to learn and free to teach.

In 1858 Chancellor Frederick A. P. Barnard laid before the Board of Trustees and the people of the state a plan for the University of Mississippi which still embodies its principal concerns and valid goals. He proposed "a university in the largest acceptation of that term, . . . an institution in which the highest learning is taught in every walk of human knowledge." Its purpose was "the high and noble work of training immortal minds to vigor and capacitating them for usefulness." Barnard saw that "the University is destined to act, invisibly it may be sometimes, but always powerfully, in every county, district and neighborhood in the State. [Only] a fraction of the people will receive their personal instruction within the University halls, yet all, without exception, will be partakers of the benefits of which the University is the fountainhead and central source." Its destiny is "to do more than any other single cause to stamp upon the intellectual character of Mississippi the impress it is to wear, to determine the respectability of the State in the eyes of mankind, to stimulate her industry, to multiply the sources of her material wealth, to elevate and purify the tastes of her people, to enlarge their capacities for happiness, and to enable them to fill up those capacities by supplying them with continually growing means of rational enjoyment."

—University of Mississippi General Catalogue, 1970

## SUGGESTIONS FOR DISCUSSION

• David Boroff offered specific standards for judging a campus culture. What standards does Solomon use to measure the cultural health of the SUNY at Buffalo campus specifically and the Buffalo community generally? What is her conclusion regarding the cultural health of both?

• Solomon believes the major educational problem was caused when the university started with an idea of what a university should be without considering the students who were to attend. What is that "idea" of a university? What other "ideas," formulas, or plans are there?

• How would you find out the "idea" of your college? Can you compare that "idea" with your views of yourself? For example, compare your recreational and cultural activities with the college's list of recreational and cultural activities. Compare your definition of the "best student" with what your teachers define as "best."

• Solomon states that SUNY at Buffalo is one prototype for America's future. Specify the elements of that prototype and discuss.

# The "Cooling-Out" Function
# in Higher Education

*Burton R. Clark*

*Burton Clark examines how a school's or even a person's self-image may hide, or at least blur, important realities. After studying the records, policies, and procedures of San Jose Junior College in California, the author developed a theory about the "hidden" social role of America's public junior colleges.*

*Clark wrote this article in 1960 for the* American Journal of Sociology.

A major problem of democratic society is inconsistency between encouragement to achieve and the realities of limited opportunity.[1] Democracy asks individuals to act as if social mobility were universally possible; status is to be won by individual effort, and rewards are to accrue to those who try. But democratic societies also need selective training institutions, and hierarchical work organizations permit increasingly fewer persons to succeed at ascending levels. Situations of opportunity are also situations of denial and failure. Thus democratic societies need not only to motivate achievement but also to mollify those denied it in order to sustain motivation in the face of disappointment and to deflect resentment. In the modern mass democracy, with its large-scale organization, elaborated ideologies of equal access and participation, and minimal commitment to social origin as basis for status, the task becomes critical. . . .

# THE ENDS-MEANS DISJUNCTURE

In American higher education the aspirations of the multitude are encouraged by "open-door" admission to public-supported colleges. The means of moving upward in status and of maintaining high status now include some years in college, and a college education is a prerequisite of the better positions in business and the professions. The trend is toward an ever tighter connection between higher education and higher occupations, as increased specialization and professionalization insure that more persons will need more preparation. The high-school graduate, seeing college as essential to success, will seek to enter some college, regardless of his record in high school.

A second and allied source of public interest in unlimited entry into college is the ideology of equal opportunity.[2] Strictly interpreted, equality of opportunity means selection according to ability, without regard to extraneous considerations. Popularly interpreted, however, equal opportunity in obtaining a college education is widely taken to mean unlimited access to some form of college: in California, for example, state educational authorities maintain that high-school graduates who cannot qualify for the state university or state college should still have the "opportunity of attending a publicly supported institution of higher education," this being "an essential part of the state's goal of guaranteeing equal educational opportunities to all its citizens."[3] To deny access to college is then to deny equal opportunity. Higher education should make a seat available without judgment on past performance.

Many other features of current American life encourage college-going. School officials are reluctant to establish early critical hurdles for the young, as is done in Europe. With little enforced screening in the pre-college years, vocational choice and educational selection are postponed to the college years or later. In addition, the United States, a wealthy country, is readily supporting a large complex of colleges, and its expanding economy requires more specialists. Recently, a national concern that manpower be fully utilized has encouraged the extending of college training to more and different kinds of students. Going to college is also in some segments of society the thing to do; as a last resort, it is more attractive than the army or a job. Thus ethical and practical urges together encourage the high-school graduate to believe that college is both a necessity and a right; similarly, parents and elected officials incline toward legislation and admission practices that insure entry for large numbers; and educational authorities find the need and justification for easy admission.

Even where pressures have been decisive in widening admission policy, however, the system of higher education has continued to be shaped partly by other interests. The practices of public colleges are influenced by the academic personnel, the organizational requirements of colleges, and external pressures other than those behind the open door. Standards of performance and graduation are maintained. A commitment to standards is encouraged by a set of values in which the status of a college, as defined by academicians and a large body of educated laymen, is closely linked to the perceived quality of faculty, student body, and curriculum. The raising of standards is supported by the faculty's desire to work with promising students and to enjoy membership in an enterprise of reputed quality—college authorities find low standards and poor students a handicap in competing with other colleges for such resources as able faculty as well as for academic status. The wish is widespread that college education be of the highest quality for the preparation of leaders in public affairs, business, and the professions. In brief, the institutional means of the students' progress toward college graduation and subsequent goals are shaped in large part by a commitment to quality embodied in college staffs, traditions, and images.

The conflict between open-door admission and performance of high quality often means a wide discrepancy between the hopes of entering students and the means of their realization. Students who pursue ends for which a college education is required but who have little academic ability gain admission into colleges only to encounter standards of performance they cannot meet. As a result, while some students of low promise are successful, for large numbers failure is inevitable and *structured*. The denial is delayed, taking place within the college instead of at the edge of the system. It requires that many colleges handle the student who intends to complete college and has been allowed to become involved but whose destiny is to fail.

## RESPONSES TO DISJUNCTURE

What is done with the student whose destiny will normally be early termination? One answer is unequivocal dismissal. This "hard" response is found in the state university that bows to pressure for broad admission but then protects standards by heavy drop-out. In the first year it weeds out many of the incompetent, who may number a third or more of the entering class.[4] The response of the college is hard in that failure is clearly defined as such. Failure is public; the student often returns home. This abrupt change in status and in access of the means of achievement may occur simultaneously in a large college or university for hundreds, and sometimes thousands, of students after the first semester and at the end of the freshman year. The delayed denial is often viewed on the outside as heartless, a slaughter of the innocents.[5] This excites public pressure and anxiety, and apparently the practice cannot be extended indefinitely as the demand for admission to college increases.

A second answer is to sidetrack unpromising students rather than have them fail. This is the "soft" response: never to dismiss a student but to provide him with an alternative. One form of it in some state universities is the detour to an extension division or a general college, which has the advantage of appearing not very different from the main road. Sometimes "easy" fields of study, such as education, business administration, and social science, are used as alternatives to dismissal.[6] The major form of the soft response is not found in the four-year college or university, however, but in the college that specializes in handling students who will soon be leaving—typically, the two-year public junior college.

In most states where the two-year college is a part of higher education, the students likely to be caught in the means-ends disjuncture are assigned to it in large numbers. In California, where there are over sixty public two-year colleges in a diversified system that includes the state university and numerous four-year state colleges, the junior college is unselective in admissions and by law, custom, and self-conception accepts all who wish to enter.[7] It is tuition-free, local, and under local control. Most of its entering students want to try for the baccalaureate degree, transferring to a "senior" college after one or two years. About two-thirds of the students in the junior colleges of the state are in programs that permit transferring; but, of these, only about one-third actually transfer to a four-year college.[8] The remainder, or two out of three of the professed transfer students, are "latent terminal students": their announced intention and program of study entails four years of college, but in reality their work terminates in the junior college. Constituting about half of all the students in the California junior colleges, and somewhere between one-third and one-half of junior college students nationally,[9] these students cannot be ignored by the colleges. Understanding their careers is important to understanding modern higher education.

## THE REORIENTING PROCESS

This type of student in the junior college is handled by being moved out of a transfer major to a one- or two-year program of vocational, business, or semiprofessional training. This calls for the relinquishing of his original intention, and he is induced to accept a substitute that has lower status in both the college and society in general.

In one junior college[10] the initial move in a cooling-out process is pre-entrance testing: low scores on achievement tests lead poorly qualified students into remedial classes. Assignment to remedial work casts doubt and slows the student's movement into bona fide transfer courses. The remedial courses are, in effect, a subcollege. The student's achievement scores are made part of a counseling folder that will become increasingly significant to him. An objective record of ability and performance begins to accumulate.

A second step is a counseling interview before the beginning of the first semester, and before all subsequent semesters for returning students. "At this interview the counselor assists the student to choose the proper courses in light of his objective, his test scores, the high school record and test records from his previous schools." [11] Assistance in choosing "the proper courses" is gentle at first. Of the common case of the student who wants to be an engineer but who is not a promising candidate, a counselor said: "I never openly countermand his choice, but edge him toward a terminal program by gradually laying out the facts of life." Counselors may become more severe later when grades provide a talking point and when the student knows that he is in trouble. In the earlier counseling the desire of the student has much weight; the counselor limits himself to giving advice and stating the probability of success. The advice is entered in the counseling record that shadows the student.

A third and major step in reorienting the latent terminal student is a special course entitled "Orientation to College," mandatory for entering students. All sections of it are taught by teacher-counselors who comprise the counseling staff, and one of its purposes is "to assist students in evaluating their own abilities, interests, and aptitudes; in assaying their vocational choices in light of this evaluation; and in making educational plans to implement their choices." A major section of it takes up vocational planning; vocational tests are given at a time when opportunities and requirements in various fields of work are discussed. The tests include the "Lee Thorpe Interest Inventory" ("given to all students for motivating a self-appraisal of vocational choice") and the "Strong Interest Inventory" ("for all who are undecided about choice or who show disparity between accomplishment and vocational choice"). Mechanical and clerical aptitude tests are taken by all. The aptitudes are directly related to the college's terminal programs, with special tests, such as a pre-engineering ability test, being given according to need. Then an "occupational paper is required of all students for their chosen occupation"; in it the student writes on the required training and education and makes a "self-appraisal of fitness."

Tests and papers are then used in class discussion and counseling interviews, in which the students themselves arrange and work with a counselor's folder and a student test profile and, in so doing, are repeatedly confronted by the accumulating evidence —the test scores, course grades, recommendations of teachers and counselors. This procedure is intended to heighten self-awareness of capacity in relation to choice and hence to strike particularly at the latent terminal student. The teacher-counselors are urged constantly to "be alert to the problem of unrealistic vocational goals" and to "help students to accept their limitations and strive for success in other worthwhile objectives that are within their grasp." The orientation class was considered a good place "to talk tough," to explain in an *impersonal* way the facts of life for the overambitious student. Talking tough to a whole group is part of a soft treatment of the individual.

Following the vocational counseling, the orientation course turns to "building an educational program," to study of the requirements for graduation of the college in transfer and terminal curriculum, and to planning of a four-semester program. The students also become acquainted with the requirements of the colleges to which they hope to transfer, here contemplating additional hurdles such as the entrance examinations of other colleges. Again, the hard facts of the road ahead are brought to bear on self-appraisal.

If he wishes, the latent terminal student may ignore the counselor's advice and the test scores. While in the counseling class, he is also in other courses, and he can wait to see what happens. Adverse counseling advice and poor test scores may not shut off his hope of completing college; when this is the case, the deterrent will be encountered in the regular classes. Here the student is divested of expectations, lingering from high school, that he will automatically pass and, hopefully, automatically be transferred. Then, receiving low grades, he is thrown back into the counseling orbit, a fourth step in his reorientation and a move justified by his actual accomplishment. The following indicates the nature of the referral system:

> *Need for Improvement Notices* are issued by instructors to students who are doing unsatisfactory work. The carbon copy of the notice is given to the counselor who will be available for conference with the student. The responsibility lies with the student to see his counselor. However, experience shows that some counselees are unable to be sufficiently self-directive so seek aid. The counselor should, in such cases, send for the student, using the Request for Conference blank. If the student fails to respond to the Request for Conference slip, this may become a disciplinary matter and should be referred to the deans.
>
> After a conference has been held, the Need for Improvement notices are filed in the student's folder. *This may be important* in case of a complaint concerning the fairness of a final grade.[12]

This directs the student to more advice and self-assessment, as soon and as often as he has classroom difficulty. The carbon-copy routine makes it certain that, if he does not seek advice, advice will seek him. The paper work and bureaucratic procedure have the purpose of recording referral and advice in black and white, where they may later be appealed to impersonally. As put in an unpublished report of the college, the overaspiring student and the one who seems to be in the wrong program require "skillful and delicate handling. An accumulation of pertinent factual information may serve to fortify the objectivity of the student-counselor relationship." While the counselor advises delicately and patiently, but persistently, the student is confronted with the record with increasing frequency.

A fifth step, one necessary for many in the throes of discouragement, is probation: "Students [whose] grade point averages fall below 2.0 [C] in any semester will, upon recommendation by the Scholarship Committee, be placed on probationary standing." A second failure places the student on second probation, and a third may mean that he will be advised to withdraw from the college altogether. The procedure is not designed to rid the college of a large number of students, for they may continue on probation for three consecutive semesters; its purpose is not to provide a status halfway out of the college but to "assist the student to seek an objective (major field) at a level on which he can succeed." [13] An important effect of probation is its slow killing-off of the lingering hopes of the most stubborn latent terminal students. A "transfer student" must have a C average to receive the Associate in Arts (a two-year degree) offered by the junior college, but no minimum average is set for terminal students. More important, four-year colleges require a C average or higher for the transfer student. Thus probationary status is the final blow to hopes of transferring and, indeed, even to graduating from the junior college under a transfer-student label. The point is reached where the student must permit himself to be reclassified or else drop out. In this college, 30 per cent of the students enrolled at the end of the spring semester, 1955–56, who returned the following fall were on probation; three out of four of these were transfer students in name.[14]

This sequence of procedures is a specific process of cooling-out;[15] its effect, at the best, is to let down hopes gently and unexplosively. Through it students who are failing or barely passing find their occupational and academic future being redefined. Along the way, teacher-counselors urge the latent terminal student to give up his plan of transferring and stand ready to console him in accepting a terminal curriculum. The drawn-out denial when it is effective is in place of a personal, hard "No"; instead, the student is brought to realize, finally, that it is best to ease himself out of the competition to transfer.

## COOLING-OUT FEATURES

In the cooling-out process in the junior college are several features which are likely to be found in other settings where failure or denial is the effect of a structured discrepancy between ends and means, the responsible operatives or "coolers" cannot leave the scene or hide their identities, and the disappointment is threatening in some way to those responsible for it. At work and in training institutions this is common. The features are:

1. *Alternative achievement.*—Substitute avenues may be made to appear not too different from what is given up, particularly as to status. The person destined to be denied or who fails is invited to interpret the second effort as more appropriate to his particular talent and is made to see that it will be the less frustrating. Here one does not fail but rectifies a mistake. The substitute status reflects less unfavorably on personal capacity than does being dismissed and forced to leave the scene. The terminal student in the junior college may appear not very different from the transfer student—an "engineering aide," for example, instead of an "engineer"—and to be proceeding to something with a status of its own. Failure in college can be treated as if it did not happen; so, too, can poor performance in industry.[16]

2. *Gradual disengagement.*—By a gradual series of steps, movement to a goal may be stalled, self-assessment encouraged, and evidence produced of performance. This leads toward the available alternatives at little cost. It also keeps the person in a counseling milieu in which advice is furnished, whether actively sought or not. Compared with the original hopes, however, it is a deteriorating situation. If the individual does not give up peacefully, he will be in trouble.

3. *Objective denial.*—Reorientation is, finally, confrontation by the facts. A record of poor performance helps to detach the organization and its agents from the emotional aspects of the cooling-out work. In a sense, the overaspiring student in the junior college confronts himself, as he lives with the accumulating

evidence, instead of the organization. The college offers opportunity; it is the record that forces denial. Record-keeping and other bureaucratic procedures appeal to universal criteria and reduce the influence of personal ties, and the personnel are thereby protected. Modern personnel record-keeping, in general, has the function of documenting denial.

4. *Agents of consolation.*—Counselors are available who are patient with the overambitious and who work to change their intentions. They believe in the value of the alternative careers, though of lower social status, and are practiced in consoling. In college and in other settings counseling is to reduce aspiration as well as to define and to help fulfill it. The teacher-counselor in the "soft" junior college is in contrast to the scholar in the "hard" college who simply gives a low grade to the failing student.

5. *Avoidance of standards.*—A cooling-out process avoids appealing to standards that are ambiguous to begin with. While a "hard" attitude toward failure generally allows a single set of criteria, a "soft" treatment assumes that many kinds of ability are valuable, each in its place. Proper classification and placement are then paramount, while standards become relative.

## IMPORTANCE OF CONCEALMENT

For an organization and its agents one dilemma of a cooling-out role is that it must be kept reasonably away from public scrutiny and not clearly perceived or understood by prospective clientele. Should it become obvious, the organization's ability to perform it would be impaired. If high-school seniors and their families were to define the junior college as a place which diverts college-bound students, a probable consequence would be a turning-away from the junior college and increased pressure for admission to the four-year colleges and universities that are otherwise protected to some degree. This would, of course, render superfluous the part now played by the junior college in the division of labor among colleges.

The cooling-out function of the junior college is kept hidden, for one thing, as other functions are highlighted. The junior college stresses "the transfer function," "the terminal function," etc., not that of transforming transfer into terminal students; indeed, it is widely identified as principally a transfer station. The other side of cooling-out is the successful performance in junior college of students who did poorly in high school or who have overcome socioeconomic handicaps, for they are drawn into higher education rather than taken out of it. Advocates of the junior college point to this salvaging of talented manpower, otherwise lost to the community and nation. It is indeed a function of the open door to let hidden talent be uncovered.

Then, too, cooling-out itself is reinterpreted so as to appeal widely. The junior college may be viewed as a place where all high-school graduates have the opportunity to explore possible careers and find the type of education appropriate to their individual ability; in short, as a place where everyone is admitted and everyone succeeds. As described by the former president of the University of California:

> A prime virtue to the junior college, I think, is that most of its students succeed in what they set out to accomplish, and cross the finish line before they grow weary of the race. After two years in a course that they have chosen, they can go out prepared for activities that satisfy them, instead of being branded as failures. Thus the broadest possible opportunity may be provided for the largest number to make an honest try at further education with some possibility of success and with no route to a desired goal completely barred to them.[17]

The students themselves help to keep this function concealed by wishful unawareness. Those who cannot enter other colleges but still hope to complete four years will be motivated at first not to admit the cooling-out process to consciousness. Once exposed to it, they again will be led not to acknowledge it, and so they are saved insult to their self-image.

In summary, the cooling-out process in higher education is one whereby systematic discrepancy between aspiration and avenue is covered over and stress for the individual and the system is minimized. The provision of readily available alternative achievements in itself is an important device for alleviating the stress consequent on failure and so preventing anomic and deviant behavior. The general result of cooling-out processes is that society can continue to encourage maximum effort without major disturbance from unfulfilled promises and expectations.

1. Revised and extended version of paper read at the Fifty-fourth Annual Meeting of the American Sociological Association, Chicago, September 3–5, 1959. I am indebted to Erving Goffman and Martin A. Trow for criticism and to Sheldon Messinger for extended conceptual and editorial comment.

"Aberrant behavior may be regarded sociologically as a symptom of dissociation between culturally prescribed aspirations and socially structured avenues for realizing these aspirations" (Robert K. Merton, "Social Structure and Anomie," in *Social Theory and Social Structure* [rev. ed.; Glencoe, Ill.: Free Press, 1957], p. 134). See also Herbert H. Hyman, "The Value Systems of Different Classes: A Social Psychological Contribution to the Analysis of Stratification," in Reinhard Bendix and Seymour M. Lipset (eds.), *Class, Status and Power: A Reader in Social Stratification* (Glencoe, Ill.: Free Press, 1953), pp. 426–42; and the papers by Robert Dubin, Richard A. Cloward, Robert K. Merton, Dorothy L. Meier, and Wendell Bell, in *American Sociological Review*, Vol. XXIV (April, 1959).

I am indebted to Erving Goffman's original statement of the cooling-out conception. See his "Cooling the Mark Out: Some Aspects of Adaptation to Failure," *Psychiatry*, XV (November, 1952), 451–63. Sheldon Messinger called the relevance of this concept to my attention.

2. Seymour Martin Lipset and Reinhard Bendix, *Social Mobility in Industrial Society* (Berkeley: University of California Press, 1959), pp. 78–101.

3. *A Study of the Need for Additional Centers of Public Higher Education in California* (Sacramento: California State Department of Education, 1957), p. 128. For somewhat similar interpretations by educators and laymen nationally see Francis J. Brown (ed.), *Approaching Equality of Opportunity in Higher Education* (Washington, D.C.: American Council on Education, 1955), and the President's Committee on Education beyond the High School, *Second Report to the President* (Washington, D.C.: Government Printing Office, 1957).

4. One national report showed that one out of eight entering students (12.5 per cent) in publicly controlled colleges does not remain beyond the first term or semester; one out of three (31 per cent) is out by the end of the first year; and about one out of two (46.6 per cent) leaves within the first two years. In state universities alone, about one out of four withdraws in the first year and 40 per cent in two years (Robert E. Iffert, *Retention and Withdrawal of College Students* [Washington, D.C.: Department of Health, Education and Welfare, 1958], pp. 15–20). Students withdraw for many reasons, but scholastic aptitude is related to their staying power: "A sizeable number of students of medium ability enter college, but. . . few if any of them remain longer than two years" (*A Restudy of the Needs of California in Higher Education* [Sacramento: California State Department of Education, 1955], p. 120).

5. Robert L. Kelly, *The American Colleges and the Social Order* (New York: Macmillan Co., 1940), pp. 220–21.

6. One study has noted that on many campuses the business school serves "as a dumping ground for students who cannot make the grade in engineering

or some branch of the liberal arts," this being a consequence of lower promotion standards than are found in most other branches of the university (Frank C. Pierson, *The Education of American Businessmen* [New York: McGraw-Hill Book Co., 1959], p. 63). Pierson also summarizes data on intelligence of students by field of study which indicate that education, business, and social science rank near the bottom in quality of students (*ibid.*, pp. 65–72).

7. Burton R. Clark, *The Open Door College: A Case Study* (New York: McGraw-Hill Book Co., 1960), pp. 44–45.

8. *Ibid.*, p. 116.

9. Leland L. Medsker, *The Junior College: Progress and Prospect* (New York: McGraw-Hill Book Co., 1960), chap. iv.

10. San Jose City College, San Jose, Calif. For the larger study see Clark, *op. cit.*

11. San Jose Junior College, Handbook for Counselors, 1957–58, p. 2. Statements in quotation marks in the next few paragraphs are cited from this.

12. *Ibid.*, p. 20.

13. Statement taken from unpublished material.

14. San Jose Junior College, "Digest of Analysis of the Records of 468 Students Placed on Probation for the Fall Semester, 1956," September 3, 1956.

15. Goffman's original statement of the concept of cooling-out referred to how the disappointing of expectations is handled by the disappointed person and especially by those responsible for the disappointment. Although his main illustration was the confidence game, where facts and potential achievement are deliberately misrepresented to the "mark" (the victim) by operators of the game, Goffman also applied the concept to failure in which those responsible act in good faith (*op. cit., passim*). "Cooling-out" is a widely useful idea when used to refer to a function that may vary in deliberateness.

16. *Ibid.*, p. 457; cf. Perrin Stryker, "How to Fire an Executive," *Fortune*, L (October, 1954), 116–17 and 178–92.

17. Robert Gordon Sproul, "Many Millions More," *Educational Record*, XXXIX (April, 1958), 102.

# The Immigrant Experience

*Richard Olivas*

I'm sitting in my history class,
The instructor commences rapping,
I'm in my U.S. History class,
and I'm on the verge of napping.

The Mayflower landed on Plymouth Rock.
Tell me more! Tell me more!
Thirteen colonies were settled.
I've heard it all before.

What did he say?
Dare I ask him to reiterate?
Oh why bother
It sounded like he said,
George Washington's my father.

I'm reluctant to believe it,
I suddenly raise my *mano*.
If George Washington's my father,
Why wasn't he Chicano?


## SUGGESTIONS FOR DISCUSSION

• If you are a junior college student, is there a "cooling-out" process at work in your school? What experiences have you had with the process at your college or during high school?

• If you are a four-year college student, describe your experiences with the techniques of selection at your college and other schools you have attended. Are they "hard" or "soft"? Are they open or concealed? Do they affect many students?

• Do you believe that all young people are entitled to a four-year college education, at public expense, since the four-year degree has replaced the high school diploma as a prerequisite for the "better positions" in business and the professions? If you were a taxpayer, and felt that higher education was a heavy burden, would you not want colleges to "cool out" or "drop out" or "flunk out" students who were "incompetent"?

• The democratic principle behind the theory of the cooling-out process is that many kinds of ability are valuable, each in its place. Theoretically, a great plumber with a high school diploma is "better" than a mediocre engineer with a college degree. Do you believe this? Does society offer more rewards to the great plumber than to the mediocre engineer? How? With social status? With money? With power?

• Does the financial necessity to limit college enrollments act, as many critics conclude, as a device for maintaining rigid social class lines? Is it an example of institutional racism? If your college has an "open door" or "special" admissions policy, does it back up these promises of equal opportunity? What facilities exist to do the job of screening students? What kinds of tests are used? What kind of help is given to students who do not use the written forms of standard English very well? Are remedial classes smaller than others? What programs exist for minority students?

• Where else in American life and institutions is the "cooling-out" process used?

• What about the "cooling-in" process? Can you give instances of it at work in schools and other institutions? Does the following excerpt from "Channeling," a Selective Service System document, exemplify such a process? *

> While the best known purpose of Selective Service is to procure manpower for the armed forces, a variety of related processes takes place outside delivery of manpower to the active armed forces. Many of these may be put under the heading of "channeling manpower." Many young men would not have pursued a higher education if there had not been a program of student deferment. Many young scientists, engineers, tool and die makers, and other possessors of scarce skills would not remain in their jobs in the defense effort if it were not for a program of occupational deferment. Even though the salary of a teacher has historically been meager, many young men remain in that job seeking the reward of deferment. The process of channeling manpower by deferment is entitled to much credit for the large amount of graduate students in technical fields and for the fact that there is not a greater shortage of teachers, engineers, and other scientists working in activities which are essential to the national interest. . . .
>
> In the Selective Service System, the term "deferment" has been used millions of times to describe the method and means used to attract to the kind of service considered to be the most important, the individuals who were not compelled to do it. The club of induction has been used to drive out of areas considered to be less important to the areas of greater importance in which deferments were given, the individuals who did not or could not participate in activities which were considered essential to the Nation.

The Selective Service System anticipates evolution in this area. It is promoting the process by granting of deferments in liberal numbers where the national need clearly would benefit. . . .

From the individual's viewpoint, he is standing in a room which has been made uncomfortably warm. Several doors are open, but they all lead to various forms of recognized, patriotic service to the Nation. Some accept the alternatives gladly—some with reluctance. The consequence is approximately the same.

* Note: The concept of channeling is no longer being practiced by the Selective Service System.

# Why We're Against the Biggees

*James S. Kunen*

*James Kunen wrote this piece for* Atlantic *magazine during his participation in the widely publicized student sit-in and strike at Columbia University in the fall of 1968. His book* The Strawberry Statement: Notes of a College Revolutionary *(1968) has been such a success (it has been made into a film as well) that some New Left radicals must wonder if Kunen himself can keep from becoming one of the "Biggees" he criticizes.*

I have surveyed the opinions of the well-intentioned American middle class regarding Columbia. That is, I have spoken to my mother about it. She's been reading the *New Republic,* and is currently fond of saying that the Columbia rebellion was set up in advance by people who are not students at Columbia, and who do not have its interests at heart. This is entirely true.

The Columbia rebellion was set in motion by a nebulous group of outsiders who are variously known as the corporate power elite, the military-industrial complex, the Establishment. A friend of mine refers to them as the Biggees.

The Biggees are a small group of men. Little else about them is known. They are probably old. They possess wealth surpassing the bounds of imagination. They have no real needs or desires, but cultivate avarice as a sort of obsessive hobby. They sit in smoke-filled rooms, so it may be presumed that they smoke cigars. In the councils of the Biggees, one might hear decisions that one thought no one could make. Buy Uruguay. Sell Bolivia. Hold India. Pollute New York. The decisions are of incomprehensible variety, but they have in common the fact that they are swiftly implemented and invariably soak the Little Man.

Sometimes the Biggees slug it out with each other, as in the gold market, where they get down to the nitty-gritty of buying and selling *money* (a commerce that no one else can understand, let alone participate in), but more often they are after *our* coin.

The Biggees lie. They shout up and down that Vitalis has $V_7$, but they don't say what $V_7$ *is*. They say that Arrid stops wetness, but they don't explain why wetness should be stopped. (I can think of a lot of things that qualify for stoppage way ahead of wetness.) They lie about little things like that, and big things like Vietnam, the ghetto, Democracy. It's all the same—truth in lending, truth in labeling, truth in government; none of them exist.

The Biggees *control*. I read a sixth-grader's history paper about the Spanish-American War. The young boy, having put away his Mattel M-16 automatic rifle for the evening to do his homework, wrote that the 1898 war was fought by America to set the poor Cubans free from tyranny. He added that America traditionally fights on the side of right for justice and freedom and therefore always wins, "like in Vietnam today." The Biggees have that kid right where they want him. They've got his mind; when he's eighteen they'll take his body.

Look around you. The Biggees are everywhere. Look in your driveway. They build cars that dissociate in three years, and they make everybody buy them, and they're in on the gas biz too, so you can forget about mileage. And no one can make them change. You get organized and ask them to please just put all bumpers at a standard level so maybe a little less than 50,000 of us will die on the roads next year, but no, they can't do it. They can't do it because it will *cost* to do it, and anyway, if all bumpers were at the same height, then there wouldn't be any choice, and that's what democracy's all about. If you didn't know that that's what democracy's all about, there are frequent ads to remind you. It seems, for instance, that in socialist countries there are only three colors of lipstick, whereas capitalism provides forty.

And with these forty shades of lipstick the Biggees turn our women into nauga-babes (vinyl girls) who in pre-fab sexiness sit tracing cheap pictures in the air with cigarettes they never make up their minds to start smoking. And, arguing about what to-do to do next, one of these naugas might be heard to say, "It's a free country."

But it isn't a free country. You can't drop out of school because you'd be drafted, and you have to study certain things to get a degree, and you have to have a degree to make it, and you have to make it to get what you want, and you can't even decide what you want, because it's all programmed into you beforehand. You can *say* whatever you want, but you won't be heard because the media control that, but if you do manage to be heard, the People won't like it, because the people have been told what to like. And if they don't like you, they might even kill you, because the government endorses killing by exemplification.

All of which brings us to Columbia, because at Columbia we're all together and we teach each other and feel strong. The Biggees are killing people in Vietnam and keeping the blacks down at home, because they have to keep some people at the bottom for their system to work, or so they thought. Now they're finding out that the downs can really screw them up bad, so they'd like to raise them just a bit, but that would certainly cost, so for the moment they'll try to keep them down by promising them rewards if they behave.

So here we all are at Columbia not comprehending this great money motivation because we didn't grow up in a depression and have always had coin and therefore don't value it as highly as we might. We're right at Harlem, so we see how it is. And we've got the draft right on us, so we know how that is. And we don't like it. We don't like it at all, because we've got a lot of life ahead of us and we're for it. Killing and dying just don't make it with us.

And lo and behold, right here at Columbia where all we young angries are seething, who should be president but Grayson Kirk, a Biggee if ever there was one. Consolidated Edison, IBM, Socony Mobil, Asia Foundation, I.D.A.—he's got an iron in every fire that's consuming us. And it turns out that Military Intelligence has offices at the university, and Electronic Research Laboratories is raking in about $5 million per annum on radar, and we're in the Institute for Defense Analysis in a big way, and the School of International Affairs is hitting it off really well with the CIA. All the while the university is systematically desiccating the integrated community of Morningside Heights, and has its eyes on land all the way over to Seventh Avenue, so that some fine day there'll be a nice white suburban buffer zone in the middle of Manhattan, which people will know, by the inevitable iron gates around it, to be Columbia.

Seeing all this, we decided to change it. Of course, if you don't like it you can leave, but if you leave you're going to run into something else you don't like, and you can't go on leaving forever because you'll run out of places to go. So we decided to change it. We petitioned, we demonstrated, we wrote letters, and we got nowhere. We weren't refused; we were ignored. So one day we went into the buildings, and one day somewhat later we were pulled out and arrested and many people were beaten. In the intervening days we were widely accused of having ourselves a good time in the buildings. We did have a good time. We had a good time because for six days we regulated our own lives and were free.

But Dr. Kirk and his associates saw that we were free and they knew of course that that sort of thing must not be permitted. They knew also that they could not deal with our demands, because that would mean a breakdown of their law and a violation of their order. So they called in the police. And they expressed regret that the police injured 150 people, and they really did regret it, because the brutal bust showed everybody how far the powerful will go to retain their power, how far they will go rather than answer a single question, rather than admit that questions can be asked.

As I write this and as you read it people are dying. So you see it isn't really a topic for suburban conversation or magazine articles. It's something that must be dealt with. That's what's happening at Columbia, not a revolution but a counterattack. We are fighting to recapture a school from business and war and rededicate it to learning and life. Right now nobody controls Columbia, but if we get it, we will never give it back. And there are 5 million college students in the country watching us. And a lot of them have just about had it with the Biggees.

Another university president with extensive business connections is Grayson Kirk of Columbia. Among other activities he helps IBM with its educational program. Reciprocally, the company gave the university $1.5 million for its current fund-raising drive. Kirk also sits on the board of Consolidated Edison; about the time Con Ed came through with a large gift, Charles F. Luce, the chairman, was made a Columbia trustee. In addition, Kirk is on the board of the Greenwich Savings Bank, two mutual funds—Dividend Shares and Nation-Wide Securities—and is a director at Socony Mobil. Kirk owns about $50,000 of stock in these companies.

—JAMES RIDGEWAY, "Universities as Big Business"

[The university's] directions have not been set as much by the university's visions of its destiny as by the external environment, including the federal government, the foundations, the surrounding and sometimes engulfing industry.

The university has been embraced and led down the garden path by its environmental suitors; it has been so attractive and so accommodating; who could resist it and why would it, in turn, want to resist?

—CLARK KERR, *The Uses of the University*

## SUGGESTIONS FOR DISCUSSION

• What is Kunen's thesis?

• Why does he bring his mother into the piece? If you did not know that this article was originally printed in a middle- and upper-middle-class adult magazine, could you find evidence in the article that Kunen has a specific age–money–life-style audience in mind?

• Is his sophisticated, bantering, and often facile style more apt to be successful with this audience than an angry tone? (Would *your* mother be more apt to read Kunen than, say, Jerry Farber, even though Farber is a faculty member and Kunen a student rebel?)

• Are the Biggees everywhere in society? If so, how do you know that they are? How much do you know about antitrust laws and the reasons for their existence? Or about the growing tendency of big corporations to buy up little companies? Or big producers to buy up little farmers? What kinds of things does Ralph Nader speak out against? Does the

Truth in Lending law relate to what Kunen is talking about? Do consumer cooperatives?

• Kunen suggests that Grayson Kirk, then president of Columbia, and "a Biggee if ever there was one—Consolidated Edison, IBM, Socony Mobil, Asia Foundation, I.D.A.," sits on the boards of business corporations because Columbia University needs corporation money and the corporations need Columbia graduates. Why does Kunen object to this university-business you-scratch-my-back-and-I'll-scratch-yours relationship? Why does he object to the university-military relationship?

• Do the Biggees control your college? What evidence is there on your campus and in your community that the military-industrial complex has any control of your college or of other colleges in your area?

• Do you know who is on the board of trustees of your college? How much do you know about them? How did they get there? What or whom do they represent? Who makes the policies regarding attendance, academic standards (grades), disqualification for rebellious conduct, and so on, for your campus? Who sets the curriculum requirements for graduation or transfer? Who determines what vocation-oriented or professional courses will be offered at your college? Does private industry give any money, directly or indirectly, to your school? How? Are there any strings attached to this money? Does the federal government, military or nonmilitary, give financial grants, with strings attached, to your college?

• Do you object to this, as does Kunen? Why? If not, why not? How might the close relationship of business and your college benefit you personally?

• Kunen says that while Columbia University is thinking big money and war, it is behaving without humanity toward the society immediately surrounding the campus, that by extending its territorial limits it is hurting people. "We are fighting to recapture a school from business and war and rededicate it to learning and life," says Kunen. Are business and war and learning and life mutually exclusive? If business and war are a part of life, should a college, as a microcosm wherein "life" is learned, exclude business and war? Or should a college be a place "to inform, enlighten, and enrich the lives of students . . . [existing] within the society as the major force to keep the society intellectually honest and politically healthy?" Should the college educate the students to be "the instruments of cultural and social change; their minds are the means through which a society seeks its own future"? (The quotes are from Harold Taylor, former president of Sarah Lawrence College.)

# 4

## CHANGE

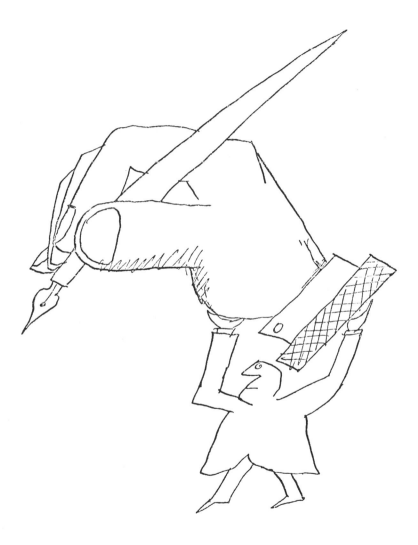

This chapter explores the potentialities, complexities, major tactics, and goals of change.

The news report from India is a reminder that student unrest isn't limited to the United States, nor are its causes always clear. The "Port Huron Statement" marks the beginning of the American student reform movement, setting forth the ideals of the movement and suggesting how students might work for them. A discussion among "representatives" of the student activists and the college establishment results in the faltering attempt at communication, "Violence and Power on Campus: A Debate." Philip Larkin's poem "Talking in Bed" suggests the difficulty of any communication, even under the best of conditions. The final piece is a detailed, subjective account of confrontation at one campus: Professor Michael Thelwell's "From Cornell: A Black Radical's Report on His Campus Struggles."

# Top Scholars Urge Inquiry into Calcutta "Orgies"

*The Times of India News Service*
*Calcutta, April 14, 1969*

A sifting and thorough inquiry into the "orgies" in parts of south Calcutta on April 6 to find out the real instigators and perpetrators of these crimes and to expose them and bring them to book has been demanded by four eminent educationists of West Bengal, including the National Professor, Mr. Satyen Bose.

It was clear, the educationists said, that this was not simply a sudden flareup of would-be entrants into the stadium getting impatient and incensed by lack of accommodation and failure of mikes, etc. It was something "deliberate and pre-planned," for visitors to musical functions do not usually carry with them bombs and crackers and petrol cans to hurt people and set cars and milk booths ablaze; "and they do not rush pell-mell assaulting women, who have to jump into the lake to escape assault and preserve their honour." In fact, several bodies had afterwards been recovered from the lake.

They alleged that ugly rumours were afloat through the city "despite the policy of hush-hush apparently followed by the authorities, the police and the Government." It was said that all this had been due to group factional rivalry, the hostile group engaging hundreds of goondas to wreck the function.

"Further, reports are rife from eyewitnesses that hundreds of saris were found the next morning strewn around the lake area; and that women, stripped naked, were seen running about seeking shelter. We do not know how far these reports are correct; but even if a hundredth part of these be true, Bengal has reason to hang its head in shame at the dishonour done to its womanhood by ruffians."

The educationists said rowdyism was now unfortunately the order of the day. But on this occasion rowdyism reached new dimensions.

# Port Huron Statement

## *Students for a Democratic Society*

*At a meeting in Port Huron, Michigan, in 1962, members of Students for a Democratic Society drafted and adopted this statement, generally considered the formal beginning of the American student reform movement. In the statement, the students set forth the social values and goals worthy of their respect and suggest means by which they and other students might work to achieve those goals.*

## INTRODUCTION: AGENDA FOR A GENERATION

We are people of this generation, bred in at least modest comfort, housed now in universities, looking uncomfortably to the world we inherit.

When we were kids the United States was the wealthiest and strongest country in the world; the only one with the atom bomb, the least scarred by modern war, an initiator of the United Nations that we thought would distribute Western influence throughout the world. Freedom and equality for each individual, government of, by, and for the people—these American values we found good, principles by which we could live as men. Many of us began maturing in complacency.

As we grew, however, our comfort was penetrated by events too troubling to dismiss. First, the permeating and victimizing fact of human degradation, symbolized by the Southern struggle against racial bigotry, compelled most of us from silence to activism. Second, the enclosing fact of the Cold War, symbolized by the presence of the Bomb, brought awareness that we ourselves, and our friends, and millions of abstract "others" we knew more directly because of our common peril, might die at any time. We might deliberately ignore, or avoid, or fail to feel all other human problems, but not these two, for these were too immediate and crushing in their impact, too challenging in the demand that we as individuals take the responsibility for encounter and resolution.

While these and other problems either directly oppressed us or rankled our consciences and became our own subjective concerns, we began to see complicated and disturbing paradoxes in our surrounding America. The declaration "all men are created equal . . ." rang hollow before the facts of Negro life in the South and the big cities of the North. The proclaimed peaceful intentions of the United States contradicted its economic and military investments in the Cold War status quo.

We witnessed, and continue to witness, other paradoxes. With nuclear energy whole cities can easily be powered, yet the dominant nation-states seem more likely to unleash destruction greater than that incurred in all wars of human history. Although our own technology is destroying old and creating new forms of social organization, men still tolerate meaningless work and idleness. While two-thirds of mankind suffers undernourishment, our own upper classes revel amidst superfluous abundance. Although world population is expected to double in forty years, the nations still tolerate anarchy as a major principle of international conduct and uncontrolled exploitation governs the sapping of the earth's physical resources. Although mankind desperately needs revolutionary leadership, America rests in national stalemate, its goals ambiguous and tradition-bound instead of informed and clear, its democratic system apathetic and manipulated rather than "of, by, and for the people."

Not only did tarnish appear on our image of American virtue, not only did disillusion occur when the hypocrisy of American ideals was discovered, but we began to sense that what we had originally seen as the American Golden Age was actually the decline of an era. The worldwide outbreak of revolution against colonialism and imperialism, the entrenchment of totalitarian states, the menace of war, overpopulation, international disorder, supertechnology—these trends were testing the tenacity of our own commitment to democracy and freedom and our abilities to visualize their application to a world in upheaval.

Our work is guided by the sense that we may be the last generation in the experiment with living. But we are a minority —the vast majority of our people regard the temporary equilibriums of our society and world as eternally functional parts. In this is perhaps the outstanding paradox: we ourselves are imbued with urgency, yet the message of our society is that there is no viable alternative to the present. Beneath the reassuring tones of the politicians, beneath the common opinion that America will "muddle through," beneath the stagnation of those who have closed their minds to the future, is the pervading feeling that there simply are no alternatives, that our times have witnessed the exhaustion not only of Utopias, but of any new departures as well. Feeling the press of complexity upon the emptiness of life, people are fearful of the thought that at any moment things might be thrust out of control. They fear change itself, since change might smash whatever invisible framework seems to hold back chaos for them now. For most Americans, all crusades are suspect, threatening. The fact that each individual sees apathy in his fellows perpetuates the common reluctance to organize for change. The dominant institutions are complex enough to blunt the minds of their potential critics, and entrenched enough to swiftly dissipate or entirely repel the energies of protest and reform, thus limiting human expectancies. Then, too, we are a materially improved society, and by our own improvements we seem to have weakened the case for further change.

Some would have us believe that Americans feel contentment amidst prosperity—but might it not better be called a glaze above deeply felt anxieties about their role in the new world? And if these anxieties produce a developed indifference to human affairs, do they not as well produce a yearning to believe there *is* an alternative to the present, that something *can* be done to change circumstances in the school, the workplaces, the bureaucracies, the government? It is to this latter yearning, at once the spark and engine of change, that we direct our present appeal. The search for truly democratic alternatives to the present, and a commitment to social experimentation with them, is a worthy and fulfilling human enterprise, one which moves us and, we hope, others today. On such a basis do we offer this document of our convictions and analysis: as an effort in understanding and changing the conditions of humanity in the late twentieth century, an effort rooted in the ancient, still unfulfilled conception of man attaining determining influence over his circumstances of life.

## VALUES

Making values explicit—an initial task in establishing alternatives—is an activity that has been devalued and corrupted. The conventional moral terms of the age, the politician moralities —"free world," "people's democracies"—reflect realities poorly, if at all, and seem to function more as ruling myths than as descriptive principles. But neither has our experience in the universities brought us moral enlightenment. Our professors and administrators sacrifice controversy to public relations; their curriculums change more slowly than the living events of the world; their skills and silence are purchased by investors in the arms race; passion is called unscholastic. The questions we might want raised—what is really important? can we live in a different and better way? if we wanted to change society, how would we do it?—are not thought to be questions of a "fruitful, empirical nature," and thus are brushed aside.

Unlike youth in other countries we are used to moral leadership being exercised and moral dimensions being clarified by our elders. But today, for us, not even the liberal and socialist preachments of the past seem adequate to the forms of the present. Consider the old slogans: Capitalism Cannot Reform Itself, United Front Against Fascism, General Strike, All Out on May Day. Or, more recently, No Cooperation with Commies and Fellow Travelers, Ideologies are Exhausted, Bipartisanship, No Utopias. These are incomplete, and there are few new prophets. It has been said that our liberal and socialist predecessors were plagued by vision without program, while our own generation is plagued by program without vision. All around us there is astute grasp of method, technique—the committee, the *ad hoc* group, the lobbyist, the hard and soft sell, the make, the projected image— but, if pressed critically, such expertise is incompetent to explain its implicit ideals. It is highly fashionable to identify oneself by old categories, or by naming a respected political figure, or by explaining "how we would vote" on various issues.

Theoretic chaos has replaced the idealistic thinking of old—

and, unable to reconstitute theoretic order, men have condemned idealism itself. Doubt has replaced hopefulness—and men act out a defeatism that is labeled realistic. The decline of utopia and hope is in fact one of the defining features of social life today. The reasons are various: the dreams of the older left were perverted by Stalinism and never recreated; the congressional stalemate makes men narrow their view of the possible; the specialization of human activity leaves little room for sweeping thought; the horrors of the twentieth century, symbolized in the gas ovens and concentration camps and atom bombs, have blasted hopefulness. To be idealistic is to be considered apocalyptic, deluded. To have no serious aspirations, on the contrary, is to be "tough-minded."

In suggesting social goals and values, therefore, we are aware of entering a sphere of some disrepute. Perhaps matured by the past, we have no sure formulas, no closed theories—but that does not mean values are beyond discussion and tentative determination. A first task of any social movement is to convince people that the search for orienting theories and the creation of human values is complex but worthwhile. We are aware that to avoid platitudes we must analyze the concrete conditions of social order. But to direct such an analysis we must use the guideposts of basic principles. Our own social values involve conceptions of human beings, human relationships, and social systems.

We regard *men* as infinitely precious and possessed of unfulfilled capacities for reason, freedom, and love. In affirming these principles we are aware of countering perhaps the dominant conceptions of man in the twentieth century: that he is a thing to be manipulated, and that he is inherently incapable of directing his own affairs. We oppose the depersonalization that reduces human beings to the status of things—if anything, the brutalities of the twentieth century teach that means and ends are intimately related, that vague appeals to "posterity" cannot justify the mutilations of the present. We oppose, too, the doctrine of human incompetence because it rests essentially on the modern fact that men have been "competently" manipulated into incompetence— we see little reason why men cannot meet with increasing skill the complexities and responsibilities of their situation, if society is organized not for minority, but for majority participation in decision-making.

Men have unrealized potential for self-cultivation, self-direction, self-understanding, and creativity. It is this potential that we regard as crucial and to which we appeal, not to the human potentiality for violence, unreason, and submission to authority. The goal of man and society should be human independence: a concern not with image or popularity but with finding a meaning in life that is personally authentic; a quality of mind not compulsively driven by a sense of powerlessness, nor one which unthinkingly adopts status values, nor one which represses all threats to its habits, but one which has full, spontaneous access to present and past experiences, one which easily unites the fragmented parts of personal history, one which openly faces problems which are troubling and unresolved; one with an intuitive awareness of possibilities, an active sense of curiosity, an ability and willingness to learn.

This kind of independence does not mean egotistic individualism—the object is not to have one's way so much as it is to have a way that is one's own. Nor do we deify man—we merely have faith in his potential.

*Human relationships* should involve fraternity and honesty. Human interdependence is contemporary fact; human brotherhood must be willed, however, as a condition of future survival and as the most appropriate form of social relations. Personal links between man and man are needed, especially to go beyond the partial and fragmentary bonds of function that bind men only as worker to worker, employer to employee, teacher to student, American to Russian.

Loneliness, estrangement, isolation describe the vast distance between man and man today. These dominant tendencies cannot be overcome by better personnel management, nor by improved gadgets, but only when a love of man overcomes the idolatrous worship of things by man. As the individualism we affirm is not egoism, the selflessness we affirm is not self-elimination. On the contrary, we believe in generosity of a kind that imprints one's unique individual qualities in the relation to other men, and to all human activity. Further, to dislike isolation is not to favor the abolition of privacy; the latter differs from isolation in that it occurs or is abolished according to individual will.

We would replace power rooted in possession, privilege, or

circumstance by power and uniqueness rooted in love, reflective-ness, reason, and creativity. As a *social system* we seek the establishment of a democracy of individual participation, governed by two central aims: that the individual share in those social decisions determining the quality and direction of his life; that society be organized to encourage independence in men and provide the media for their common participation.

In a participatory democracy, the political life would be based in several root principles:

that decision-making of basic social consequence be carried on by public groupings;

that politics be seen positively, as the art of collectively creating an acceptable pattern of social relations;

that politics has the function of bringing people out of isolation and into community, thus being a necessary, though not sufficient, means of finding meaning in personal life;

that the political order should serve to clarify problems in a way instrumental to their solution; it should provide outlets for the expression of personal grievance and aspiration; opposing views should be organized so as to illuminate choices and facilitate the attainment of goals; channels should be commonly available to relate men to knowledge and to power so that private problems—from bad recreation facilities to personal alienation—are formulated as general issues.

The economic sphere would have as its basis the principles:

that work should involve incentives worthier than money or survival. It should be educative, not stultifying; creative, not mechanical; self-directed, not manipulated, encouraging independence, a respect for others, a sense of dignity and a willingness to accept social responsibility, since it is this experience that has crucial influence on habits, perceptions and individual ethics;

that the economic experience is so personally decisive that the individual must share in its full determination;

that the economy itself is of such social importance that its major resources and means of production should be open to democratic participation and subject to democratic social regulation.

Like the political and economic ones, major social institutions—cultural, educational, rehabilitative, and others—should be generally organized with the well-being and dignity of man as the essential measure of success.

In social change or interchange, we find violence to be abhorrent because it requires generally the transformation of the target, be it a human being or a community of people, into a depersonalized object of hate. It is imperative that the means of violence be abolished and the institutions—local, national, international—that encourage nonviolence as a condition of conflict be developed.

These are our central values, in skeletal form. It remains vital to understand their denial or attainment in the context of the modern world.

## THE STUDENTS

In the last few years, thousands of American students demonstrated that they at least felt the urgency of the times. They moved actively and directly against racial injustices, the threat of war, violations of individual rights of conscience, and, less frequently, against economic manipulation. They succeeded in restoring a small measure of controversy to the campuses after the stillness of the McCarthy period. They succeeded, too, in gaining some concessions from the people and institutions they opposed, especially in the fight against racial bigotry.

The significance of these scattered movements lies not in their success or failure in gaining objectives—at least not yet. Nor does the significance lie in the intellectual "competence" or "maturity" of the students involved—as some pedantic elders allege. The significance is in the fact that the students are breaking the crust of apathy and overcoming the inner alienation that remain the defining characteristics of American college life.

If student movements for change are still rarities on the campus scene, what is commonplace there? The real campus, the familiar campus, is a place of private people, engaged in their notorious "inner emigration." It is a place of commitment to business-as-usual, getting ahead, playing it cool. It is a place of mass affirmation of the Twist, but mass reluctance toward the controversial public stance. Rules are accepted as "inevitable," bureaucracy as "just circumstances," irrelevance as "scholarship," selflessness as "martyrdom," politics as "just another way to make people, and an unprofitable one, too."

Almost no students value activity as citizens. Passive in public, they are hardly more idealistic in arranging their private lives: Gallup concludes they will settle for "low success, and won't risk high failure." There is not much willingness to take risks (not even in business), no setting of dangerous goals, no real conception of personal identity except one manufactured in the image of others, no real urge for personal fulfillment except to be almost as successful as the very successful people. Attention is being paid to social status (the quality of shirt collars, meeting people, getting wives or husbands, making solid contacts for later on); much, too, is paid to academic status (grades, honors, the med school rat race). But neglected generally is real intellectual status, the personal cultivation of the mind.

Look beyond the campus, to America itself. That student life is more intellectual, and perhaps more comfortable, does not obscure the fact that the fundamental qualities of life on the campus reflect the habits of society at large. The fraternity president is seen at the junior manager levels; the sorority queen has gone to Grosse Pointe; the serious poet burns for a place, any place, to work; the once-serious and never-serious poets work at the advertising agencies. The desperation of people threatened by forces about which they know little and of which they can say less, the cheerful emptiness of people giving up all hope of changing things, the faceless ones polled by Gallup who listed "international affairs" fourteenth on their list of problems but who also expected thermonuclear war in the next few years—in these and other forms, Americans are in withdrawal from public life, from any collective effort at directing their own affairs.

Some regard these national doldrums as a sign of healthy approval of the established order, but is it approval by consent or by manipulated acquiescence? Others declare that the people are withdrawn because compelling issues are fast disappearing; perhaps there are fewer breadlines in America, but is Jim Crow gone, is there enough work and is work more fulfilling, is world war a diminishing threat, and what of the revolutionary new peoples? Still others think the national quietude is a necessary consequence of the need for elites to resolve complex and specialized problems of modern industrial society. But, then, why should business elites help decide foreign policy, and who controls the elites anyway, and are they solving mankind's problems? Others finally shrug knowingly and announce that full democracy never worked anywhere in the past—but why lump qualitatively different civilizations together, and how can a social order work well if its best thinkers are skeptics, and is man really doomed forever to the domination of today?

There are no convincing apologies for the contemporary malaise. . . . The apathy is, first, subjective—the felt powerlessness of ordinary people, the resignation before the enormity of events. But subjective apathy is encouraged by the objective American situation—the actual separation of people from power, from relevant knowledge, from pinnacles of decision-making. Just as the university influences the student way of life, so do major social institutions create the circumstances in which the isolated citizen will try hopelessly to understand his world and himself.

The very isolation of the individual—from power and community and ability to aspire—means the rise of a democracy without publics. With the great mass of people structurally remote and psychologically hesitant with respect to democratic institutions, those institutions themselves attenuate and become, in a fashion of the vicious circle, progressively less accessible to those few who aspire to serious participation in social affairs. The vital democratic connection between community and leadership, between the mass and the several elites, has been so wrenched and perverted that disastrous policies go unchallenged time and again. . . .

The first effort, then, should be to state a vision: What is the perimeter of human possibility in this epoch? . . . The second effort, if we are to be politically responsible, is to evaluate the prospects for obtaining at least a substantial part of that vision in our epoch: What are the social forces that exist, or that must exist, if we are to be successful? And what role have we ourselves to play as a social force?

# THE CAMPUS REVOLT

"Students don't even give a damn about the apathy," one has said. Apathy toward apathy begets a privately constructed universe, a place of systematic study schedules, two nights each week for beer, a girl or two, and early marriage; a framework infused with personality, warmth, and under control, no matter how unsatisfying otherwise.

Under these conditions university life loses all relevance to some. Four hundred thousand of our classmates leave college every year.

But apathy is not simply an attitude; it is a product of social institutions, and of the structure and organization of higher education itself. The extracurricular life is ordered according to *in loco parentis* theory, which ratifies the administration as the moral guardian of the young.

The accompanying "let's pretend" theory of student extracurricular affairs validates student government as a training center for those who want to spend their lives in political pretense, and discourages initiative from the more articulate, honest, and sensitive students. The bounds and style of controversy are delimited before controversy begins. The university "prepares" the student for "citizenship" through perpetual rehearsals and, usually, through emasculation of what creative spirit there is in the individual.

The academic life contains reinforcing counterparts to the way in which extracurricular life is organized. The academic world is founded on a teacher-student relation analogous to the parent-child relation which characterizes *in loco parentis*. Further, academia includes a radical separation of the student from the material of study. That which is studied, the social reality, is "objectified" to sterility, dividing the student from life—just as he is restrained in active involvement by the deans controlling student government. The specialization of function and knowledge, admittedly necessary to our complex technological and social structure, has produced an exaggerated compartmentalization of study and understanding. This has contributed to an overly parochial view, by faculty, of the role of its research and scholarship; to a discontinuous and truncated understanding, by students, of the surrounding social order; and to a loss of personal attachment, by nearly all, to the worth of study as a humanistic enterprise.

There is, finally, the cumbersome academic bureaucracy extending throughout the academic as well as the extracurricular structures, contributing to the sense of outer complexity and inner powerlessness that transforms the honest searching of many students to a ratification of convention and, worse, to a numbness to present and future catastrophes. The size and financing systems of the university enhance the permanent trusteeship of the administrative bureaucracy, their power leading to a shift within the university toward the value standards of business and the administrative mentality. Huge foundations and other private financial interests shape the under-financed colleges and universities, not only making them more commercial, but less disposed to diagnose society critically, less open to dissent. Many social and physical scientists, neglecting the liberating heritage of higher learning, develop "human relations" or "morale-producing" techniques for the corporate economy, while others exercise their intellectual skills to accelerate the arms race.

The university is located in a permanent position of social influence. Its educational function makes it indispensable and automatically makes it a crucial institution in the formation of social attitudes. In an unbelievably complicated world, it is the central institution for organizing, evaluating, and transmitting knowledge. . . . Social relevance, the accessibility to knowledge, and internal openness—these together make the university a potential base and agency in the movement of social change.

1. Any new left in America must be, in large measure, a left with real intellectual skills, committed to deliberativeness, honesty, and reflection as working tools. The university permits the political life to be an adjunct to the academic one, and action to be informed by reason.

2. A new left must be distributed in significant social roles throughout the country. The universities are distributed in such a manner.

3. A new left must consist of younger people who matured in the post-war world, and must be directed to the recruitment of younger people. The university is an obvious beginning point.

4. A new left must include liberals and socialists, the former for their relevance, the latter for their sense of thoroughgoing reforms in the system. The university is a more sensible place than a political party for these two traditions to begin to discuss their differences and look for political synthesis.

5. A new left must start controversy across the land, if national policies and national apathy are to be reversed. The ideal university is a community of controversy, within itself and in its effects on communities beyond.

6. A new left must transform modern complexity into issues that can be understood and felt close-up by every human being. It must give form to the feelings of helplessness and indifference, so that people may see the political, social, and economic sources of their private troubles and organize to change society. In a time of supposed prosperity, moral complacency, and political manipulation, a new left cannot rely on only aching stomachs to be the engine force of social reform. The case for change, for alternatives that will involve uncomfortable personal efforts, must be argued as never before. The university is a relevant place for all these activities.

But we need not indulge in illusions: The university system cannot complete a movement of ordinary people making demands for a better life. From its schools and colleges across the nation, a militant left might awaken its allies, and by beginning the process toward peace, civil rights, and labor struggles, reinsert theory and idealism where too often reign confusion and political barter. The power of students and faculty united is not only potential; it has shown its actuality in the South, and in the reform movements of the North.

To turn these possibilities into realities will involve national efforts at university reform by an alliance of students and faculty. They must wrest control of the educational process from the administrative bureaucracy. They must make fraternal and functional contact with allies in labor, civil rights, and other liberal forces outside the campus. They must import major public issues into the curriculum. . . . They must make debate and controversy, not dull pedantic cant, the common style for educational life. They must consciously build a base for their assault upon the loci of power.

As students for a democratic society, we are committed to stimulating this kind of social movement, this kind of vision and program in campus and community across the country. If we appear to seek the unattainable as it has been said, then let it be known that we do so to avoid the unimaginable.

## SUGGESTIONS FOR DISCUSSION

• The group of idealistic students who wrote this Statement in 1962 viewed America as "stagnating" and most Americans as holding "the common opinion that America will 'muddle through,'" closing their minds to the future and offering no "viable alternatives to the present." "Our times," said the students, "have witnessed the exhaustion not only of Utopias, but of any new departures as well." What evidence do the student writers offer of the "stagnation" and "closed minds" they speak of? Are their examples still valid today? What "viable alternatives" do they suggest? Is their use of the word "Utopias" indicative of their idealism? Does exhaustion of Utopias necessarily, in their terms, mean the impossibility of a changed future?

• Much of the discussion in the "Port Huron Statement" is about values. The students say that our conventional moral terms "reflect reality poorly, if at all, and seem to function more as ruling myths than as descriptive principles." What are these "ruling myths" which have little relation to reality but which constitute our morality or values system? Discuss the relationship between the myths revealed in Chapter 1 and our present stated values.

• Do you feel, as do the students who drafted the Statement, that the "fundamental qualities of life on the campus reflect the habits of society at large"; in other words, that the college is a moral microcosm as well as a socioeconomic-political one?

• Are there people "on the make" (like Blackburn in Trilling's short story) on your campus? Are there "desperate" students "threatened by forces about which they know little and of which they can say less"? Are there students with "cheerful emptiness" and no hope of changing or desire to change things? What other values, or lack of them, do you observe on your campus which reflect society at large?

• The Statement says the university is a relevant place where, according to the students, a new left with viable alternatives to offer can be developed. Could a new left offering viable alternatives be created on your campus? If so, what positive indications for change, as outlined in the statement, exist on your campus? If not, what conditions prevail on your campus which would make the creation of a new left impossible? If one were to be created, would you join? Would you agree that "the ideal university is a community of controversy, within itself and in its effects on communities beyond"? Can you think of practical, concrete ways for a university movement to move out into the community and act to reform?

• Assume that you agree with the first part of the Statement: America is bereft of moral values matching reality and has no new ideas for the future. Are there ways other than the six points in the Statement (all of which call for involving the college or university in leadership or controversy) that the campus can effect change? Or should change be effected in the larger community, while the college remains aloof and educates in the traditional way?

# Violence and Power
# on Campus: A Debate

## Morris Abram, Seymour Lipset, Michael Rossman and Michael Vozick

*This arranged debate obviously does not succeed as a considered deliberation of a question: each speaker appears to be more interested in espousing his own cause than in genuinely exchanging ideas or arguing and offering proof for his position. The piece, then, stands as an example of noncommunication, which frequently takes place when representatives of certain positions are called on to "perform," rather than people with differing ideas being called on to consider their ideas together. Both Michael Rossman and Michael Vozick have been with the National Student Association; Rossman was a member of the steering committee of the Berkeley Free Speech Movement, and Vozick was one of the founders of the student-run Experimental College at San Francisco State College. Lipset is professor of Sociology at Howard University, and Abram is former president of Brandeis University. The debate was tape recorded and printed by the editors of* Change *magazine for the March/April 1969 issue.*

LIPSET: One of the problems with the student activists is that many of them completely misunderstand the power structure of the university. If I had to estimate the distribution of power in the good universities, I'd say 95 percent of the internal, on-campus power is in the faculty's hands, and maybe 5 percent or less is in the hands of the president and the trustees. From what I know of Berkeley, I'd say the biggest single structural change that's occurred there since the Free Speech Movement of 1964, particularly among the social sciences, is that the faculty is teach-

246

ing much less. This is an example of the unanticipated consequences resulting from social action. The students, by revolting, helped the faculty by increasing their bargaining power.

vozick: At Columbia, it's going to go even further; there is going to be a shift in the focus of power from administration toward faculty. Kirk really did have a much larger voice than any future administration at Columbia is going to have.

The question is, then, is there any behavior of which we are capable that would tend to empower students? First, to give the individual student a greater control over his own education. And second, to give students collectively complete power over their own social rules, and some power to influence the direction of the curriculum. In form, in liberal rhetoric, students have the power to decide whether or not to go to any college, and therefore, to make or break any institution. But because of a whole catalog of psychosocial phenomena, that power is not empirically present. The pressures on a student to join this culture by going to college are enormous. If the sharing of decisions with students is a hopeless cause, then those students who wish to participate in the control of their learning environments must organize in opposition to the powers-that-be on campus. So for me, the issue is whether the powers-that-be are capable of constructive abdication, or whether they have to be destroyed.

rossman: In its essential aspects I don't think the university is set up as an institution which *can* change. The university shares in common with other institutions of society the fact that it lacks an explicit sub-institution or mechanism which permits institutional change, and this has been coming out in Berkeley. Since 1964, the University of California has not significantly changed as an institution, has not shown itself capable of generating any mechanism which can make any significant change. It has improved the status of the faculty, but it cannot and will not and chooses not to empower the students.

abram: I think it's quite difficult to get changes in these relationships, even changes of a less fundamental nature. I decided that at Brandeis we ought to have a university council in which faculty, students and administration would debate the next steps in the development of the university. Now, I didn't want to choose faculty representatives, and I didn't want to choose student representatives, so I proposed that there be open elections for seats on this council. And I couldn't get either the faculty or the student representative bodies interested in having these elections.

VOZICK: Perhaps there is little in the experience of the individual student or the individual faculty member who was asked to vote in the elections that would indicate to him that you meant what you said.

ABRAM: I don't know what you mean. If I say let us have elections, faculty vote for faculty, students vote for students, this to me is participatory democracy. They could have run anyone they wanted.

VOZICK: One of the problems of my adult life is that I have been unable to develop confidence in the electoral process of the society that I'm in. It has to do with the behavior evidenced by those who participate in the structures of government. There is nothing in the experience of most students at a university which indicates to them that when the president says, "I want you to elect people and I'm going to empower them" that he means it. I'm not saying *you* didn't mean it. I'm just saying there's . . .

ABRAM: I never fooled them. I said they would be *advisory*. But questions as to the government of the university . . .

VOZICK: The problem that I would have in voting for an advisor is that I would want to know that the advisor had the capacity to advise with such power that he who was being advised would have to listen. And I know few such people, fewer still who would be willing to accept such a role.

LIPSET: I spent ten years working at the University of California where the faculty has had more formal power, where the faculty has had the most formal system of self-government, than faculties at any other major American university. There had been a faculty revolution in 1919 which resulted in an academic senate with enormous power. But what this produced was rule by the faculty "mediocracy." Most faculty members who were seriously interested in their research or teaching wouldn't serve on the large number of very time-consuming faculty committees which were set up to administer this self-government system. Conversely, other faculty—frequently the least scholarly ones—spent most of their working lives serving on committees. And California administrators have constantly deferred to these professional committeemen as if they were the esteemed leaders of the faculty. Most deans appointed at Berkeley were chosen on the recommendations of these highly unrepresentative committeemen. This is the system which is called faculty democracy at Berkeley.

Harvard is less democratic on a formal constitutional level than Berkeley. There are no elections to any faculty committee, and there are, in fact, far fewer faculty committees. Yet the Harvard administration, like all administrations in good universities, must clear all important decisions with the leaders of the faculty. No administrator could take any major action without doing this. When necessary, major faculty serve on key committees at Harvard, because committee service is not a life's work. In California, the administrators were often consulting and acting on the advice of the local campus politicians who really had no influence over the faculty as a whole.

I think one of Berkeley's problems was that it had too weak an administration, not too strong a one. . . .

Now, I am not arguing against faculty power on crucial matters—the faculty in any case retains control in all good schools over such important issues as faculty hiring, curriculum, and research policies. Rather, I am saying that an elaborate, formal system of faculty self-government means that the faculty's official representatives usually are self-elected, unrepresentative, weak people. Hence when a crisis occurs and the administration consults such faculty committeemen, it gets the opinions of men who are often out of touch with the more significant faculty. In a less institutionalized system, the administration must co-opt representative faculty into its councils or face the prospect of repudiation by the faculty.

ABRAM: I would no more think of making a fundamental decision about Brandeis without sounding out students and without sounding out faculty. I think it would be absurd to do so, particularly as a new president. But the point I would like to make is that I honestly feel that there is possibly in me and in maybe many other presidents and administrations an open-mindedness that does not exist in some of the more imbedded institutions of the university, including the faculty. For example, I do not know how one meets the problems of relevance in education without some interdepartmental appointments. But you try to make one and there will be resistance from the faculty.

LIPSET: I wouldn't bother trying.

ABRAM: You're right. I have frequently said, for example, that it might be difficult today to get Adolf Berle on the faculty of a great university in the field of economics. Although he is a great man who has made important and far-reaching contributions in his field, he may not fit into the niche of a particular economics department. His scope of interest and expertise would extend far beyond a departmental range.

LIPSET: You're talking here about the problem of faculty self-government. But compare its results to that of trade unions. As we all know, there are a lot of things that trade unions do which are not very good as viewed by the stndards of the general polity; for example, their racial discrimination, their economic selfishness, their lack of concern for community welfare. But unions are usually representing the will of their members in such actions. It is important to recognize that a democratic sub-unit which is relatively homogeneous will often engage in actions which, from the point of view of the larger society, are immoral or at least very selfish. Now, university faculties are fundamentally self-interested, exactly like union members. Democratizing faculty government is not going to produce a group of professors who are more concerned with what students want. Administrators, as a group, in fact, are generally much more interested in students than faculties are.

ABRAM: What I'm concerned about is the tendency of this new generation to approach every problem as if it had to be solved on the basis of power. I think it can be solved on the basis of reason, at least within a university. I've been a lawyer all my life. I have been in courtroom after courtroom in which I had no power of confrontation, which seems to be the new mystique or the new power or the new mode. All I had was the power of logic. There were no legions or divisions behind me. The lawyer on the other side had none either. My problem in understanding many of today's youth is that they start from the assumption that there must be some kind of battalions behind them—other than the force of their own logic. My life has been one of entering situations in which a neutral person must be convinced by the force of logic and ideas. I have never felt that I had to have "lawyer power" in the sense of a battalion of militiamen behind me, or a mob, or anything like that, in order to convince the court.

Students today talk to me in terms of the need to keep the student body unified on all issues, which, by the way, I think is anathema to a university. To have unified opinion, monolithic opinion, on *all* issues in a university seems to me to be contrary to the nature of the university and its mission. At any rate, students today somewhat amaze me when they say they feel the need of power when dealing with the faculty or with me because if they have ideas, I'm perfectly willing to listen.

ROSSMAN: Wait. You talk about logic and the power of logic. Now I really feel bitter. I—like Vozick, I am sure—was brought up buying lock, stock and barrel the academic ideology about a rational world and rational men. It was a long time before I found out about Yeats' "weasels fighting in a hole." There's a difference between an intellectual—which is a term I use as a sneer word—and the *working* intellectual. All the ideas about change and what to do are there already. I sit and think about what I'd like to do, what I'd like to see—it's all been written down 47 different times. You find it in Goodman; I can go back 92 years and find it in Dewey.

The trouble with the bloody university professors is that they don't understand the difference between an idea and its translation into social reality. They have no idea how to translate their ideas into social realities, and so they sit on their fannies, thinking nice ideas, putting them down in books, reading them to kids later on. It seems to me that the universities are not changing. You can see that we're heading straight for the culture breaking up and smashing up because it does not know how to change. Example: At Berkeley, how many faculty members, how many of the most prestigious intellectuals in the bloody country, came down and studied the FSM? At most, two faculty members made a direct study of the people involved. Generally, the faculty avoided us because there were these crowds of people there. They made these huge detours around the campus. They got very mad; they wouldn't come and listen. But if you want to learn about change, then you go and you talk to people who want to make change. You don't sit back and make intellectual formulations about it. The university is going to break wide open because it cannot change, and because the people in it are desperate for some kind of change which will accommodate their changing human reality. Because the university lacks any kind of mechanism for change, it is going to break violently—it *is* breaking violently. Violence exists because we live in a culture of violence, and also, for the first time in history, this is a culture which is addicted to chronic change, which generates its own progressive obsolescence. We need a new kind of cultural institution directly responsible for the health of change in the rest of the culture's institutions. Because we lack it, our culture is going to split up the middle. And it's going to be a violent split.

ABRAM: You critics are saying that the university is more important than its supporters say it is. Those of you who criticize the university are saying, frequently in unacceptable ways: "Our society is in deep trouble. The university has the capacity to redeem or reform society if only the university reforms itself." It is a compliment to the university that men in these times should crystallize their attention, anxieties, frustrations and anger on the university. But I would suggest that those who strike at the university strike at it purely because it's the closest institution and the most vulnerable institution to strike at.

ROSSMAN: That's untrue.

ABRAM: And I would suggest that it is probably the most fragile of all institutions.

ROSSMAN: That's not true either.

ABRAM: If you really want to change society, there are ways to do it within the system. How many voters have you registered, Michael? Not one, and you never will. Now, I am, as you are, a critic of the present society, but I would suggest that I've done a lot more about it than you have. I'll tell you why. I felt that the state of Georgia was in a dreadful condition by virtue of the fact that it did not have democracy there—it had a county-unit election system. I spent fourteen years in the courts and in elections to get rid of the unit system, and we won. I have spent a great deal of time in voter registration projects, which have registered 500,000 blacks in the South. But you people don't spend any time using the system to change the system. My feeling is that maybe the system won't work, but it's time to try it.

VOZICK: I respect you, and your work, and your position. And I think that the role you played in the speech you just made is essentially destructive and violent.

ROSSMAN: I'm not impressed. I don't think you know much about social change.

ABRAM: Some of us have produced a lot more than you have.

ROSSMAN: I don't think you've produced as much as I will. Let me say, first, why I think the university is important.

ABRAM: I think it's important, too. But I think you attack it because it's vulnerable.

ROSSMAN: That's not true. I think it's important—and an inherently violent institution. The university is not a place where information is exchanged; the university is a place where, increasingly, essentially all of the culture's main class spend a critical part of their development in a total life environment. The university is important because the culture assigns to it large numbers of its most important people for their last critical stage of maturation. Second, America is a deeply violent culture, and the university is an essential microcosm of America; the university is deeply violent. The central instrument of violence in American culture is not physical violence; it's the word. We are violent to each other in almost no other way, and therefore the central institutions of violence in America are those which deal with the word and with the killing abstraction. Advertising media are one example; the university is another. The university may be the central institution of violence in America.

ABRAM: Explain that.

ROSSMAN: Consider the standard classroom. I see two elements that testify to the violence that goes on there daily. One is boredom. Every student knows that almost all classes are just a drag, man, that's why so many universities still function with formal or informal restrictions designed to take punitive action against students if they escape the classroom.

ABRAM: You say boredom is violent? I'm opposed to boredom, but I don't think it's violent.

ROSSMAN: Stand and learn: If you listen to the silence that obtains in the standard classroom and compare that with the vitality of the people in there, it seems to me that you have to have an extraordinarily oppressive social context to reduce them to this silence of boredom, which in individual psychological cases is well established as being anger which will not permit itself to be expressed, anger that is so great that it is inexpressible. Therefore, I say the classroom is a hotbed of anger. Secondly, consider grades. I believe essentially that every student who comes into college—and I don't just mean Berkeley—if placed in a free and freeing environment, is capable of doing work which you would appropriately call 'A' work. One reason kids get bad grades is because that's a socially acceptable way of expressing their hostility.

ABRAM: Have you made a study of this, or is this *ex cathedra?*

ROSSMAN: This is the best understanding I have of the environment I grew up in. I say this anger and this hostility are indices that enormous violence is begun in the classroom, and one of the first things that happens when you lift the lid, one of the first things that happens when you relax the authority in the classroom, is that an enormous amount of visible anger boils over between people, between students and professors.

ABRAM: How do you know this?

VOZICK: That experience is widely shared, even if it's not written in the journals you respect most. And one of the most intriguing problems of this culture is that there is a whole new body of knowledge appearing which no one cares to put in the academic journals.

ROSSMAN: My last point: What are the significant technologies of social change in this day and age? I would much rather run a community FM station than have total control of four elections. I'm dead serious. What you have to do is change the way people perceive, think and express—that's where the root change comes. You give me control of what happens in the classroom, baby, you let me write and speak and touch people in such a fashion that it changes classroom relations and basic authority relations, and I'll give you the entire electoral system. You aren't going to have a chance: I'm going to have your kids. And I'm going to make your kids able to talk to each other in such a way that they're capable for the first time of coping with democracy on a mass scale. You're just messing around with the surface of social change. I'm going to have more of an impact on this country than you will unless I die at an early age, which is quite possible, in the streets of some city or on some campus, at the hands of that authority complex which does not release control, which marches into Czechoslovakia, which marches into Chicago and which shuts live speech out of the classroom.

ABRAM: Let me put this to you, Michael. If the faculty are as you have described them, then the problem is to break their authoritarian power in the classroom, is that right?

ROSSMAN: The place where the action is, is the classroom. The classroom is the arena of teacher power. In exchange for subscribing to the entire social system that exists in the departments, which is hierarchical and bureaucratic, the professor gets his piece of territory, and nobody comes and meddles with it. He's got a private, fragmented space. Professors don't help each other; professors don't criticize each other. Now the question of true empowerment, I think, ultimately centers in the heart of the learning process. True empowerment in the classroom means that the student can flexibly and ultimately shape his own education. You have a live human being there; he's got his own individual learning style, his own individual set of difficulties, his own set of needs, wishes, perspectives. The educative process must be made relative to and inclusive of that. Yet in the standard classroom now, 98 percent of the time is spent on the nominal material and content; and almost none on the way the live people there relate to one another, and within themselves, in the process of learning. For me, what it comes down to is making the deepest possible change in the social relationship obtaining in the classroom.

The thing which characterizes the classroom as a microcosm of all American society is authority. In this culture, authority is hierarchical, based on punishment and reward, and defined by role rather than relevance; it is not oriented at all to giving up control. There is one model of authority which permeates American society and which lends the characteristic definition to all its institutions. The teacher in the classroom, the cop on the street, the United States acting as policeman to the world, the father acting as parent to the child: these models are all the same in their essential elements. And so to make a real change in the classroom, if you're going to have a really flexible learning situation, you have to have a new notion of authority. So to make a real change in the university ultimately involves nothing smaller or less grandiose than moving to a radically new social system, in fact a radically new culture, both within the classroom and in the whole.

LIPSET: If I may interrupt, Michael, I would say that you're asking from the university something which it can't give. What you want is right but you're trying to get it in the wrong way, or at least you're trying to get it by focusing on single institutions.

Take the problem of faculty. If you consider the first-rate universities where presumably the students and faculty both are of a fairly high caliber, the faculty have been hired for their ability to do important research. There is nothing which can be done that's going to make them more concerned with teaching than research. If they drop research for teaching, they and their institutions would no longer be considered first-rate by the rest of the academic world. The reward system used everywhere in the world assigns prestige, and income, to institutions and individuals who are leaders in scholarship. You can't expect to change the system in any given school, because if you succeed in getting any one university to put pressure on its scholars to emphasize teaching, they'll just quit—there are plenty of other universities which will give higher salaries and lighter teaching loads to recruit prestigious scholars. Anything which interferes with the scholarly atmosphere of a university, including political turmoil, reduces the ability of schools to retain or hire men with scholarly interests.

ABRAM: I've had some say that to me.

VOZICK: I disagree . . .

LIPSET: Okay, disagree. The French events started at Nanterre, in the sociology department. There were four professors of sociology at Nanterre last year, the only place in France that has a department of sociology. You know how many there are right now? Zero. All four of them left or applied for transfer. Berkeley also has lost many faculty since 1964. Its rate of resignation among senior faculty, particularly in the social sciences, has been far higher than before the FSM. Berlin, the principal center of student unrest in Germany, has lost many professors since the disturbances started there in 1966.

VOZICK: I think the distinction between scholarship and teaching which has come to characterize the American educational establishment is self-destructive in a way which is obscenely degrading. It is degrading to any scholar and it is degrading to the responsibility that every man has to pass his knowledge on to the next generation. The problem is that the institutions of higher education have no respect for the acts of teaching and learning, which are their ostensible purposes.

LIPSET: You're wrong, you're totally wrong. The United States needs research institutes; it also needs schools. What we've done is to tack one on to the other. As we've changed to a more technological society, we've turned our best universities into major research institutes, while also keeping them as institutions of teaching and learning. It's not obscene. The problem is we have combined two different functions in one place, and that we reward one—scholarship—much more than the other—teaching. The reason for this is simple; scholarly prestige is ranked on a national, even international, basis, and is a relatively scarce commodity, while teaching cannot be so ranked—its prestige is local and does not travel—and hence does not have anything approaching the same scarcity value.

VOZICK: What is obscene is the idea that one can separate the creation of new knowledge from the transmission of knowledge.

LIPSET: You can't.

VOZICK: Right, but in the way prestige is granted in American institutions it is separated. For helping a student to actually learn, one gets little credit; for publishing a thick paper, one gets a great deal of credit, and this is a root problem.

ABRAM: I want to ask both Michaels a question: To what extent, in their judgment, will violence pay off in the reform of an institution—the university—which is, it seems to me, screaming for reform?

VOZICK: The first point that must be clear, difficult as it is to accept, is that violence is the norm of the university today. The violence takes a psychological form, that of someone controlling the environment in which you exist, preventing you from expressing yourself. Students cannot undo the violence that already exists, although some are trying to do that. One can no longer expect that the violence will simply disappear. The question is whether initiating more violence will do any good. It is my personal experience that it is unwise to initiate more violence in a violent situation; that what we are called on to do for spiritual reasons, if no other, is to simply present, in rooms like this, as clearly as we can, the most deeply striking thoughts and feelings that we have.

In this room I feel that I have tried, and that the effort has been quite inadequate.

ABRAM: You know you may be wrong.

VOZICK: I may be wrong . . .

ABRAM: So if a person doesn't understand you, does that give you the right to use violence?

VOZICK: I will only use violence at that point when I have no other alternative.

ABRAM: To do what? To get your way?

VOZICK: To try to generate an environment in which it is possible for me and others to live.

ABRAM: In *your* judgment?

VOZICK: In my judgment. It is only my judgment that I have to rely on whether I am alive or not.

ABRAM: Is it your position that if you should determine that despite the fact that there's been no violation of your person or of your rights according to law, that if you feel oppressed, you have the right to use violence, the right to assault?

VOZICK: Stop, stop. The problem is in the way you perceive structures in your mind around the word "assault."

ABRAM: I meant in the legal sense.

VOZICK: But I cannot accept your language fully.

ABRAM: Then each of us has the right, without regard to any system of rights and duties that hold society together, to decide at what point we will use violence?

VOZICK: Do you recognize the violence you're doing to me?

ABRAM: . . . Despite the fact that under any kind of objective norm, the other man has not used violence or any illegal measure against you?

VOZICK: The whole . . .

ABRAM: We each judge our own cause?

VOZICK: The ordinary, everyday academic America that educated me at the Bronx High School of Science, at Columbia University, at Johns Hopkins, appeared to me, when I started to become an adult, as deeply assaulting. The form that the assault took—the first form that became clear to me—was around the words *socialism* and *socialized medicine,* in that I had believed that socialism and particularly socialized medicine were inherently evil, unfair and unreasonable.

ABRAM: I was taught that but I didn't believe it.

VOZICK: Okay. But the dilemma is that I did. And the people that I feel my deepest allegiance to grew up believing that the American myth that they were taught was right, and are discovering by experience that it wasn't. And what I see happening is that an enormous force is appearing on the scene, a force of young people sharing a consciousness. It seems to me that if turned to violent ends it could be destructive, but it does not seem to me that it must be, nor does it seem to me that it basically is being turned to violent ends. When I talk with the young people in America, with whom I share that consciousness, I find that they are seeking alternatives that are not violent, but that what they are meeting are cold eyes and "mature wisdom" from scholars and administrators who are telling them that they are deeply wrong. And this is violating their sense of consciousness, violating

their sense of being whole human beings. And they are trying . . .

ABRAM: Mike, I'm not all that much older than you, and I was
at Nuremberg, and I want to tell you our society has deep faults,
like every society. Terrible paradoxes, racism, hatred, poverty,
ignorance. The tragedy is that it has all these things and it ought
not to have any of them, because this is the one society, and the
one time in the history of the world—truly, the first—which can
provide a decent life for everybody. It is a veritable cornucopia,
an economic machine that can do anything we want it to. And
we ruin it. We misapply the resources, we misdirect its energies,
and all of that. But, Michael, the difference between you and me
is that I have no illusions about the possibility of you and your
friends producing the perfect society, any more than I or my
friends have produced it. And if we let this beast of violence loose
in the street, there are more people who are prepared to use
violence for bad means—bad as measured by *your* definition—
than for good means—measured by your definition.

And if that beast gets loose, you are going to be devoured
first, and I'm going to be devoured second.

ROSSMAN: When I stop listening to the words in my head and
listen to my stomach, I'm oppressed by a deep sadness here. I've
never lifted a hand in physical anger since the third grade, yet I
have an impulse to take two of these glasses, knock them together
and use the shards to cut your throat. And you would look at me,
angrily or pitiably, and say, "But I never done you no wrong."
The difference between you and me is that we are both equally
violent persons, and that I am deeply conscious of it. The difference between us is that I am terribly conscious of my violence,
and you are, with pitiful blindness, unconscious of yours.

The question of violence and change on the bloody campus
is a fake question; it's an absolutely fake question. The basic
coin and trade on your campus is violence. The first step I can
see toward making this clear is to make anger in public places, to
make it clear what's going on underneath the bright intellectual
formations. All the kids on the campuses are doing is making the
first step toward a constructive theory of change, acting in such
a fashion that the violence which is continual and implicit and

permeating in all the processes of the university, suddenly, finally, becomes revealed in an actual physical form to the intellectuals who cannot bloody well recognize it now. So your question, *Is violence good for making change on the campus?*, is a totally delusive question. It's based on a very dangerously limited perception of where violence actually exists. But I would fall into its trap very directly and say: "Yes, blow up the administration hall. Yes, do that in the classroom which causes the teacher to get angry, or rather to display his intrinsic anger in a less polite form, which makes him lose that suave, cultivated control." Because the first step in finding out how to move from where we are is seeing clearly where we are.

America is violent. The fact is that America is now setting up to kill her children, as you learn if you go around this country with long hair, which makes you a new kind of nigger and a genuinely new kind of underclass. America's nature, the university's nature, are becoming visible. I don't know how to move from here, but I know that the way to start moving is to start seeing really clearly the nature of what is, to scrape your mind free of intellectual formulations of the past. If violence, when seen from a narrow, old cultural view, is one of the consequences, that saddens me, but it does not cause me pain.

The function the Berkeley FSM phenomenon served for the entire country was to clarify that change is not forthcoming in the institutions. The most eloquent lesson in Berkeley is that there's been *no* significant institutional change. For me, a young man with only one life to live, that tells me where it's at with change in this culture. It tells me you don't try to work to change the institutions in any recognizable fashion; you take the children over, you go build new institutions.

# Talking in Bed

*Philip Larkin*

Talking in bed ought to be easiest,
Lying together there goes back so far,
An emblem of two people being honest.

Yet more and more time passes silently.
Outside, the wind's incomplete unrest
Builds and disperses clouds about the sky,

And dark towns heap up on the horizon.
None of this cares for us. Nothing shows why
At this unique distance from isolation

It becomes still more difficult to find
Words at once true and kind,
Or not untrue and not unkind.

# "Without Law, the University Is a Sitting Duck . . ."

The two statements below by university presidents take on added significance in view of the following circumstances: Harris Wofford, one-time special assistant to President Kennedy on civil rights, was arrested in Chicago in August 1969 for participating in a silent march protesting police brutality at the Democratic Convention. He has insisted on a trial by jury. One of the character witnesses who will testify on his behalf is the Rev. Theodore M. Hesburgh of Notre Dame.

There seems to be a current myth that university members are not responsible to the law, and that somehow the law is the enemy, particularly those whom society has constituted to uphold and enforce the law. I would like to insist that all of us are responsible to the duly constituted laws of this university community and to all of the laws of the land. There is no other guarantee of civilization versus the jungle or mob rule, here or elsewhere.

If someone invades your home, do you dialogue with him or call the law? Without the law, the university is a sitting duck for any small group from outside or inside that wishes to destroy it, to incapacitate it, to terrorize it at whim. The argument goes— or has gone—invoke the law and you lose the university community. My only response is that without the law you may well lose the university—and, beyond that, the larger society that supports it and that is most deeply wounded when law is no longer respected, bringing an end to everyone's most cherished rights.

THEODORE M. HESBURGH, C.S.C.
President,
University of Notre Dame.

When the President of Cornell is assaulted physically by a student and the rule of two-by-fours takes over the public platform, which is what happened in Ithaca recently, those of us who protested lawless police violence in Selma and in Chicago have a duty to act just as promptly and strongly against lawless student violence. When necessary, as it was at Cornell, we must be prepared to enforce the rule of reason, by university action, by court injunction, and even by criminal prosecution of those who turn to force. That is unfortunate but not frightening.

What we should fear and the students should learn to fear is the temptation to try to decide issues by force. Persuasion is our profession, and we should know—as we hope the destructive minority will learn—that the old law of an eye for an eye leaves everyone blind.

So we must not surrender to force—that would truly be the

# COME!

Have tea and talk with us

⇨ SUNDAY 3 P.M.

Join students & faculty in the courtyard

of the Stanford Applied Electronics Laboratory


as guests of


Stanford Students Sitting-in

treason of the intellectuals. We must argue against and stand against those demands that seem unreasonable and wrong, and propose alternatives that make sense. We must find the ways to turn destruction into dialogue, confrontation into education, heat into light.

HARRIS WOFFORD, JR.,
President,
N. Y. State University College,
Old Westbury.

---

*SUGGESTIONS FOR DISCUSSION*

• What definitions of "violence" are stated or implied in the discussion? How does the fact that "violence" is given more than one definition make communication within the group difficult, if not impossible? If you had set up this debate, how would you have defined the term in order to get some real communication going?

• Are differing definitions of "power" and "authority" also responsible for the breakdown of the discussion?

• How well does each of the four participants succeed in clarifying the larger issues of power, authority, and violence, and the interrelationships of those issues, on campus? Michael Rossman says, "The thing which characterizes the classroom as a microcosm of all American society is authority." Does he develop his thesis adequately? In other words, what connections does he make between the authority found in the classroom and the authority found in American society? Are his connections logical and valid? When he says that the teacher (as an authority figure) is the equivalent of "the United States acting as policeman to the world," is he talking from an emotional or a rational point of view? Presumably, the American electorate can decide on a "new notion of authority" which would change America's international role. Can the student decide on a "new notion of authority" to change the concept of authority in the classroom? Does Rossman or Vozick express any ideas about how this change may be effected? (Did Farber offer any ideas?) Can you impeach a teacher?

• If violence can take a psychological form, as Rossman and Vozick contend, how can it—rather than physical violence—be used to achieve political and social ends? For instance, how can psychological violence, as Rossman and Vozick define it, be used to end the rule of the authoritarian teacher or the authoritarian administrator who hires the teacher? Does this ever come up in the debate?

# From Cornell: A Black Radical's Report on His Campus Struggles

*Michael Thelwell*

*Michael Thelwell teaches black literature at Cornell. He was a contributor to the book* William Styron's Nat Turner: Ten Black Writers Respond. *This report, obviously written from the black point of view, appeared in the July 1969 issue of* Ramparts *magazine.*

*"All sho'nuff dialogue come from the barrel of a gun."*—JUNEBUG J. JONES, CORNELL UNIVERSITY ADDRESS 21ST (DAY AFTER THE OCCUPATION OF WILLARD STRAIGHT HALL).

*"If, as we are constantly being told, there is a white power structure at this university, then it had damned well better start acting like one."*—VISITING PROFESSOR (WHITE), CORNELL UNIVERSITY, MAY 1ST.

If Sunday were not a "slow" news day, and if Americans—particularly white Americans—did not have an obsessional love-fear-guilt thing about guns, James A. Perkins, the president of Cornell University, would be resting more easily tonight. In fact he might have good reason to be downright pleased with himself and his administration. But for those two factors, Perkins would be able to point to the fact that Cornell was successfully weathering a potentially violent confrontation with its black students and their SDS supporters without large-scale destruction of property, massive police violence, or the "shutting-down" of the university's functions by dissident students—none of which Harvard, Columbia or Berkeley was able to avoid.

But Sunday *is* a slow news day and white America's guilt-ridden fascination with guns becomes paranoid hysteria when those guns are in the hands of young blacks. And the idea—greatly exaggerated by the way—that any part of the white society's governing institutions, even something as innocuous as a university, has "capitulated" or "surrendered" to those armed blacks evokes the beginning of the end, the specter of a black take-over, and blows white America's collective mind. So Perkins' regime, which was—until the appearance of the guns and what they refer to as "that damned picture"—one of the most skillful exponents of anticipatory compromise, has been shaken to the point where friend and critic give it no better than a 50–50 chance of survival. If the Perkins regime falls, it will be because the press said he "capitulated" to armed blacks—and to capitulate is unforgivable, even if the blacks were right and, as far as anyone could tell, quite determined to fight in dead earnest for their position.

The establishment has many strategies and tactics for dealing with dissent, but its ultimate weapon is violence. (There was no violence at Cornell, but nobody seems to remember that.) Short of violence, the establishment has minor ploys like transforming issues of principle into issues of etiquette (it is bad form for students to disrupt violently the Vice President's speech, even though a rotten egg is not a fire bomb and the Vice President *is* the spokesman for a policy of genocide in Viet-Nam). Another name for this is, of course, hypocrisy, and it is this process at work which has made the focal issue at Cornell the question of guns in the hands of the blacks. But the press in its foolish search for sensationalism has stumbled onto a question which may become crucial for the foreseeable future: *What if blacks and radicals generally refuse to concede the exclusive right to violence to the establishment?*

Traditionally, when the establishment calls for dialogue and negotiation it means *limited* dialogue. That is, it will, as my students say, "dialogue with" you until it grows weary or impatient, at which point the language of dialogue becomes the language of the nightstick and the Marines. This certainly has been the nature of all black dialogue with white America in the past. University administrations, despite their loud appeals to reasonable and civilized discourse, have reserved their right to "invoke cloture" by way of the machinery of violence that the system places at their disposal. It is only because the dissenters have tacitly conceded them this prerogative that the violence on university campuses has been "limited," if one considers broken heads and backs to be "limited" violence. Under the pressure of the situation the Cornell blacks were forced to take that option away from Perkins, and faced him with the necessity of choosing between equal negotiation or unlimited violence.

Negotiation from a position of equality becomes, in the language of the establishment, "capitulation." This is what got the trustees, the state legislature, the governor, and the conservative faculty up-tight: the recognition that the rules had been changed and that their traditional position of paternalistic power supported by the threat of violence was not operative. For the first time in four months the university had to *listen* to the blacks; all along they had been pretending to listen. Faced with the alternative of doing either a little "capitulation" or a little killing, they chose to negotiate for real—what is an appropriate response in Harlem, Watts, Newark, or Saigon is clearly inappropriate on an Ivy League campus. The black students violated not only the civilized proprieties but also the notion of aesthetic distance, the notion that white American violence should be kept as far as possible from suburbia.

It is ironic that—with the exception of an episode in which the occupied building was invaded by fraternity jocks intent on acting out their red-blooded white American male fantasies— the Cornell incident was totally nonviolent. To what extent was this due to the presence of those guns? It is not by any means *certain* that, had they not been present, Perkins, under pressure from trustees, faculty and alumni, would have unleashed the cops to break black heads. That this did not happen at Cornell may not be due solely to the presence of those guns, but the black students feel that in this case, at least, the basic effect of the guns was to prevent violence. It is a sad commentary on the society and the university that they are probably right.

Given the relatively peaceful and nondestructive nature of the incident and the fact that the black students emphasized their intention to use their guns only in the event of physical danger to the black women in the building, and that they did not threaten, coerce or intimidate anyone at gunpoint, the response of certain hysterics on the faculty (located interestingly enough in the upper echelons of the history and government departments) is significant.

These gentlemen claim to be hopelessly compromised, that the university is in ruins and chaos, and that "academic freedom" has been ravished—presumably by the phallic rifle barrels. Obviously they are speaking in terms of high and lofty principle, as they must be speaking symbolically when they say that the administration has surrendered and there is "no authority" at Cornell, since the school seems to be functioning no less efficiently than it was before. What does my colleague mean—he is a civilized and humane man—when he calls Perkins a "spineless jellyfish" and calls for the "white power structure to start acting like one"? Would they really have preferred a shoot-out? And to maintain what principle?—their own notion of their privileged class position protected by the coercive machinery of the state?

What exactly is the "trust" that they accuse Perkins of violating? That he did not swiftly and forcibly put the blacks in their place? How? None of these men have, as far as I can see, said a mumbling word against police violence at Harvard. Guns in the hands of the ROTC on this campus, on the hips of the campus cops, and in the hands of certain fraternities who had been arming themselves—this was a matter of public knowledge for weeks—do not seem to concern them. It is no wonder that "liberal" and "intellectual" have become dirty words in the minds of the young.

Given the peaceful nature of the confrontation, the agitation of these men is understandable only in the context of the entire controversy. The "trust" whose violation they bemoan is simply the racist principle that they and their class have the prerogative to run black people's lives. Because underneath the labyrinthine swirls of red tape, due process and rhetoric on both sides, that is what the ultimate issue is. The actual, specific issues that triggered the confrontation are quite trivial.

Here is an abbreviated version of how the issues developed. When James A. Perkins, a Philadelphia Quaker of liberal pretensions, gained the presidency in 1963, he took over a university that embodied, as do most American universities, the best and worst of American society. One thing it did not have was a race problem, since there were virtually no blacks (about six per class year or no more than 24 at any one time). Besides, the few Negroes who were present at that time, rather than preparing the university for what was to come, probably misled them. These were middle-class, "integrated" blacks who were upwardly mobile and who wanted to fit in and belong.

A committee was set up to finance and recruit black students at Cornell and in 1965 a group of 39 arrived. Contrary to popular racist myth, the black students at Cornell were not "so badly prepared as to be unable to handle the academic load," which is a reason given by certain journalists for the agitation. Prior to the "troubles," this first group, which will graduate this year, had lost only three students, and only one for academic reasons. The psychological burdens are far greater than the academic ones, as we shall see.

What was expected, of course, was that these favored blacks would adjust, adapt, and integrate themselves into the life of the campus, happily, gratefully—and uncritically. At the end of four years they would emerge with the skills, manners and attitudes necessary to usher them into the middle-class world of affluence and gracious living. The only problems anyone visualized in that age of innocence were social ones, like what to do about fraternities that discriminated. (Cornell, with some 60 Greek-letter organizations, has not been quite able to shake its reputation as a winter playground for the sons and daughters of the eastern establishment.) But at first even the fraternities cooperated, sponsoring a "soul of blackness week" and setting up a committee to help black prospects cope with the intricacies of "rushing."

For a while everything went according to script. The notion that this almost lily-white institution, which had been conceived, structured, and had functioned without any thought to the educational needs of the black community, would have to undergo very basic adjustments if it were to be really responsive to the practical and psychological needs of blacks, was apparently as unthinkable as any serious suggestion that God might be black. The fact that with three exceptions, and those in the professional schools, the faculty was lily-white and that no courses *at all* dealing *specifically* with the black experience were offered, seems to have escaped notice. Truly Cornell's small black community was without history or identity so far as the institution was concerned.

As the black population grew—it now numbers about 250—the sounds from the black community changed. Blacks began to perceive that integration was not liberation. Cultural integrity for the black community became a goal and instead of white tolerance and liberal sympathy, black folks were talking about Black Power, and not only that but by any means necessary.

Nationally the black community had stopped asking and started demanding. *They* would make the decisions affecting their lives, and *they,* for the first time in their history, would define the terms of their relationship to the white society. Junebug Jabbo Jones—may his tribe increase—the peripatetic black sage who is a legend in his own time, told a gathering of black Ivy Leaguers that "Harvard, Princeton and Yale had ruined more good niggers than whiskey and dope together," and he received a standing ovation.

At Cornell, blacks began to examine their historical situation and the motives of their benefactors. What was the intent of the decision that had brought them to Cornell? Who had made it and who supplied the money? Had white folks suddenly got religion or did the riots have anything to do with it? Were black students in fact partners and beneficiaries in the exploitation of other blacks here and in the Third World? More important, would their education lead them to a never-never-land suspended between the two communities?

They started talking about the role of a class-oriented, culturally chauvinistic, white educational system in dividing the black community and siphoning off and co-opting its leadership. More than that, they saw the well-meaning but somewhat self-congratulatory publicity that the university was sending out (in fairness it was mainly to alumni for purposes of funding the project) as reducing them to laboratory specimens and evidence of the school's new morality.

They demanded an Afro-American studies program from the university shortly after the King assassination. It seems that the students had no clear idea of what the form and structure of such a program should be. But how in reality could they be expected to, given the educational system to which they were accustomed? Some faculty members, for reasons of politics, internal and general, expressed skepticism or outright hostility. But the administration, sensing the temper of the students, set up a committee to give shape to the idea.

This committee, under Professor Chandler Morse, set about its work in a methodical and cautious manner, genuinely concerned, I believe, with exploring all possibilities in order to set up a program that would not be vulnerable to sniping from the established departments nor offensive to even the most conservative sensibility, and which would also satisfy the blacks. This proved impossible, particularly since the no longer diffident blacks were definitely not interested in avoiding any of those contingencies.

Not much of a tangible nature had happened by November of 1969, and the blacks, suspecting that they were witnessing still another example of honky "tricknology," got restive.

They were simultaneously experiencing some guilt at either having "escaped" the ghetto or, in some cases, never having experienced it. This was exacerbated by a steady stream of black speakers and ideologically articulate students who challenged the group's presence on the white campus as opposed to "working" in the community or at a black school.

Thus the Afro-American studies program became very important as a tangible sign that they were not being "co-opted" and seduced by the Man's system. But to be that, the program had to be free of domination, control, and influence, overt or covert, from and by whites.

Within the Afro organization sentiment for an autonomous black college developed; the group occupied the office of the committee chairman and declared the committee dissolved. This did not sit well with a great many faculty members.

In support of a number of political demands the organization began a series of noisy, disruptive and admittedly abrasive —but essentially nonviolent—demonstrations. To emphasize the need for black courses and materials they took a number of books from the library shelves and, finding them irrelevant, tossed them in a heap on the floor. To dramatize their demand for separate eating facilities they danced on tables in the cafeteria at lunch hour. They disrupted the clinic in demanding a black psychiatrist. And when the promised building to house the activities around the program did not materialize, they took over a building and evicted the whites, giving them three minutes to leave. They still have that building, and when the university did not furnish it as rapidly as they wished, a task force liberated furniture from other campus buildings. Now faculty and students alike were murmuring that it was time to teach the blacks a lesson.

When a small group ran through the administration building and into Perkins' office brandishing toy guns (they were obviously on some revolutionary fantasy of their own), it was clear to many whites that they had gone too far. By this time black-white tension was quite high.

The demands were not what was at issue—since even critics had to admit that they were justified, and with each demonstration the speed of administrative implementation perceptibly increased. The sentiment among some whites, mostly faculty, was that the blacks had to be disciplined. Consequently, charges were brought against six brothers for the toy gun incident and the liberation of the furniture.

Despite repeated urgings, promises of merely "symbolic" punishment, and later warnings and threats of suspension, the six refused to appear before the disciplinary committee. Now all the time this committee was saying informally that the charges themselves were not too "serious" they were also threatening suspension for nonappearance. So the issue was clearly the validation of the judiciary by the appearance of the six, not the charges (especially since the committee's mandate provided no mechanism for judgment in absentia).

During this period there was a symposium on South Africa. Cornell did own stock in Chase Manhattan and several other companies involved in business in South Africa, and Perkins himself—a perfect liberal—was on the Chase Manhattan board. (He is also chairman of the board of the United Negro College Fund.) Because of these connections, the black students felt that Perkins was hardly qualified morally or politically to introduce the speakers in the final session.

They planned to disrupt the meeting but one brother got

carried away and seized Perkins by the scruff of the neck. (The brother was agitated at the prospect of his scholarship money possibly originating in South African slave labor. The contradictions for black people on a white campus are indeed great.) Anyway, that broke the dam and sentiment was now quite high for swift and irrevocable discipline for blacks. Meanwhile, the six brothers were still adamant.

At the point where the six were to be suspended, 150 blacks appeared before the committee and informed them that the miscreants were not present and would not appear because:

1. The actions against only six constituted selective reprisal and were clearly intended as political intimidation.

2. By insisting on their appearance and hinting at light penalties, the committee was acting out a charade, the purpose of which was a symbolic lynching to appease "racist" elements on the campus.

3. The committee, as an agent of the university, had no legitimacy to judge political actions directed against the university.

4. As a lily-white committee, it was not a jury of any black's peers and was thus illegitimate.

5. As long as black people were in the institution it was necessary for them to reserve the right of political action as a group, and since the six were the agents of the entire body, the entire body was culpable. But they were not about to relegate to whites the right to control the political activities of blacks made necessary by "lingering vestiges of white racism."

The committee—a joint student-faculty affair—saw fit to make no judgment and passed the buck to the Faculty Committee on Student Affairs. This committee examined the Afro-American position and found no merit therein. The six were instructed to appear and did not. At this point the issue became one of conflicts of autonomy. The blacks were trapped in a position of having to back up their statement, and their definition of their "right to political action." The faculty committee —beneath BOMFOG* rhetoric dripping with words like "sensitivity," "understanding," and "sympathy"—was affirming its right to judge blacks for political actions. It is thus primarily

* Brotherhood-of-Man-Fatherhood-of-God.

*A Black Radical's Report on His Campus Struggles*    279

responsible for creating the situation that the administration then had to deal with.

Pointing to the precedent of labor-management arbitration, the blacks said they wanted neither sympathy, understanding nor sensitivity, but an objective judiciary committee made up of people independent of the university to judge political actions of blacks.

At this point, the action thickens—three white students are discovered beaten up on campus, one of them quite seriously. The allegation was made by one that his assailant(s) were black. The Daily Sun, the campus newspaper, printed a hasty and ill-advised editorial implying that their policy of collective responsibility for political acts made all blacks in the Afro-American Society responsible and that they should "ferret out" the assailants and hand them over. It is not clear that the assailants were in fact black or that, if they were, they were in fact students. But the editorial, hysterical in tone and quite vituperative, was a clear call to white vigilantism. No one on the faculty pointed this out, nor were any voices raised about the prejudicial nature of the Sun's assumptions.

The blacks received word that some fraternities and individual white students were purchasing arms in Ithaca. The blacks followed suit. The matter of the six had now dragged on for over two months and, given the added tension of the muggings, the nerves of both blacks and whites were frayed. But the whites outnumbered the blacks 14,000 to 250. Both sides seemed unable to dismount from the principled positions which they were riding to what seemed an inevitable confrontation.

The judiciary committee suddenly discovered that suspension was not inevitable after all and that they *could* judge the six in absentia. Two months earlier, this decision might have averted trouble. But when they handed down the reprimands, which are purely formal anyway, the atmosphere of heightened tension made it a provocation to both black and white.

That night a cross was burned, by person or persons unknown, at the black women's cooperative house. When the campus police came, they were unable to stay because of a series of false fire alarms that were being triggered all over the campus. The blacks found both actions equally provocative. The cross speaks for itself and the police action seemed indicative of a callous, even racist, disregard for the safety of black women.

This was Thursday night. The coming weekend was parents' weekend and the blacks moved to occupy Willard Straight Hall, which was to be the focus of activities. When the fraternity men forced their way in, and the blacks heard radio reports concerning five carloads of armed whites (which never materialized, however), they sent out and got their guns.

The rest is history—the arrival of the mass media, the picture of armed blacks leaving the building and the agreement with the administration in which the reprimands were rescinded and promises of legal assistance and no criminal action were made to the blacks. It is this agreement that the faculty found so distasteful.

It is impossible to say for certain just which principles the faculty imagined themselves to be preserving. In the beginning, the black students would probably have settled for a lifting of the suspension threat. As the issue developed and frustrations increased, however, the question became in their minds one of their ultimate powerlessness and what they saw as the university's willingness and ability to assert its power over their lives arbitrarily, however veiled and mild the manifestation of that power. This appeared to them to be simply a new style of paternalism which their new-found concept of black independence forced them to resist. It is interesting that having resisted so successfully and with élan, they now evince a new spirit and unity that is much less up-tight and beleaguered.

The Afro association has now become the Black United Front, and the American blacks are entering into negotiations with Puerto Ricans, American Indians, West Indians and African brothers and inviting them to use the facilities of the liberated building which has now become the Third World Center.

The white students, as a consequence of the "dialogue" which followed the incident, are also much less up-tight than before. It is interesting that while the administration, for reasons of public safety as they put it, made disarmament the first priority, the white students to whom I spoke felt that as long as the blacks pledged to use their guns only in self-defense, and as long as the university, as one administrator said, "could not be responsible for conditions in the general society" that might threaten blacks (some claim to be still receiving threatening phone calls), they saw no reason why the blacks should be forced to disarm. The generation gap again? But it is clear why the administration's priorities are different from the students'.

This is a division which is symptomatic of much more; as long as the universities continue to embody within themselves the best and worst aspects of the society, it will continue. At their best the universities, and particularly the private ones, have represented, however marginally, a tradition of decency and a principled resistance to know-nothingism, political orthodoxy and repression in the general society. Witness the McCarthy era and the movement against Viet-Nam that was launched from American campuses. By expressing a perception of the possibility of man, they have been the incubators of a generation of audacious, impatient, morally committed and idealistic young radicals not committed to the excesses of folly, pride, greed, moral flatulence and violent exploitation that mark their society's relationship to the poor and powerless at home and abroad.

But at their worst, the universities are the agents and beneficiaries of exactly these forces. Without the technical systems and personnel they provide, Viet-Nam would be possible but not easy. Too often the privileged and smug faculty mandarins are flattered to supply the intellectual underpinnings for economic and political imperialism, and are able to coexist with racism in the society and to perpetuate it in the curricula. They grow affluent and powerful by supplying tax and moral loopholes for the heavily burdened pocketbooks and consciences of the rich. And despite their frequent and loud appeals for reasoned discourse as the avenue to "orderly change," they are ultimately no less coercive, inflexible, manipulative, undemocratic and elitist than the class which they serve and whose interests they maintain while professing to scorn its values. As long as this duality continues, the conflict can only intensify. And the society is certainly more violent than the most revolution-intoxicated student can even imagine.

• Thelwell calls white America's fascination with guns "guilt-ridden." Does he explain why he uses that adjective? Can you explain why he does? Does his charge, in the same paragraph, that "guns in the hands of young blacks" cause "paranoid hysteria" in whites remind you of anything James Baldwin said about white paranoia (in Chapter 1)? If his statement about "guns in the hands of young blacks" is true, and not a rhetorical device, why are young blacks put in the army and trained to be skilled gunmen?

• Has the establishment the "exclusive right to violence," as Thelwell charges? (The college establishment's right to call in the National Guard, for instance, or the national establishment's right to start a war?) How does he define "violence"? (Recall the limited quality of the debate in this chapter, partly because there was no agreement on a definition of "violence.")

• Thelwell says: "It is a sad commentary on the society and the university that they [the black students at Cornell] are probably right [that] the basic effect of the guns on campus was to prevent violence." Does Thelwell develop this thesis? Do you believe that the threat of violence, on or off campus, might prevent violence?

• Thelwell repeatedly talks about the nonviolent nature of the Cornell struggle, but admits, at one point in his essay, that "the black students . . . planned to disrupt the meeting but one brother got carried away and seized Perkins by the scruff of the neck." Does this statement deny his thesis? Would former Brandeis president Abram define this act as violence? Would Rossman or Vozick? Would you?

• On November 6, 1967, a year before the violent strike at San Francisco State which catapulted S. I. Hayakawa to power, the white editor of the *Daily Gater*, San Francisco State's student paper, was beaten in the newspaper's offices by members of the Black Student Union, who claimed that the paper's news coverage of the Black Student Union was inaccurate and implicitly racist. A year later, the student editor, formerly regarded as a conservative, looked on the "*Gater* incident" differently. In *Crisis*, a publication on the 1968 San Francisco State strike, he is quoted as saying:

> It took me a while, but I really learned something from the beating I took. I learned that violence can be a very normal, human reaction. My own reaction to the beating [an editorial calling for the expulsion of the BSU] was also very normal. I had been kicked in the head, and I reacted by

striking back with that editorial. I figure my attackers had been kicked in the head, too—probably literally in a lot of instances, and certainly figuratively.

He also commented:

Both the students and the administration are operating at the lowest human level. It's the "I'm right, you're wrong" attitude. Each side has set up ultimatums to which the other side can't accede. So now everybody's hating the other guy's image and it's turned into an issue of who is strongest. And naturally, nobody wants to be proven weak. If there was really respect for the other people's ideas, there would be no ultimatums.

The editor admits that violence is normal. Does he, or does Thelwell, offer any alternatives to the use of this "normal human reaction"?

• Thelwell says, in recording the history of blacks at Cornell, that "they began to perceive that integration was not liberation." This perception, and his question, "Would their education lead them to a never-never-land suspended between the two communities?" has been repeated by minorities on campuses across the country: blacks, Chicanos, Oriental Americans, Puerto Ricans, women. Demands have, in some instances, led to programs in Black Studies, Asian Studies, and the like, that is, special programs for minorities within white campuses. At one community college campus, a minority of militant students successfully demanded that *all* students be *required* to take an ethnic studies course. Do you think students should be able to make such demands? Are they more or less able than the administration and faculty to propose curriculum?

• How can students know what curriculum would best prepare them for the off-campus world? Do segregated or special programs have limited usefulness? Is there a distinction between curriculum demands and the kinds of "political" demands cited by Thelwell in regard to the university's treatment of six black students who were to be suspended? According to Thelwell, the Cornell administration reacted to all demands in much the same manner.

• Thelwell's piece is a report on the tactics of the black students as opposed to the tactics of the administration. How do you define "tactic"? Evaluate the specific tactics of students currently working for changes on your campus and at other schools. (Note the polite invitation for tea and talk issued by Stanford students, reprinted on page 265, as *one* tactic of a campus struggle; these same students also blocked traffic and fought with the off-campus tactical police squad.)

• Thelwell implies that the public press was guilty of exaggerating the Cornell situation, leading the public to hysterical fear, and limiting the possibilities for any negotiated settlement. ("That damned picture," incidentally, won the young AP photographer who took it, Steve Starr, a Pulitzer prize. Starr, well under thirty, was something of a campus radical himself while attending California State College at San Jose and was disciplined for importing the Berkeley Free Speech Movement to a campus not yet caught up in turmoil.) Thelwell also accuses the Cornell campus paper of exaggeration. What role does (or should) the press play in reporting and creating tactics? Mark Rudd, one of the major participants in a strike at Columbia University, reports his feelings about the coverage of the strike by the press:

> Since journalists lack the tools to report events outside the accepted limits of action and thought, and since many newspapers are committed to an ideological position, as in the liberal *New York Times*, the truth of the Columbia rebellion had a hard time coming through.
>
> The press created two predominant symbols of the strike, both of which helped to divert attention from the issues. The first is that of the strike leaders as a symbol of the strike, i.e., focusing attention on my actions, words, past history, creating stories about plots, "Maoist cores," etc., all of which masks the political significance of the strike. . . . The other symbol of the strike dwelt on by the press and others was our tactics. To them, minority action in seizing buildings constituted an absolute crime. This became the major issue of the strike, at least to those who obtained their information from the press.

• Do you know of situations in which the press has made a person the symbol of an issue? Do you know of situations in which the action has been emphasized at the expense of the fuller context of an issue? Is it naive to expect the press to be fair? Are these problems more common in newspapers or on television? What is the responsibility of the reader or viewer?

• Harvey Yorke, Director of Public Affairs at San Francisco State College, had this to say about the effects of the news media on the 1968–69 crisis on his campus:

> On the subject of television, the question is raised frequently whether some of the mass action and violence may have been averted if the cameras were not present. The answer seems to be in the nature of the crisis and the plans

of its perpetrators. Essentially this was an internal crisis, with many implications for the outside community. From the beginning the plan seemed to be to cripple the instructional process, to create broad interest in the issues and to force action by the college administration and higher authorities. Thus, it seems, television and the other news media were incidental to the objectives of the strikers. What happened, whether by plan or not, is that the extensive television coverage focused on the violence which could be photographed easily instead of the issues which are not photographable and a large share of public opinion was thus formed. The same results probably would have been evident without television, but after a longer period of time.

Newspapers probably had more influence on the course of events during the crisis than most people realize. Most of us view them merely as recorders of events. We see them as daily history in print and exert enormous amounts of energy to be sure our positions and facts reach the editors in time for the early editions. But what few people realize is that the newspapers were virtually the only medium of communication among contending groups for most of the crisis period.

Yorke called the San Francisco State crisis a "family affair." To what extent would you want the press involved in your "family affairs"? Should there be limits on TV coverage of school crises as there now are on court trials?

# 5

## PROGRAMS
## AND
## PROPOSALS

Chapter 5 offers for analysis and comparison seven very different programs and proposals for changing the teaching-learning process. These are specific proposals by educational critic Paul Goodman, who would, among other things, do away with high schools; by social scientist and Harvard professor David Riesman, who suggests that more rigid, not more flexible, formal academic standards should be demanded by women; and by Antioch professor Judson Jerome, who would abolish traditional colleges in favor of noncollege "institutes."

The Nairobi College Planning Committee reports on their experiment in community education for blacks; Elizabeth Sewell on Bensalem College, a small living-education program within the traditional structure of Fordham University; Joseph Tussman on a highly structured experimental two-year program based on a curriculum of "required" reading along with writing and discussion; and Barrie Zwicker on Rochdale College in Toronto, a totally student-operated college.

The seven programs and proposals selected for this chapter do not represent a bias toward any particular solution or solutions to the educational crises of today. They were chosen because they indicate the many different ways in which students, teachers, and administrators are trying to reshape education. They offer the reader a chance to compare and contrast ideas as well as activities, exploring alternatives in education that are directly parallel to alternatives in the larger society, where everything from total anarchy to total repression has been tried at one time or another and in one place or another.

The chapter makes clear that there is no *single* solution to the problems in education, any more than there is a *single* solution to the problems in society, and that education experiments are in as much danger of failing to achieve idealistic goals as are social experiments: Rochdale College was founded in a mood of complete student freedom from teachers, grades, and most of all, administrators; it was soon foundering in its own top-heavy administrative set-up. This is little different from new left, or black militant, or other revolutionary anti-establishment groups

291

in society who are seeking individual freedom, and who all too frequently establish a structured organization which permits its members little individuality or freedom.

There are, too, numerous experiments—both unstructured and authoritarian—going on at the kindergarten through high school level, in both public and private schools, suggesting that in the broadest sense society is struggling to find new mediums between authority and freedom, between freedom and license, and that the world of education is a mirror, a microcosm, of that struggle.

# The Present Moment
# in Progressive Education

*Paul Goodman*

*Paul Goodman is a writer, lecturer, and former teacher who has for many years advocated (and in some instances practiced) major reforms in American education. He has taught at the University of Chicago, the Manumit School of Progressive Education, and Black Mountain College in North Carolina and has been a lecturer at the student-run Experimental College at San Francisco State College. He has also practiced as a lay psychotherapist with the New York Institute for Gestalt Therapy. His writings include* The Community of Scholars, Compulsory Education, The Society I Live in Is Mine, *and* Growing Up Absurd *(all nonfiction);* Making Do *and other novels; several plays; and a large number of essays.*

*The following selection appeared in* The New York Review of Books, *April 1969.*

It is possible that the chief problem in the coming generation will be survival, whether from nuclear bombs, genocide, ecological disaster, or mass starvation and endless wars. If so, this is the present task of pedagogy. There already exist wilderness schools for self-reliance and it has been proposed to train guerrillas in schools in Harlem. The delicately interlocking technologies of the world indeed seem to be over-extended and terribly vulnerable, and the breakdown could be pretty total. But let us fantasize that this view is not realistic.

My own thinking is that

(1) Incidental education, taking part in the on-going activities of society, should be the chief means of learning.

(2) Most high schools should be eliminated, with other kinds of communities of youth taking over their sociable functions.

(3) College training should generally follow, not precede, entry into the professions.

(4) The chief task of educators is to see to it that the activities of society provide incidental education, if necessary inventing new useful activities offering new educational opportunities.

(5) The purpose of elementary pedagogy, through age twelve, is to protect children's free growth, since our community and families both pressure them too much and do not attend to them enough.

Let me review the arguments for this program. We must drastically cut back the schooling because the present extended tutelage is against nature and arrests growth. The effort to channel growing up according to a preconceived curriculum and method discourages and wastes many of the best human powers to learn and cope. Schooling does not prepare for real performance; it is largely carried on for its own sake. Only a small fraction, the "academically talented"—between 10 and 15 percent according to Conant—thrive in this useless activity without being bored or harmed by it. It isolates the young from the older generation and alienates them.

On the other hand, it makes no sense for many of the brightest and most sensitive young simply to drop out or confront society with hostility. This cannot lead to social reconstruction. The complicated and confusing conditions of modern times need knowledge and fresh thought, and therefore long acquaintance and participation precisely by the young. Young radicals seem to think that mere political change will solve the chief problems, or that they will solve themselves after political change, but this is a delusion. The problems of urbanization, technology, and ecology have not been faced by any political group. The educational systems of other advanced countries are no better than ours, and the young are equally dissenting. Finally, it has been my Calvinistic, and Aristotelian, experience that most people cannot organize their lives without productive activity (though, of course, not necessarily paid activity); and the actual professions, services, industries, arts and sciences are the arena in which they should be working. Radical politics and doing one's thing are careers for very few.

As it is, however, the actual activities of American society either exclude the young, or corrupt them, or exploit them. Here is the task for educators. We must make the rules of licensing and hiring realistic to the actual work and get rid of mandarin requirements. We must design apprenticeships that are not exploitative. Society desperately needs much work that is not now done, both intellectual and manual, in urban renewal, ecology, communications, and the arts, and all these could make use of young people. Many such enterprises are best organized by young people themselves, like most of the community development and community action Vocations for Social Change. Little think tanks, like the Oceanic Institute at Makapuu Point or the Institute for Policy Studies in Washington, which are not fussy about diplomas, have provided excellent spots for the young. Our aim should be to multiply the paths of growing up, with opportunity to start again, cross over, take a moratorium, travel, work on one's own. To insure freedom of option and that the young can maintain and express their critical attitude, all adolescents should be guaranteed a living. (The present cost of high schooling would almost provide this.)

The advantage of making education less academic has, of course, occurred to many school people. There are a myriad of programs to open the school to the world by (1) importing outside professionals, artists in residence, gurus, mothers, dropouts as teachers' aides; and (2) giving academic credit for work-study, community action, writing novels, service in mental hospitals, junior year abroad, and other kinds of released time. Naturally I am enthusiastic for this development and only want it to go the small further step of abolishing the present school establishment instead of aggrandizing it.

Conversely, there is a movement in the United States, as in China and Cuba, for adolescent years to be devoted to public service, and this is fine if the service is not compulsory and regimenting.

It is possible for every education to be tailor-made according to each youth's developing interest and choice. Choices along the way will be very often ill-conceived and wasteful, but they will express desire and immediately meet reality, and therefore they should converge to finding the right vocation more quickly than by any other course. Vocation is what one is good at and can do, what uses a reasonable amount of one's powers, and gives one a useful occupation in a community that is one's own. The right use of the majority of the people would make a stable society far more efficient than our own. And those who have peculiar excellences are more likely to find their own further way when they have entry by doing something they can do and being accepted.

Academic schooling can be chosen by those with academic talents, and such schools are better off unencumbered by sullen uninterested bodies. But the main use of academic teaching is for those already busy in sciences and professions, who need academic courses along the way. Cooper Union in New York City used to fulfill this function very well. And in this context of need, there can finally be the proper use of new pedagogic technology, as a means of learning at one's own time, whereas at present this technology makes the school experience still more rigid and impersonal.

Of course, in this set-up employers would themselves provide ancillary academic training, especially if they had to pay for it anyway, instead of using parents' and taxpayers' money. In my opinion, this ancillary rather than prior schooling would do more than any other single thing to give black, rural, and other "culturally deprived" youth a fairer entry and chance for advancement, since what is to be learned is objective and functional and does not depend on the abstract school style. As we have seen, *on the job* there is no correlation between competence and years of prior schooling.

But this leads to another problem. Educationally, schooling on the job is usually superior, but the political and moral consequences of such a system are ambiguous and need more analysis than I can give them here. At present, a youth is hired for actual credentials, if not actual skill; this is alienating to him as a person, but it also allows a measure of free-market democracy. If he is to be schooled on the job, however, he must be hired for his promise and attended to as a person; this is less alienating, but it can lead to company paternalism, like Japanese capitalism, or like Fidel Castro's Marxist vision of farm and factory-based schools (recently reported in *New Left Notes*). On the other hand, *if the young have options and can organize and criticize,* on-the-job education is the quickest way to workers' management which, in my opinion, is the only effective democracy.

University education—liberal arts and the principles of the professions—is for adults who already know something, who have something to philosophize. Otherwise, as Plato pointed out, it is just verbalizing.

To provide a protective and life-nourishing environment for children up through twelve, Summerhill is an adequate model. I think it can be easily adapted to urban conditions if we include houses of refuge for children to resort to, when necessary, to escape parental and neighborhood tyranny or terror. Probably an even better model would be the Athenian pedagogue, touring the city with his charges; but for this the streets and working-places of the city must be made safer and more available than is likely. (The prerequisite of city-planning is for the children to be able to use the city, for no city is governable if it does not grow citizens who feel it is theirs.) The goal of elementary pedagogy is a very modest one: it is for a small child, under his own steam, to poke interestedly into whatever goes on and to be able, by observation, questions, and practical imitation, to get something out of it in his own terms. In our society this happens pretty well at home up to age four, but after that it becomes forbiddingly difficult.

I have often spelled out this program of incidental education, and found no takers. Curiously, I get the most respectful if wistful attention at teachers' colleges, even though what I propose is quite impossible under present administration. Teachers know how much they are wasting the children's time of life, and they understand that my proposals are fairly conservative, whereas our present schooling is a new mushroom. In general audiences, the response is incredulity. Against all evidence, people are convinced that what we do must make sense, or is inevitable. It does not help if I point out that in dollars and cents it might be cheaper, and it would certainly be more productive in tangible goods and services, to eliminate most schools and make the community and the work that goes on in it more educational. Yet the majority in a general audience are willing to say that they themselves got very little out of *their* school years. Occasionally an old reactionary businessman agrees with me enthusiastically, that book-learning isn't worth a penny; or an old socialist agrees, because he thinks you have to get your books the hard way.

Among radical students, I am met by a sullen silence. They want Student Power and are unwilling to answer whether they are authentically students at all. That's not where it's at. (I think they're brainwashed.) Instead of "Student Power," however, what they should be demanding is a more open entry into society, spending the education money more usefully, licensing and hiring without irrelevant diplomas, and so forth. And there *is* an authentic demand for Young People's Power, their right to take part in initiating and deciding the functions of society that concern them—as well, of course, as governing their own lives, which are nobody else's business. Bear in mind that we are speaking of ages seventeen to twenty-five, when at all other times the young would already have been launched in the real world. The young have the right to power because they are numerous and are directly affected by what goes on, but especially because their new point of view is indispensable to cope with changing conditions, they themselves being part of the changing conditions. This is why Jefferson urged us to adopt a new constitution every generation.

Perhaps the chief advantage of incidental education rather than schooling is that the young can then carry on their movement informed and programmatic, grounded in experience and competence, whereas "Student Power," grounded in a phony situation, is usually symbolic and often mere spite.

Finally, let me go back to a very old-fashioned topic of educational theory, how to transmit Culture with a big C, the greatness of Man. This is no longer discussed by conventional educators and it was never much discussed by progressive educators, though Dewey took it increasingly seriously in his later years. In our generation, it is a critical problem, yet I cannot think of a way to solve it. Perhaps it is useful to try to define it.

The physical environment and social culture force themselves on us, and the young are bound to grow up to them well or badly. They always fundamentally determine the curriculum in formal schooling; but even if there is no schooling at all, they are the focus of children's attention and interest; they are what is there. Dewey's maxim is a good one: there is no need to bother about curriculum, for whatever a child turns to is potentially educative and, with good management, one thing leads to another. Even skills that are considered essential prerequisites, like reading, will be learned spontaneously in normal urban and suburban conditions.

But humane culture is not what is obviously there for a child, and in our times it is less and less so. In the environment there is little spirit of a long proud tradition, with heroes and martyrs. For instance, though there is a plethora of concerts and records, art museums, planetariums, and child-encyclopedias, the disinterested ideals of science and art are hardly mentioned and do not seem to operate publicly at all, and the sacredness of these ideals no longer exists even on college campuses. Almost no young person of college age believes that there are autonomous professionals or has even heard of such a thing. Great souls of the past do not speak to a young person as persons like himself, once he learns their language, nor does he bother to learn their language. The old conflicts of history do not seem to have been human conflicts, nor are they of any interest.

The young have strong feelings for honesty, frankness, loyalty, fairness, affection, freedom, and other virtues of generous natures. They quickly resent the hypocrisy of politicians, administrators, and parents who mouth big abstractions and act badly or pettily. But in fact, they themselves—like most politicians and administrators and many parents—seem to have forgotten the concrete reality of ideals like magnanimity, compassion, honor, consistency, civil liberty, integrity, justice—*ruat coelum,* and unpalatable truth, all of which are not gut feelings and are often not pragmatic, but are maintained to create and re-create Mankind. Naturally, without these ideals and their always possible and often actual conflict, there is no tragedy. Most young persons seem to disbelieve that tragedy exists; they always interpret impasse as timidity, and casuistry as finking out. I am often astonished by their physical courage, but I am only rarely moved by their moral courage.

Their ignorance has advantages. The bother with transmitting humane culture is that it must be re-created in spirit, or it is a dead weight upon present spirit, and it does produce timidity and hypocrisy. Then it is better forgotten. Certainly the attempt to teach it by courses in school or by sermons like this, is a disaster. Presumably it was kept going by the living example of a large number of people who took it seriously and leavened society, but now there seems to be a discontinuity. It has been said that the thread really snapped during the First World War, during the Spanish War, with the gas-chambers and Atom-bombs, etc., etc. I have often suggested that the logical way to teach the humanities, for instance, would be for some of us to picket the TV stations in despair; but we are tired, and anyway, when we have done similar things students put their own rather than different interpretations on it. We try to purge the university of military projects, but students attack the physical research itself that could be abused (and is even bound to be abused), as if science were not necessarily a risky adventure. They don't see that this is a tragic dilemma. They seem quite willing—though battening on them in the United States—to write off Western science and civil law.

Yet apart from the spirit congealed in them, we do not really have our sciences and arts, professions and civic institutions. It is inauthentic merely to use the products and survivals, and I don't think we can in fact work Western civilization without its vivifying tradition. The simplest reason that cities are ungovernable is that there aren't enough citizens; this happened during the Roman Empire too. It is conceivable that the so-called Third World can adapt our technology and reinterpret it according to other ideals, as was supposed to be the theme of the conference in Havana against Cultural Imperialism; but I read dozens of papers and did not find a single new proposition. Anyway, this does nothing for us. Here at home it is poignant what marvels some people expect from the revival of African masks.

A young fellow is singing a song attacking the technological way of life, but he is accompanying it on an electric guitar plugged into the infra-structure; and the rhythm and harmony are phony mountain-music popularized by Stalinists in the Thirties to give themselves an American image, and which cannot cohere with a contemporary poem. But I can't make him see why this won't do. I can't make clear to a young lady at the Antioch-Putney School of Education that a child has an historical human right to know that there is a tie between Venus and the Sun and thanks to Newton we know its equation, which is even more beautiful than the Evening Star; it is *not* a matter of taste whether he knows this or not. Yet she's right, for if it's not his thing, it's pointless to show it to him, as it is to her.

It seems to me that, ignorant of the inspiration and grandeur of our civilization, though somewhat aware of its brutality and terror, the young are patsies for the "inevitabilities" of modern times. If they cannot take on our only world appreciatively and very critically, they can only confront her or be servile to her and then she is too powerful for any of us.

Margaret Mead says, truly, that young people are in modern times like native sons, whereas we others use the technology gingerly and talk like foreign-born. I am often pleased at how competent my young friend proves to be; my apprehension for him is usually groundless. But he is swamped by presentness. Since there is no background or structure, everything is equivalent and superficial. He can repair the TV but he thinks the picture is real (Marshall McLuhan doesn't help). He says my lecture blew his mind and I am flattered till he tells me that L. Ron Hubbard's metempsychosis in Hellenistic Sardinia blew his mind; I wonder if he has any mind to blow.

I sometimes have the eerie feeling that there are around the world, a few dozen of Plato's guardians, ecologists and psychosomatic physicians, who with worried brows are trying to save mankind from destroying itself. This is a sorry situation for Jeffersonian anarchists like myself who think we ought to fend for ourselves. The young are quick to point out the mess that we have made, but I don't see that they really care about that, as if it were not their mankind. Rather, I see them with the Christmas astronauts flying toward the moon and seeing the Earth shining below: it is as if they are about to abandon an old house and therefore it makes no difference if they litter it with beer cans. These are bad thoughts.

But I have occasionally had a good educational experience in the Draft Resistance movement. The resisters are exceptionally virtuous young men and they are earnest about the fix they are in, that makes them liable to two to five years in jail. Then it is remarkable how, guided by a few Socratic questions, they come to remember the ideas of Allegiance, Sovereignty, Legitimacy, Exile, and bitter Patriotism, which cannot be taught in college courses in political science. It is a model of incidental learning of the humanities, but I am uneasy to generalize from it.

# An Interview
# with David Riesman

*Maria Wilhelm*

*David Riesman, writer* (The Lonely Crowd), *social scientist, lawyer, and Harvard professor, here reflects on the expectations of women today and the educational limitations placed on them. He is interviewed by Maria Wilhelm for the March 1971 issue of* Family Circle *magazine.*

*Interviews, whether on television or in newspapers or magazines, are a special form of communication. In interviews the perceptions of the interviewer frequently control the responses of the interviewed. Here, Maria Wilhelm's questions and statements reflect her conclusions about the female readers of her magazine; Riesman's answers attempt to reach beyond these limitations.*

"Yes, I strongly believe that women have heightened expectations today. Your possibilities for a full and meaningful life are greater now than they ever have been."

David Riesman, professor of social sciences at Harvard, settled back in his chair and glanced out the window. His best seller of the '50s, *The Lonely Crowd,* was a penetrating study of life changes for the individual in America today, changes that are now taking place at an even faster rate.

"What exactly do you mean?" I asked. "All we hear today is that women must realize their potential to be equals with men, if they are going to be happy and fulfilled, both as individuals and as a group."

Riesman's strong, handsome face broke into a quick half-smile: "That's a very limited view, though I am a sympathizer with the Women's Liberation Movement in many respects.

Women's needs have changed enormously in many ways, as they have become increasingly aware of themselves. Not only are women 37 percent of the work force, but what they need from men is changing. Not too long ago, a woman's security came to a large extent from being married (the acceptable state) and being supported. If that support was steady, her expectations were fulfilled. Now, with so many women working, this need is shifting to one for emotional support, for an understanding give-and-take. And as the situation has improved for women, so have their expectations. Yet, there's the rub—because it's very easy to fall into the trap of unrealistic expectations. The trick in life is to find your own level and live it to the fullest.

"You know, it seems to me there's a widespread belief that we can achieve a constant intensity of living. It's got to be the most—you've got to do your thing to the fullest or you're not with it. This notion puts a fantastic demand on life, and life just can't live up to the billing.

"Let me explain by telling you about a situation I run into all the time. You know what most students are pushing for now: 'Get rid of grades, required courses and exams. Just give a pass or fail—we don't need the old-fashioned degree.' Well, the girls want to follow suit, but they shouldn't because they still have to prove themselves in a man's world. They still need that document that says they can do what a man can do, or that they are well-equipped for specific work. Because it still *is* a man's world, a man can afford to skip around in his jobs, at least when he's young. But a girl needs standards to prove she's good at whatever she does, from practical nursing to being a news reporter. I tell my girl students their demand should be for more seriousness—not for kicking over all the traces. Insist on a semiprofessional degree that guarantees you the right to a teaching or editing job; not just a B.A. in literature and the promise that a year or two at secretarial school will give you a job in a publishing house.

"If you want to break stereotypes, break the one that women are no good at science. That's sheer nonsense. Ranging from engineering to lab work, women could be every bit as good as men—but how many women engineers do we have? And while we're on the subject of stereotypes, one of my quarrels with Women's Lib is their hang-up here. They are snobs about women's traditional caretaking jobs. Nursing, for instance, is well-suited to lots of women. Instead of running it down as an inferior career in which women will be downtrodden, insist it be upgraded to the respectable level it should be. Long before Women's Lib, women have been insecure about the worth of nursing. Radcliffe used to offer a program in it, and they should again."

That half-smile flickered across his face again, and he ruefully rubbed his iron-gray hair. "Do you know how the girls react to this advice? They get plain mad—they want to do what the boys are doing; they just can't understand timing is all-important and you can jump over steps only as far as your legs will carry you."

I laughed. "When I went to school, English literature was big for girls, and we all saw ourselves as instant editors after we graduated." Riesman nodded: "And what a limited expectation that was. If girls must study literature, they should specialize— study Japanese or Yugoslav literature, develop a skill and create the demand. Face up to the fact that the world is still unfair, and that you need protection in culture as well as contraception. You can't aspire to the relaxed, nonrivalrous groups boys are experimenting with—*not yet*—because you are still rivaling for equality."

"May I interrupt and go back to something you said earlier? Your point about emotional support interests me; we've always thought of the ideal woman as wife-sweetheart-mother, the warm shelter after a hard day."

"Yes," Riesman answered, "and part of your heightened expectations has to be that as you reach an occupational par with men you begin to develop some of their needs. And will men be able to meet your new needs? That's a good question. To be supportive doesn't mean to be fatherly, obviously, but it is a sensitive part of the male-female relationship that has traditionally been the woman's role. In time, as the roles equalize, I think this understanding will materialize. For the present, women may be able to ease the loneliness they feel in their new role by closer communication with other women. I'm sure this is part of the reason that Women's Lib is catching on so fast—not just the fight for equality."

"Professor Riesman, what about the girl who can't go to college or maybe doesn't want to?"

"I think you should use whatever education you get to test and expand your capacities. A good, well-planned high school education can provide a satisfying life. Let's go back to expectations. They become unrealistic and unattainable when they are not appropriate to a given set of circumstances. A particular category of work can be eminently satisfying or disastrously frustrating. The college girl who winds up as a secretary often isn't realizing the capacities she's been trained for. That doesn't mean the job of secretary is inferior. It's a fine job; it can be very interesting in terms of content—it provides contact with all kinds of people. Being a check-out clerk in a supermarket can have its satisfactions, too.

"My quarrel with high school education is that it doesn't go far enough toward opening doors for a range of jobs and experiences a capable student should be exposed to. As I said before, the trick in life is to find your own level and live it to the fullest, but this can't be imposed on you. You have to discover it and you can't do that without exposure to alternatives.

"Let's be specific. Helen, who's a second-year high school student, has an aptitude for math—only neither her teacher nor her counselor (who is probably ill-equipped) recognizes this; or if they do, they don't see the potentialities for her future. If Helen went on to take algebra and trigonometry, she could qualify for CPA or bookkeeping training, and accountant work is both remunerative and flexible. Or, if she did work as a check-out clerk in a supermarket in her spare time, she might work herself into a good front office job. Take languages. If a girl were encouraged to stick with French or Spanish for three years, instead of home economics, she could become a highly paid bilingual secretary."

We were both silent for a few moments. My reverie was interrupted by Riesman's calm voice saying, "You're damned if you do and you're damned if you don't." I guess my startled expression reflected my puzzlement.

"Look, women today are damned if they are docile and damned if they're not. Let me tell you about another situation I'm familiar with—college teaching. If girls are outstanding scholars, there are professors who distrust them and put them down as being bitchy or castrating. On the other hand, these professors don't want to teach in schools that aren't co-ed because they prefer the stimulation and combativeness of male students, and mistakenly interpret quiet, responsive listening by females as passive docility."

"Would you say things are going to get worse before they get better?"

Riesman nodded. "It may seem so now, but changes are being made that have excellent long-run possibilities of cooling the friction between the sexes. First of all, though, I think the primary need is for full employment. As long as people—men among themselves or men versus women—are competing for the same knowledge, there's bound to be trouble.

"But beyond that, I think we're going to find peace in a partial exchange of roles. Let men do some of the things that women do, and vice versa—start now giving children new models of the expanded roles men and women can play both at work and at home. I mentioned women engineers and science teachers. I think that men should be teaching art and literature to fourth-graders, or they might even be kindergarten teachers. Obviously, I am not talking about losing sexual identity but about breaking down some of the rigid and unnecessary imposed sexual differences. This goes back to my earlier point that a woman—or a man—has to define what he or she can do as an individual. If a boy would be happy as a secretary and a woman as a policewoman, they should do their thing without regard to what was thought right in the past."

"But when women intrude on men's jobs they're accused of being aggressive and unfeminine and most of us resent these labels—nor do we want to be unfeminine."

"Well, I said before, you're damned if you do and you're damned if you don't—but I think this could be a stage toward a much more equitable society. Women are right to insist on equity, not to hold back. To some degree it's a question of patience and timing, of persistence without steamrollering."

Our dialogue was getting to the nitty gritty with my next question: "Women usually don't like to work for women—whether in services or an office. Why do you think this is so and, more important, what can women do to change this?"

"I haven't said much about Women's Lib, but in this respect I think it's going to be a very positive force. Let's face it, it *is* a male-oriented world and it is a plain fact that women respond to men and are traditionally used to subordinating themselves, if necessary, to a male. But the Women's Lib groups seem to be creating a sense of solidarity among women, they are beginning to regard each other as colleagues. There is a lot more sympathy being shown toward those who haven't made it, and less envy toward those who have. If women are going to be authority figures, other women will have to accept and help them in this role.

"The more we get a mix of roles, the less you're going to hear the remark, 'I hate working for a woman.' Mix it up, break the stereotypes. President Franklin Roosevelt was considered very progressive when he made Frances Perkins Secretary of Labor; I think he should have made a woman Secretary of the Navy. Elinore Herrick did a fine job with the Dodd Shipyards during World War II, for example.

"It's a very different situation in Asia and even in Europe. Women are accepted in top jobs by men—look at Indira Gandhi —but the answer is that Asia and Europe were and still are class societies, and America never has been. Women like Mrs. Gandhi are capable, of course, but they got where they are because they also belonged to the ruling class and, so, were accepted as leaders. The fact that they are aristocracy is more important than their sex."

Next I turned to something that affects almost all of us, whether we work or not: "Will the heightened expectations of women affect marriage as an institution?"

"Oh, but I think marriage has already changed a great deal," Riesman replied quickly, "and I certainly think it will change more. Sharing of responsibilities is much greater now than it ever has been, and not just among professionals who both work. It goes beyond being willing to baby-sit one night a week while the wife goes to bingo, her card club or whatever. I see many men in automatic laundries and supermarkets, and look at the male students walking around with babies piggyback in these new baby carriers. You never saw this 20 years ago. Men are cooking, too, and not just as the occasional gourmet or the backyard grill chef. They do it as matter-of-factly as they stack the dishwasher, while the wife catches up on monthly bills—if she's better at bookkeeping than he is.

"I think, though, that the high rate of divorce is testimony to a continuing idealism about marriage which has nothing to do with the collision of traditional male-female roles. I mean idealism in the true sense of the word—a desire to attain perfection, the ideal. Formerly, it was expected that a man would come home and settle down to his paper and beer or radio or whatever he did for relaxation. Now many women want a reaction or an interaction, and this may be more than most men are capable of providing in our present society. You might call this a 'need for tenderness'—something it was formerly expected women gave to men and children. In time men may develop this responsiveness—of course, some have it now and have had through the ages—but, meanwhile, groups like Women's Lib may provide the emotional support and understanding contemporary women need as they move into the crowd."

Professor Riesman had been very courteous and he never once looked at his watch. I didn't dare look at mine because I knew well over an hour had passed. When I had approached him about an interview for *Family Circle,* he said he'd be delighted to talk to its readers. These are the young people, he pointed out, who are most involved in today's fast-moving world. I decided to risk one more question.

"What about the woman who doesn't need to work and doesn't want to; what outlets does she have for fulfillment other than her house and children—and maybe she doesn't have children or they have flown the coop?"

"When I wrote *The Lonely Crowd* 20 years ago, I had an idea that women should put more emphasis on play. I meant that I didn't think their liberation would come from a culturally defined job, and that maybe by going to work they were simply adding to their own domestic problems all the anxieties men endure at work.

"But I've changed my mind about that. I've come to the conclusion that if work isn't serious and demanding, whatever it is, nonwork just isn't as rewarding—one becomes simply a consumer of leisure time. Let's not forget that lots of housewives really enjoy their work and get as much feeling of satisfaction and pleasure from it as a secretary, laborer, doctor or artist.

"But, whether they realize it or not, women who have no function feel parasitic, and this is one of my arguments with Women's Lib, as I've said. They turn up their noses at lots of occupations on the grounds that these are inferior to what men do. Wouldn't it be better to keep a library open extra hours a week than to take that attitude? There are both paid and volunteer jobs of that kind that go begging—where a girl could occupy her time meaningfully and find stimulation in talking to other people. Then the hours that she puts her feet up and reads a magazine would seem a lot more pleasurable and she would anticipate her leisure.

"Not everyone is a PTA or community-action type; even fewer are interested in local politics, though if they forced themselves to go to some meetings and hearings they might find a brand-new interest. And I believe women are bound to become more and more political animals, which is all to the good, if our so-called natural goals are to be reshaped to meet what women want—peace and a chance for their children to survive and live well.

"Maybe what I'm saying is that women ought to connect in some way with a group other than the family. In our fluid world it is just too risky to depend only on this for security and happiness through self-realization."

# Toward an Ideal College

*Judson Jerome*

*Poet and teacher Judson Jerome has had a long-time, active interest in educational reform. Dr. Jerome is on the faculty of the new branch campus of Antioch College in the "planned" city of Columbia, Maryland. This article was published in* The Humanist *magazine's March/April 1969 issue.*

When the Rouse Corporation, developers of a planned city that is already emerging at Columbia, Maryland, invited Antioch College to suggest a plan for a college, a number of us—Antioch faculty and students—began to dream. A loosely formed committee met; we aired our dissatisfactions with available educational institutions and our notions of how they might be changed. But this essay is by no means a committee report. It represents purely my own thoughts about what is presently wrong with colleges and how an educational facility at Columbia (I hesitate to call it a college—and certainly refrain from calling it "liberal arts") might avoid them. These thoughts are those that have survived critical discussion in the committee; and I have some confidence that at least this general approach will be reflected in the design that is finally suggested.

I will start with discontents, what I call the four diseases of American education today: compartmentalism, sequentialism, essentialism, and credentialism. This is a process of clearing the field, undermining many of the assumptions we bring to education as preparation for building anew.

(a) *Compartmentalism*—the notion that knowledge can be sorted and filed in areas, departments, disciplines, and courses:

The model of education is that of the bottling works, filling each container, stamping on a cap. Scholars or scientists accumulate and verify data, sorting it into appropriate pigeonholes. They become experts regarding the contents of their particular pigeonhole. Education is a kind of training or programming: A student is "exposed" to the contents of various pigeonholes. Each expert stresses the worth of his own field. Both the experts and the students become fragmented. Integration of knowledge and experience is left to the uncertain processes of the individual nervous system.

Today students are talking about "getting themselves together." We are recognizing, finally, that the integrative process requires conscious attention—and may, indeed, be the central educational need. That is, instead of thinking of education as systematic exposure to a variety of specialties, we should think of it as active integration of specialties. Instead of worrying about acquiring knowledge, we should think of using it—and acquiring more when there is a clear and definite need. I do not mean exclusively a "vocational" need—though I believe it is time we got over our snobbery about vocational education. Basically I mean the need of every man to have his own life make sense to him, to find some coherency in his human experience.

The hope of filling each citizen's head with at least a sampling of the important fields of knowledge is a vain one at best in this era of knowledge explosion. Before the invention of banks each man stored his own wealth—and carried much of it on his back. In Samuel Pepys's diary, at the time of the great London fire of 1666, the private burgher was much concerned about his "plate," literally silver plates and utensils that represented his savings and that had to be buried in the garden before he fled his burning house. In those days much of a man's wealth went into his garments—and he sometimes walked the streets wearing several layers of wool simply because that was the simplest and safest way of guarding his holdings. Today all a man needs is a pocket to carry his credit card; so fluid have our economic processes become that even the checkbook is out-of-date.

In education we still proceed as though the individual head were the best bank—and we carry our layers of resources around with us, even to bed. If we thought of education as learning to use knowledge rather than getting it, if we concerned ourselves with developing ready access to the world bank, if we measured people less by what they knew than by what they could do, we might free them, permit them to get themselves together—and we might begin to solve some of the problems that beset our culture.

Compartmentalism is passive; it receives without digesting. I have heard that computers sometimes break down from a kind of psychosis called "information overload." We are systematically clogging minds with discrete bits of information and leaving it to the students to discover if and where these bits may be converted into active functions in their lives. We are like secretaries who believe problems disappear if one knows where to file them. Our cabinets bulge—and we founder in a polluted world, not knowing how to use what we know. This comes from our habit of emphasizing "content" in education, of regarding our job as educators as one of putting things into people rather than one of evoking what they know and are and what they are capable of becoming.

(b) *Sequentialism*—the notion that there is, if we could only find it, one right linear order in which things can best be learned or done: The myth is that in each compartment of knowledge there are "fundamentals," that step one must precede step two. Our language is shot through with notions of levels, progression, advancement, and often these terms reflect no reality other than our own conditioning.

I believe that sequentialism has something to do with habit, as well as our desire that others suffer what we have suffered, that they pay their dues. It is not unlike the indignation one used to hear from middle-class people who saw forests of television aerials over ghettos or Negroes driving Cadillacs. Men who carried spears are now flying jets in Nigeria. Like it or not, we must accept the fact that there are short cuts to industrialization, that nations build atomic weapons without having taken all our required courses, just as we must accept the fact that young people emerge from their media-choked homes with more information and more life experience (albeit vicarious) than many of us have in middle age. There are thousands of routes to learning, and the young are swarming into the modern world like the throngs that stormed the Winter Palace. It is pathetic to think of some teacher telling students that they cannot go on until they have passed Algebra I.

We need—and are learning how to achieve—instant fluency in languages, instant industrialization, instant alteration of ancient cultural patterns. One of the most interesting developments is the proliferation of various kinds of encounter groups, achieving instant intimacy, instant honesty, perhaps instant friendship, instant courtship. Everywhere we are seeing more evidence of quantum leaps in our culture that seem to belie the need we have always assumed of intervening steps, of continuity. And we hardly know how to live in the simultaneity that is appearing. Riots break out in China, New York, and Rome as though they had more to do with phases of the moon than what we have assumed to be social causes and effects. Perhaps the species is developing some more sophisticated kind of communication that bypasses words—such as that which enables a cloud of gnats to maintain flight formation over the evening water. Waves of information, gestalt perception, leaps, conversion, "vibes" . . . these terms are appearing everywhere as we struggle to comprehend our present experience and to liberate ourselves from the sequential modes in which we were trained.

(c) *Essentialism*—the notion that we can decide (as members of a community, as parents, as educators, as elders) what is "essential" that a person know: Compulsory education, required courses, general education—all these educational formulations are based on the essentialist premise that the tribe defines the initiation rites. All served some useful social function in the past, but it is becoming clear today that they are elitist, conformist, and unrealistic. One wonders whether literacy, which has long served as an index of civilization, can be defended as essential for citizenship in a world where such vast proportions of critical communication do not require reading and writing. When we add to literacy the strange variety of other skills and areas of knowledge that we have argued a person should master before being granted a diploma, the absurdity of our design becomes apparent. If we forgot about the number of units of world history, foreign language, mathematics, driver training, sex education, use of mass media, and computer programming, we might more nearly approximate the essential areas of education of the average citizen.

If we add to that list urban affairs, race conflict, the military-industrial complex, the uses of atomic power, and a few other such subjects, we could perhaps prepare citizens to read *Look* magazine. But I am not suggesting that we bring essentialism up to date. Above all we should see the futility of the effort to define what is basic, the cultural bias that lies behind most of our concepts of essential education, and—with mass education—the deadening effect of standardization in textbooks, course structures, sequences—the classroom conformity and depersonalization in the name of objectivity and standards. Essentialism is a doctrine of programming, of conditioning citizens to the regulations of mass society. Once we thought of it in terms of the need for an educated electorate in a democracy. Now I think it is becoming evident that it produces not independent thinkers but zombies, the "good" student being the one who attends, performs on schedule, learns what is taught, and does not rock the boat with questions about what lies beyond the curriculum.

(d) *Credentialism*—the notion that we can meaningfully certify things about people, about what they can do and what they know: This myth leads directly to the authority hangup— the disastrous confusion between authority as special knowledge and authority as power. Our system is now a complex of authorizations on the basis of credentials—and the credentials are, for the most part, either bogus or trivial.

What do we mean when we label someone? I am a poet. That sentence may mean that I have written and published poetry— something that can be verified—but to express that better I might say I *was* a poet. Whether I *am* a poet and will be one tomorrow remains to be seen each time I roll paper into the typewriter with the intention of writing a poem. "I am a Ph.D." is a much less meaningful statement. It gives you no assurance that there is anything in particular that I know or can do (except, probably, read and write English). Yet the statement is accepted as much more factual than "I am a poet," and it gives me tremendous influence over the lives of people. It gives me the authority to prescribe what they will do and to punish them, if I choose, for what they think.

Credentialism works into our minds and filters through our structures like cancer. Degree requirements are its most concrete manifestation. Compulsion and education are as contradictory as compulsion and love, yet most of our educational activity is conducted by means of the dynamics of compulsion. Credentials lure people into easing demands on themselves: If they have the document and have met the standards, they are largely relieved of the necessity of growing and doing, of proving themselves in each engagement, of questioning their own authenticity, of justifying their demands on others. And yet we stack our diplomas together like a house of cards that becomes magically transformed into a prison. Students are locked into their seats by our diplomas when there are no other chains. Why do they not rebel more furiously than they have? Because they want diplomas. It is a game invented for Parker Brothers by Franz Kafka. Compartmentalism, sequentialism, essentialism, and credentialism—these constitute the anti-life in our system, the slow replacement, molecule by molecule, of organic tissue by solid rock.

## II

If, then, one had a clean slate on which to diagram a new system, how would he begin? I believe that an educational institution primarily for young adults (old enough to be free from parental custody, young enough to be unencumbered with dependents) has a twin mission: to enable people to free themselves from their miseducation in the past and to enable them to develop ability for self-determination and survival in the only available world. On the horizon, like the glow of dawn, is the possibility that our institution might enable them to achieve more than that —what progressive educators are calling ecstasy. But it is probably much too soon to expect an institution in our society to stipulate ecstasy as an educational aim.

We need to create the opportunity for young adults to get, as one student put it, "un-hungup." Patterns of dependency, conformity, misdirected rebelliousness, and self-hatred have already been ingrained. And our problem is compounded by the fact that there is no way to "teach" people to be independent, self-directed, self-fulfilling. All we can do is provide the setting and support that may enable this transformation to take place.

I believe it would be a great mistake for a college to relinquish its parietal function, for we know that most education on campuses takes place in peer relationships and in the living situation as significantly opposed to the classroom. I would be tempted to say that living in college residences ought to be required, except that I believe nothing should be required. And the residences provided by the college should be almost the opposite of the dormitories traditionally provided: They should encourage interaction between the sexes and provide settings of privacy, informality, and great personal choice in life style. They should encourage some sense of community with others, be small enough so that the residents know one another well, large enough so that no one is trapped by too limited a set of relationships. Though it is important that young adults learn to relate successfully to their own age group, it is also important that there be some vertical range in the ages of people with whom they live: Children and older adults should be part of the community.

I am thinking of complexes of apartments housing no more than about a hundred individuals in each complex. Most apartments would be for two or three people, but some would be for one person, others for larger groups such as families. Housing should not be assigned but chosen—and available on the same basis to students and faculty. Each complex should have common rooms, a small auditorium, green space, and recreational facilities. Each apartment should be connected by closed circuit systems to the information and resources centers of the college.

Some faculty in each complex should have, as their primary educational responsibility, the charge of fostering the use of the living environment for learning. They should sponsor group activities, help people with similar interests get together, bring in resources (i.e., visitors, programs, exhibits, books) that are relevant to the learning needs of the residents. Their role is consciously therapeutic: They strive to create the conditions under which people can be liberated from their mental obstacles to learning. It should be understood that students will spend a great deal of time, as much time as needed, in the residential setting and the activities associated with it. This is no less a legitimate part of their education than time spent in the institutes, on jobs, or in other learning situations. In fact, because of society's tendency to think otherwise, some special emphasis upon the validity and necessity of residential or environmental education may be necessary. The residence is home, and home is, in large part, the center of our lives. "Leisure" is a pejorative word today, but in the future that may be the principal business of many of us. It is important that we be able to conduct ourselves well alone, in free time, and in intimate relationships with others.

But it is premature to gear ourselves for a society of leisure. Truly independent people are those who are freed not merely to do what they like but those who are in some sense self-supporting. "Self-supporting" means, of course, deriving support from others in some mutual relationship; the individual avails himself of the services of others by serving them. In that context of mutual dependency, freedom is possible only to the extent that the individual has as wide a range as possible of competencies, so that he may choose the ways in which he will serve and so that he can choose the services of others that will enable him to pursue his purposes. At the very least, a person who has been to this college should be able to cope—to perform real tasks in the world, to support himself not because he has a diploma but because he has developed marketable, effective skills. In this respect liberal-arts colleges are usually deficient because of basically elitist orientation that disdains application.

Therefore, as an alternative to departmental structure, the chief organizational units of the college should be problem-oriented institutes in such areas as race and poverty, communications, education, human development, urban studies, arts and society, and pollution. Though institutes suggest specialization and compartmentalism, each would, in fact, address a cross-section of human problems, and the institutes would be forced to rely on one another for information, ideas, and energy in attacking practical issues. As social problems change, the problems addressed by the institutes would continually change, requiring new personnel, now foci of interest.

Each institute would have three components: research, application, and education. Unlike departments, institutes can seek funds for their programs and broker their services for actual social needs. The programs they undertake in research and application should be designed in ways that permit the easy absorption of unskilled and unlearned students into their tasks. That is, "undergraduates" should be able to learn by participation even at the expense of some inefficiency in the operations.

In addition to the institutes, the college would make educational use of other functioning organizations in the community (i.e., factories, theaters, schools, publishing plants, churches), and it might, in fact, manage some such organizations, staffing them chiefly with students. That is, the college would conceive of itself primarily as an agency to get students into situations in which they can learn, to facilitate their learning there, and to provide the resources for study in greater depth than regular employees, scholars, or researchers are likely to discover. Because students would move fluidly from one institute or organization to another, have the stimulation of an enriched living and learning environment and free time to explore, think, and study, they would acquire not only the skills necessary to perform tasks but the perspective to see those tasks in relationship to the whole complex of social needs and their personal needs.

For most of the work students do in the institutes or on jobs in organizations, they should be paid—at a rate that would enable them to subsist in the college without outside support. Perhaps it would be possible—and desirable—to standardize the rate of pay throughout the system, so that a student "earns" as much working in a theater or reading philosophy as on a job in a biochemical laboratory or in business. Moreover, it might be advisable to handle this "salary" in such a way that no money changes hands, but the salary is applied to residential costs by a transfer on the books. It may be educationally advisable to insist that he *not* receive support directly from his parents or other outside sources. Rather, his parents might be encouraged to donate to the institution as a whole and therefore indirectly increase the rate of remuneration to all students.

One of the faculty in the student's residential complex would serve as his adviser, a guide to the array of educational possibilities in the college as a whole. He might study independently, work in one or more of the institutes, take a part-time job in one of the cooperating organizations, engage in projects or study ventures with other students or resident faculty—in short use the enriched environment in whatever way seems most relevant to his intellectual and personal growth. Movement of people among available learning slots in the institutes and on jobs would be coordinated by a computerized reservation system such as is used by motels and airlines. Dossiers of recommendations could be accumulated by the students or by a central office; letters collected there from supervisors would testify to the exact nature and quality of the student's performance in various areas of work or study, and these would be the student's chief demonstration to graduate schools or employers of the content of his education. Standardized examinations would be available, administered by the college at the student's request, if he chose to collect that kind of data about himself for the information of others.

Since at the present time the social demand for degrees is so great that a person is handicapped without one, and since there should be no penalty on a person who educates himself at this college rather than another, a process would be established for granting a degree, though no student is compelled to become a degree candidate. Such a degree program would have a residential stipulation (i.e., a minimum of three years of full-time participation in the college program). The student himself should define his objectives, the means by which he seeks to achieve them, and the evidence he wishes to submit of accomplishment. A staff or faculty committee would advise him in the formation of his plans, review his achievements, and write a descriptive paragraph to appear on the individual degree that indicates the student's aims, his accomplishments, and the committee's judgment as to their quality. Thus the degree would mean no more nor less than it said on its face—and one might hope that in time even this degree would wither away.

Thus the institution would consist of overlapping networks —of residences designed for educational purposes and of opportunities for direct engagements with real problems in the world. The units in the network (the residential complexes, the institutes) would be as autonomous as possible in governance, budgeting, formation and pursuit of goals. Since the networks would be compounded of modular units, they can be infinitely expanded, the size of the college being a reflection of what the traffic will bear. The central administration would be an agency, a device for enabling education to occur. It would operate central learning resources centers, recreational facilities, public relations, recruitment, and admissions and other such college-wide functions. It would initiate institutes and residential units, decide when these should be phased out or replaced, and help find appropriate staff.

To those who think of education as doing things to other people's minds these flexible networks will not sound like a college at all. "Why, that is just living," one person responded when I revealed my educational design. This is true—just living, in an environment in which there is a conscious effort to remove barriers to learning and growth, in which the machines have plastic housing to reveal their working parts, in which the individual is nurtured like a plant rather than conditioned to a maze (as a mouse might be by electric shocks). The aims of this college would be to develop originality, independence, competence in coping, to release human potential. That is a vision of excellence that sounds very strange in our present educational world.

# Nairobi College

*The Planning Committee
of Nairobi College*

*Nairobi College is located in the predominantly black community of
East Palo Alto, California. It opened in September 1969, following a
year of turmoil at the local public junior college centering around an
educational program for minority students.*

Nairobi College is designed to produce the leaders so desperately needed by communities of color. Leadership training at Nairobi is not a matter of learning leadership skills in a vacuum. Nairobi College students are constantly involved in the administration, governance, and planning of their education, their communities, and the future of their people. Leaders are trained by assuming the responsibilities of leadership while learning the specific skills and techniques necessary to build communities. Nairobi College students are self-selective just as leaders are self-selective. Those who wish to become the builders of tomorrow's communities of color are provided with the skills they need. A leader is a person who wants to lead and has the skills to do so.

If a student accepts the philosophy of the college and is willing to assume the responsibility of community work and self-development that the philosophy incurs, he is accepted into the college without consideration of his previous academic training. It is the belief of the college that it is precisely those with great leadership potential who are frequently excluded from education and who therefore come to Nairobi least equipped to pursue their goals. It is the function of the college to furnish leadership abilities while equipping students with the education they previously have been excluded from.

The Nairobi College Board of Trustees is an illustration of the College's belief in self-determination for peoples of color and in learning to lead by leading. Members of the Board equally represent students, faculty, and community members from each of the communities, being served by the College. Student representatives: two Black, two Brown (including Native Americans), and two Asian, are elected by the students; faculty representatives with the same racial composition are elected by the faculty; community representatives, appointed by the student members of the Board.

## GOALS OF NAIROBI COLLEGE

Briefly the goals of the Nairobi College curriculum are:

1. To make its students and faculty aware of the problems of the communities of color.

2. To make students and faculty aware of the institutional racism of the society that oppresses them.

3. To develop a revolutionary spirit among its members through a program of enlightenment and involvement.

4. To develop basic skills, other skills, and a communal spirit among its students and faculty.

5. To make its students and faculty aware of the history of Black people.

6. To impart to students and faculty a correct knowledge of the history of other people of color.

7. To develop a dedication to the rebuilding of the communities of color among its students and faculty.

8. To make its students and faculty aware of the basis for unity among people of color.

These goals are measurable. They can be used as a basis for evaluation of student and faculty who leave Nairobi College and go to other schools or to the non-white community. Undoubtedly, they will be modified and added to in the future, but at present, they represent a sound set of goals to shoot for. Nairobi College is dedicated to the task of making them realizable.

## COMMUNITY CONTROL

Members of the Board are aided in their policy-making decisions by an advisory committee composed of those individuals with influence, expertise, or wealth who generally serve on college boards of trustees, the National Advisory Committee, and by an Advisory Committee composed of friends of the College active in service to the communities which the College serves, the Community Advisory Committee. Both of these committees serve in the advisory capacity only.

In addition to being well represented on the Board of Trustees, students sit on all College committees and have full voting power in these committees. They are involved in all levels of decision-making within the College. They interview potential instructors and control hiring. They serve on the curriculum committee and play a large part in developing courses for the College. They are involved in contacting social agencies and in developing and coordinating the work of students in these agencies.

## THE COMMUNITY IS THE CAMPUS

Nairobi is truly a college without walls. The community is its campus. Courses are conducted in churches, existing schools, faculty homes, recreation centers, and social service agencies. To preserve its identity with the community and to prevent the formation of a separate, walled institution, the College will not build a campus in the traditional sense. As buildings are constructed, they will relate to the needs of the total community. The College library will be the community library; the College theatre will be the community theatre. Students, then, will always be in and of the community they intend to serve, continually involved in the development of skills to solve problems and to change aspirations into programs.

No student will be dehumanized by being forced to forget his brothers while he improves himself. His personal development will constantly be a reflection of the development of his community and his fellow man.

## COMMUNITY SERVICE

Every full time student is required to work in the community. He may choose from a wide variety of community agencies and a wider variety of tasks. He may develop a new agency in cooperation with other students. Students serve as teacher aides in elementary schools, planners and workers for Municipal Council, skilled and unskilled workers for the community health center, and counselors for legal aid. Whatever his interests, the student is encouraged to create a program of service which will further his skills while serving his people.

## CURRICULUM AND INSTRUCTION

Nairobi College offers courses which are traditional and non-traditional in subject matter. Course offerings are currently available for fall and winter quarters. At the moment, Nairobi is a four year college offering only two years of instruction. Its courses are partially designed to enable students to transfer easily into four year schools of their choice. Courses and instructional method are primarily designed to complement the goals of the College. Educators and students have long been concerned that while preaching Democracy, most institutions practice and therefore teach something quite different. Nairobi College has thrown out the lecture method so that students learn through interaction with each other and faculty. Students within a quarter of transferring to a four year institution who need to know how to function well in lecture-recitation classes are counseled to take a course at a nearby institution. Several students take courses at Stanford University under an agreement developed between Nairobi and Stanford allowing students to take courses at Stanford free of charge. Many attend nearby junior colleges: College of San Mateo, Cañada, Foothill.

In addition to removing the faculty authoritarian figure, the keeper and dispenser of knowledge, the Nairobi family and students are involved in other changes in instructional method which reflect directly on learned behavior. For example, schools stress cooperation as a value and teach competitiveness. Helping a fellow student learn in most school situations is called cheating. Early in the educational process a student is taught that the way to success, a four point average, is seeing to it that no one else in the class knows as much as he does. Students are taught to withhold information and ideas in discussion so that they may triumph on examinations. Grading on a curve, punitive grading, closed book examinations, and a classroom designed with rows of students facing a teacher, all teach students to be competitive, to improve themselves at the expense of others.

At Nairobi, classes have been known to redirect their attention for a three hour session to bring a late-comer up to date on what the class is doing. Students learn and reinforce their learning by teaching others. When students cooperate, ask for a group rather than individual grading, and become genuinely responsible for each other's learning, all members of a class learn more. Even more important, at the same time they learn to aid rather than to destroy each other.

In the first quarter, students in a reading and linguistics course requested that an eleven-year-old in the community who had been severely damaged by the school system and who could not read at all be invited to join their class. Because there is no ridicule of him, because each member of the class believes he will learn to read and takes responsibility for his learning, he will learn to read. Just as important, each student in the class will learn more about reading through teaching the eleven-year-old and more about psychology through watching his growth away from being withdrawn, scared, and inhibited toward being accepting of his own value as a human being.

Throughout the country, students are crying for relevance. They are asking that they not be asked to store unrelated knowledge computer-style until some future date when knowledge may or may not aid them in the tasks they select. At Nairobi the task precedes the learning. A student who wants to rebuild his community so that the structures fit and enhance the life styles of those who live and work in them may be placed in an architect's office for a quarter observing and doing a variety of tasks. He learns, immediately, what he does not know, that he must take more mathematics, more sociology. As a result of his experience in the architectural office, he has a realistic view of his vocational goal and begins to develop a program to reach that goal. That same student might work in a city planner's office during his third quarter and with a contractor during his fourth. Job placements have been and are being developed with companies and firms throughout the Peninsula to provide all Nairobi students with first hand knowledge of vocational choices.

---

There is only one comment which I hope will remain true at Venceremos: that the College will remain an instrument for social change—*an integration of theory and practice* that is not afraid to bite the apple to find out what it tastes like and that it is not afraid to abolish the social structures that stand in the way of true Self-Determination for *la Raza*.

This is California, Aztlan, not London, England. Our Brown Beautiful Nation wants our land, our food, housing, education, medical care, clothes, good roads, our own cops. And we!! *We* will determine for ourselves how we are going to run things. That is it, that's what we are all about; Brown Berets, United Farm Workers, Crusade for Justice, Venceremos College, that is what it is all about.

—AARON MANGANIELLO
Director, Venceremos College
Redwood City, California

# Space for Something Else:
# Bensalem

*Elizabeth Sewell*

*Teacher and writer Elizabeth Sewell is the former Director of Fordham University's experimental college, Bensalem. Her informal report on the College's founding year was written in 1968 and has been widely distributed by the United States National Student Association.*

I am writing this in the pause between the end of Bensalem's first year and the beginning of its second. We begin again on Monday next, in three days time, with the arrival of our next group of students, sixteen men and fourteen women. Thirty last year, thirty this year, thirty—if all goes well—next year, and that will bring us to our full size, for we are working on the basis of a three-year B.A., not a four-year one, with summers included. I am writing in the morning of a cool gray Bronx day, sitting on the bed which does duty for a couch in the living room of my apartment in our communal building. Windows are open, the roar of Fordham Road comes in, there are sounds from the apartment building which backs on to ours, someone's record player is busy (ours or theirs? Probably ours), people are stirring in the building; some of our second-year students are with us, and the new students are moving in bit by bit this week, as are the resident faculty. One has a sense of a center of activity, of things getting going, nothing clear yet but all sorts of possibilities. It is cheerful and scaring, one of the many paradoxes that go into life here.

Bensalem, this activity, is the Experimental College which

Fordham University set going last year. It came from ideas which Father Leo McLaughlin, S.J., our present President, and I had back in 1965, and probably long before that though they weren't articulated and directed until then. There is not, and has never been, a set of theories behind this experiment: rather, a very strong sense that higher education in America cannot go on much longer in the way it is going now (clear enough by 1965 and a lot clearer since), and a readiness to make, within Fordham, a space for something else.

What we had in mind took shape as a small residential college where students and their faculty would live together, and by that living and working and thinking would try to find out what education really is and could be, here and now. ("Relevance," that much used word, belongs here perhaps.) Our terms of reference were that we were to be free of requirements, curricula, grades, examinations, credits. Each student plans his or her own course of study, and has a faculty advisor who can offer help or advice when needed, but one of whose main functions is that there should be one faculty member at least among us who really knows and understands what Student X or Student Y is doing. Programs have already proved enormously varied, ranging from theology to working in a storefront school in Harlem, from Icelandic to being active in the Yippie movement. Any of our students may register for courses at "big Fordham," which incidentally is just across the road from the apartment house where Bensalem finds itself this year, but this is at their choice, i.e., they do not have to. Some interesting things have happened here: some of our students—freshmen, straight from high school—being admitted to upperclass courses or graduate courses on big campus, and holding their own well; or a student whom we accepted, whose formal grades and College Board scores and so on were far below Fordham's cut-off point, doing very creditably indeed in regular Fordham classes. All the facilities of the university are at their disposal, and beyond that, those of the neighboring community, which is out-and-out city, with all those urban problems so much to the forefront now; and beyond that again, all of New York City; and beyond that, the world, or as much of it as can yet be absorbed and taken as real by young Americans who still seem to find it hard, even with all the restlessness and discontent with their own society which they exhibit, to see much beyond it. There is a lot of space here, and much of it we have hardly even thought of moving into as yet. We hope to do more during the coming year.

People always ask what kind of faculty and students come to us, so let me deal with that next. The original faculty in the planning and opening stages were nearly all young friends of mine, collected from the very various places in the United States where I have held teaching jobs over the last fifteen years. They were mostly at the pre-Ph.D. or just-post-Ph.D. stage, and that has held good this year too, though we have gone out this time for a broader range of discipline, including our first scientist. The youthfulness is important, I feel too, partly for flexibility but partly also for sheer survival. Now about the students—all were, and are, volunteers of course, and this year the number asking to come rose considerably. When considering applications we are, I suppose, looking for a certain kind of discontent and independence, people ready to take responsibility for shaping their own studies and making their own choices, about day-to-day living as well as longer-term matters. It is important too that our students should have thought a bit about communal living, its reality and difficulty as well as the advantages it can have. The key to the actual admission process is a longish interview, conducted by one faculty member and two students, these groups rotating. We emerged last year with a fairly varied group, which seemed right. We can afford, being the kind of place we are, to take risks, and certainly our students have to take them too, simply by coming to us, for, "something else" as we are, we are by no means safe. The President of Fordham University says that Bensalem students will receive Fordham B.A.s after three years of satisfactory work, but our future bristles, very properly, with questions and questionableness. What constitutes satisfactory work on our terms, which are far from those of a standard degree? What is success in Bensalem, or failure? How does a student measure or determine his progress, and how does anyone else do so? We ask all our students to keep careful records, and we take counsel from the other experimental colleges of which there are scores now all over the country; but if students seeking entry to Bensalem indicate a desire for safe progress to some unimpeachable Graduate School above all else, we are liable to advise them to go elsewhere. We do believe, though, that our students will be accepted in graduate schools, and in any case somebody has to do something about graduate education in this country, and soon. There's another area where things cannot go on as they now are, but this is not Bensalem's business immediately. (Talking of risks, the parents of our students have to take them too, and we realize and respect this.)

If I seem to be talking rather negatively, about risks and unsafety and so on, it is because this has been a real part of our experience this last year. You think genuinely that you want freedom, removal of traditional forms, space in which to try new things; but when you have them you may discover as we did, faculty and students, that into that space you bring also a good deal of fear. If I had to characterize our worst enemy during this first year of ours, I would say it was fear and mistrust. Simply by committing ourselves to Bensalem and what it implied, we had moved out of the tidy delimited ordered world (even if that order was constraining and often illusory) we had lived in for most of our lives. Like the seafarers in Bacon's *New Atlantis*, lost in mid-ocean till they came to the island called Bensalem on which they landed and found a welcome (this is where our name comes from, by the way), we had really left the known and familiar behind us. Many of the young people found it at first very hard to function in a world of space where the choices were theirs, instead of the familiar educational boxes, and social rules, into which high school and home and the traditional set-up of a freshman year in college put you. Faculty moved from the specialized tasks of a standard university teaching post into total immersion in the world of present-day eighteen-year-olds, an astonishingly disconcerting experience from which, by the way, the traditional freshman classroom is designed to protect you; they discovered also that they had each, turn by turn, to take on an almost unlimited number of functions for which they had neither training nor special aptitude. Besides being instructor they found themselves acting as administrator from time to time, counselor, dean of discipline, fellow-student alongside the students in some of the seminars, conducted by visiting faculty or students themselves, which go on in Bensalem. In all these things we were all amateurs, and made a lot of mistakes, as also in the reshaping of our relationships to one another. We have all emerged very considerably changed by the year now behind us;

changed in some respects for the better, I hope, but changed certainly.

Some people might be feeling at this point that much of this could have been foreseen; that by careful planning, educational and social, this could have been largely eliminated. I understand the feeling, but I think not. We in fact planned scarcely at all before we began, on an instinct that "that which is creative must create itself" and I do not, after a year, feel differently, although I think this summer will be steadier than last, largely because of the presence of what are now our second-year students. In this kind of enterprise one has to be ready to grope and prophesy one's way forward rather than to plan beforehand, I believe, and on Monday next we shall meet with all our students and begin that odd living process again, for the forthcoming year.

At least by now we know a little more about the areas we have to deal with, and the questions we have to address ourselves to. We realized that we were to consider or reconsider education; and with this from the start, as the second pole of Bensalem's interest and activity, was the idea of community, of what a "learning community" might be. There was a third too, which I for one was less clear about when we began, which was what I might call "government." The authority-based, from-the-top-down kind of government in colleges and universities (perhaps in schools as well?) is plainly over, and we had to learn how to order ourselves, students and faculty together, on some basis of mutual consent.

The three together, education, community and government, proved quite a mouthful. I have said a good deal about education already, and will not add to that here. Community exercised our minds all year, and still does, as indeed it should. We learned fast that just living together in our apartment house did not constitute us a community; we were more of a conglomeration much of the time, with all the predictable personal hostilities, and the close and loving friendships too, liable to arise in what is after all a gathering of individualists. We kept holding meetings about "community"—why had we not attained it (whatever it was)? How and in what ways could we do better? Halfway through the year it began to seem as if Bensalem was polarizing around the two poles, as I had always seen them, of our endeavor, education on one side and community on the other, with some of us apparently going all out for the one at the expense of the other, so that in-groups began to form and people drew away from one another with a certain suspicion and uneasiness. In the end this shifting and fermenting has produced a positive result, for a small group of students and one faculty member who want to form a closer intentional community, which they envisage as continuing after their years at Bensalem proper are over, have moved out and rented a big house this year where they can really put their thoughts and desires into practice, and we hope to learn a great deal from what they learn there. Experiment should breed experiment, and it interests me greatly that we shall already have to start thinking now about how one holds a scattered community together, since Bensalem is in two bits and may well be in more before we've done. I feel sure this is important, because this is how, it seems to me, many a community of the future is going to have to work, and we may as well begin now to learn how to manage networks of this sort, geographically separated, perhaps world-wide, but forming a new and real kind of extended organism.

Connected with both the above, education and community, is what I am calling government, and here too we had plenty of ups and downs. How, in a group where one is trying to reach a consensus, can one arrive at decisions? Especially the hard and unpleasant ones involving people? What about minority opinions? Voting and the standard so-called democratic procedures did not feel right to us, and we grope after something else, and shall go on doing so this coming year. Hard and long and frustrating as the process often is, difficult as I sometimes find my position as Chairman where I am bound to hold myself responsible for the decisions and actions of this group of people, faculty and students, Bensalem, over which I have no authority in the old sense of the word and agree that it is right that I should have none, this too seems to me important, for we are going to need to know in educational institutions other than this small place how to manage in these circumstances, how perhaps to invent some altogether new form of managing these things and to learn to acquire the attitudes and willingnesses that go with this as yet undiscovered and plainly urgent way of working. A "we," at least, not the distressing "we" and "they" which seems so characteristic of this area, and indeed of all internal university situations just now.

None of this, needless to say, is peculiar to us. Other people are working at these same things, with us, all over the place now. Breathing in the space between last year and the coming one, one is aware of a number of thoughts, or perhaps of feelings rather than thoughts which is one reason why this activity of Bensalem has not been easy to set out here in prose; it goes better into poetry which is the form in which I have mostly reported on it thus far. Also I have the sense that each Bensalemite, if asked to write on what I have been dealing with here, would have written something very different; and perhaps that is good. There is a feeling of astonishment, at our survival, at the persistence and enthusiasm of our students, present and to come, at the fact that the faculty, despite the enormous demands made on them, are back for more. There is a feeling, too, and a very strong one underneath all the questions and anxieties, that what we are attempting here is in the right direction. I have not thought it necessary to argue here the case for change in education, or for experiments, of many kinds, to meet student demands, not just the vocal ones but the inarticulate wretchedness and despair which walks about, embodied, on campus after campus nowadays. Events speak loud enough to this point. Interdisciplinary skills, free choice of programs, independent study, a relating of learning to one's own life and that of "the great city of the world" in Bacon's phrase, an attempt at some better society however small its beginnings, the doing away with competitiveness and the substitution of cooperation as far as possible, the sharing and spreading of decision—a king and responsibility—that is the way it is going to go. Bensalem is not a "model" and very far from a Utopia. But it is and remains a space for that process, now seemingly world-wide among the young and the ready-to-move, a space for something else than we now have; maybe, all in all, a space for hope.

# Experiment at Berkeley

*Joseph Tussman*

*The Tussman Experimental Program at the Berkeley campus of the University of California was born in the mid-1960's, about the same time that Mario Savio and others were making demands for free speech and free choice in the university programs. This program is "radical" in a way that Savio and his followers would not accept: it is a prescribed, rigidly academic approach to reading, writing, and discussion. Dr. Tussman, a professor of Philosophy at the university and the director of the experiment, asserts that "Minds are not made free by being left alone. Nor are students." The following is a reprint of the "Plan of the Program" given to students considering the program.*

The Program is an attempt to provide a coherent scheme of liberal education for the first two undergraduate years—a time during which the student is not yet pursuing a "major." The structure of the program is quite unlike the traditional one, but it has a structure of its own, which governs the educational life of its faculty and its students. It is not organized in terms of courses or academic subjects. It is, instead, based on a common, required curriculum—a program of reading, writing, and discussion.

The core of the program is a sequence of reading. The reading not only poses a number of persistent problems but serves as a focus for writing and discussion. In general, the readings themselves cluster about some periods in Western civilization during which a major crisis evokes a broad range of thoughtful and creative response. During the first year the focus is on Greece during the Peloponnesian wars and on seventeenth-century England. The second year focuses on America.

## THE READINGS

The reading list is deceptively short. But we believe in reading a few great works in depth rather than reading a great many things in haste. The reading experience in the program is quite unlike what one has generally encountered in his earlier education. If, for example, we "read" the *Iliad* for a two-week period this is almost the equivalent, in time, of an entire quarter course. But the work is concentrated and undistracted since, generally, we are reading only one thing at a time. Thus, one can read the *Iliad*, in a preliminary way, in several days; but that reading only scratches the surface, and we must learn how to get beyond that with the aid of discussion, writing, rereading and rereading.

Generally, we do not require or even advise the reading of secondary works or scholarly commentary, although students may, of course, do so if they have time. While two weeks may, at the outset, seem to be a long time to spend on the *Iliad*, the time will, at the end, seem all too short. If we are working properly, every book will be laid aside with regret.

## WRITING

We approach writing with the conviction that a student can hardly do too much of it. The program policy is that the student should write every day for the entire two-year period. The theory is not that we are out to produce "writers," but that writing as a habitual exercise calls on us to develop clarity, coherence, and other powers of analysis and expression, and contributes to our capacity to read perceptively and to engage in fruitful discussion.

The writing program will normally be coordinated with the reading and will involve:

(1) Formal papers—about five each quarter—on topics and in a form to be assigned by the faculty.

(2) A log or journal in which each student is to write every day. This should be a page or two which develops some idea raised by the reading or in seminar or lecture. The log is to be available for faculty scrutiny on appropriate occasions.

## DISCUSSION

Students, in seminar groups of eight, will meet twice each week—once with a faculty member present and once without. The discussion is to be focused on the questions or problems raised by the reading. Discussion is a difficult art with a complex moral and intellectual structure. It involves listening and responding as well as speaking. It calls for judgment about significance and relevance, and it requires adequate preparation. The seminars can be a stimulating and exciting aspect of the program.

## LECTURES

Twice a week (Tuesday and Thursday, 10–12) the student body and faculty assemble for something like a general lecture-discussion session. Sometimes a faculty member may deliver a lecture or speak for a half hour or more. On other occasions a number of faculty members may have a panel discussion. There will usually be questions from students, and responses. Sometimes we will have a guest lecturer.

Again, the "lectures" will be related to the reading. The purpose is not to give background information or to explain the reading but rather to deepen the issues, to offer suggestive interpretations, and generally to spark consideration of fundamental problems.

## CONFERENCES

Each student will have a different faculty member as his seminar leader or instructor each quarter. The instructor will read and comment on the papers and may, from time to time, hold individual conferences. These conferences may occur either on the initiative of the instructor or of the student—as needed rather than on a regularly scheduled basis.

## INFORMAL ACTIVITY

The house, which has been assigned to the program for its exclusive use, is the physical center for most of our activity. Faculty offices are located there, and seminars are held there.

But, in addition, it is available for a wide range of informal uses by members of the program. Coffee is available at all hours, the lounge is pleasant and convenient for conversation, and a quiet reading room is available.

It is hoped that the house will be used by the students for a variety of appropriate informal activities—morning, afternoon, and evening.

It should be noted that the general resources of the University are available for students in the Program—libraries, gymnasia and sport facilities, lectures, concerts—and it is expected that our students will live fairly active lives.

## THE SUBJECT

Since we do not organize our work in terms of such familiar fields or disciplines as economics, sociology, political science, history, or literature, it is difficult to give a simple answer to the question, "But what are you studying?" Nor is it quite accurate to say that the program is "interdisciplinary." We are concerned with certain fundamental human problems, although it would seem pretentious to say that we are studying the problems of freedom, order, justice, authority, conscience, war, rebellion, and tyranny. But these, among others, are problems with which the Greeks struggled; they are problems which dominate the mind and spirit of seventeenth-century England; they constitute, in some mysterious sense, the American agenda; they are problems we grapple with as we try to create a significant life in this time and this place. This, as we see it, is the "subject" of liberal education; this is what the reading is about.

## SOME GENERAL OBSERVATIONS

Of course, formal assignments or activities, crucial as they are, constitute only a minimal aspect of education. They are the necessary ceremony or ritual which aid in the development of the appropriate habit or cast of mind. They are to be taken religiously—that is, seriously—but for anyone in search of education they do not define the limits of his work. The student is the ultimate steward of his energies; the institution can guide, encourage, advise, and sustain. But it cannot simply *give* him his education.

The program frees the student from many of the prods and checks to which he has become accustomed. There are no examinations; the pass–not pass system can remove much of the competitive grade pressure; the small number of formal "classes" gives him a great deal of unscheduled time. He will have to learn to use his time and energy fruitfully in an environment full of random excitement, enticement, and distraction.

To enroll in the program is to assume certain commitments. It is to become one of a group seeking to create a learning community, to engage in a common intellectual life. Education is not entirely a private matter; it is a social enterprise. And it has its obligations. Thus, for example, every student is expected—required—to attend every formally scheduled meeting, lecture, or seminar; to do the reading carefully and thoroughly, to turn in promptly papers which represent his best efforts. The freedom which we cultivate is the freedom of mastery, not of impulse.

## Calendar for First Year, Readings
### (Three 10-Week Quarters)

*Fall Quarter*

1. Homer's *Iliad*
2. *Iliad*
3. Homer's *Odyssey*; Xenephon's *Anabasis*; Hesiod's *Works and Days*
4. Thucydides' *Peloponnesian War* ⎤ Supplemented by selected
5. *Peloponnesian War* ⎬ lives from Plutarch and
6. *Peloponnesian War* ⎦ comedies by Aristophanes
7. Aeschylus' *Oresteia*
8. Sophocles' Three Theban Plays
9. Euripides' *The Bacchae*
10. Plato's *Apology* and *Crito*

## Winter Quarter

1. Plato's *Gorgias*
2. Plato's *Republic*
3. *Republic*
4. *Republic*
5. Bible ⎱
6. Bible ⎬ Selections from the King James version
7. Bible ⎰
8. Shakespeare's *King Lear*
9. Machiavelli's *The Prince*
10. (Short Quarter)

## Spring Quarter

1. Milton's *Paradise Lost*
2. *Paradise Lost*
3. Hobbes's *Leviathan*
4. *Leviathan*
5. *Leviathan*
6. J. S. Mill's *On Liberty*
7. *On Liberty*
8. Arnold's *Culture and Anarchy*
9. *Culture and Anarchy*
10. General Review

## Readings for Second Year

(This list is tentative, and probably incomplete. The sequence is subject to change.)

## Fall Quarter

Henry Adams                     *The U.S. in 1880*
The Flag Salute Cases           U.S. Supreme Court
*The Federalist Papers* and The Constitution
*McCulloch v. Maryland*         (John Marshall)

| Calhoun | *Disquisitions on Government* |
| Edmund Burke | *Selections* |

## Winter Quarter

Supreme Court cases on church & state, conscience, freedom
Thoreau (selections)

| Meiklejohn | *Political Freedom* |

## Spring Quarter

Marx (selections)
Freud (selected works)
*The Education of Henry Adams*
*The Autobiography of Lincoln Steffens*
*The Autobiography of Malcolm X*

| Meiklejohn | *Education Between Two Worlds* |

# Rochdale:
# The Ultimate Freedom

*Barrie Zwicker*

*Barrie Zwicker has reported on education for the* Toronto Daily Star *and has served on the staff of the Province of Ontario Council for the Arts. This article appeared in the November–December 1969 issue of* Change *magazine.*

It's not easy to get a grip on Rochdale College. I hope this isn't taken entirely as a plea for sympathy for the writer, which partly it is. But Rochdale doesn't lend itself to polite discourse or even, really, to print.

Rochdale is an experimental, residential free university, run by students and housed in a $5.8-million, student-owned, eighteen-story building in downtown Toronto. Of the more than three hundred free universities on this continent, Rochdale is perhaps the most ambitious. It opened last year with good press, high ideals and its building unfinished. It now houses about one thousand persons—fewer than one-third of them original residents—of unusual diversity, especially in dress, background and education. Little formal learning is taking place there.

The reality of Rochdale—the graffiti, the open use of drugs, the sounds, smells, conversational styles and way of life— shatters most conventional yardsticks by which colleges are measured: degrees offered, faculty renown, quality of student clientele, facilities, course descriptions. It will, if it survives, be measured in part by the attainments of its alumni, a criterion also applied to conventional universities. Otherwise it is the antithesis of their image. Unconventional dress is the norm; bizarre behavior is tolerated; until recently chaos was honored over *any* substantial rule. (How else explain that one "head of security" for the Rochdale building was a "biker" [a motorcycle gang member] addicted to pink shirts and tough talk?)

Some writers have rummaged deep into a Kandy Kolored incense-filled urn of psychedelic modifiers in an attempt to zap their readers with Rochdale. I was asked to write "a tough, concise portrait of Rochdale and its student-faculty clientele." After a year's acquaintance with Rochdale, I still haven't one of those. Rochdale rejects labels as a faulty vending machine rejects coins. Rochdale does not comprise a "hard" story.

The place offers no degrees, cannot be said to be recognized academically (although two students were given credit for their Rochdale work at a department of Simon Fraser University), has no faculty and few courses which last very long. Programs for screening applicants come and go. One scheme was to have one person, by more or less common consent, do all the interviewing and use his judgment. The day I talked with him about his criteria, in an off-campus attic with eighteenth-century atmosphere, his first words were, "Have some dope," as he offered me a smoldering corncob pipe. Five or six others, relaxed around a heavy rectangular wooden table, were bathed in near silence. One, wearing heavy boots, absently and expertly drew a haunting, muted melody out of a beaten-up concert guitar. I settled as unobtrusively as possible into a deep chair and tried not to disturb the luxuriousness of the occasion. "I just use my judgment, like anyone else would," the admissions officer said, before taking another long drag from the pipe. Had he turned anyone down? "Yes, three." Why? "Because they would have been complete disasters." A girl offered a more particular explanation: "If someone comes in waving a gun, you turn him down."

As President Claude Bissell of the University of Toronto says, it is too early to tell about Rochdale. Serious students of the phenomenon agree that the first year is a shakedown for such an institution and that the second year will be telling. Rochdale is fascinating; it could be significant. Already there are signs that certain arts—music, weaving, sculpture, drama— may flourish well, that Rochdale may produce more humane, more socially-conscious graduates, that it may have lessons to teach about the place of drugs in the society of the future. There are dark omens, too. Tough elements have infiltrated; some carry guns; hard dope, such as heroin, has been pushed; motorcycle gangs like the Detroit Renegades have paid visits. Over the summer a much harder policy toward such activities developed, and at the time of writing Rochdale is cleaner and "straighter" than it probably has ever been.

More than any other university I know, Rochdale is its students. More than any other university I know, Rochdale is about the outside world, because the strongest thread of commonality among Rochdalers is that they have rejected the world. Rochdale is pervaded with reaction to that world. Therein lies its fascination, its promise, and perhaps the seeds of its dissolution. The joys and problems that consume the energies of Rochdale are primarily those of human interaction, rather than learning in the conventional sense. The question, then, is: How relevant to life in the remainder of the twentieth century will the learning-by-living offered by Rochdale turn out to be?

The name "Rochdale" comes down through the years from 1844, when twenty-eight workers in the little town of Rochdale, England, formed one of the world's first consumer cooperatives and laid down the tenets of cooperativism. In 1936 a divinity student, inspired by a Student Christian Movement conference in Indianapolis, established a student-owned and operated residence in Toronto. By 1945 that house had grown, after several evolutions, into Campus Co-operative Residence Inc.; it owned ten houses near Toronto University, and by 1968 it had four hundred members, most of them students at the University of Toronto, living in thirty-one buildings.

In 1965 the Canadian government, recognizing a serious shortage of student housing, passed legislation enabling the Crown-owned Central Mortgage and Housing Corporation to loan up to 90 percent of the cost of cooperative student dormitories. During the following two years, the education committee of Campus Co-op was in a state of ferment about the purposes of university life. The debate focused on the proposal to create Rochdale. Those who conceived Rochdale, including doctors of philosophy, faculty members and doctoral candidates, were very much of the intellectual community, although profoundly ill-at-ease in the conventional university setting. They also were the heirs of thirty-two years' successful experience in student-operated college living quarters.

A Statement of Aims[1] was approved in principle by the Rochdale Council in November 1966, and these aims were further articulated in the charter[2] granted by the Ontario Provincial Secretary and Minister of Citizenship on July 17, 1967. Financial and construction arrangements were made,[3] and although the building was not completed in time for the September 1968 opening, people began moving in.

This is not an insignificant point, as anyone who has lived in a partially-finished building or one being renovated can testify. Residents wove their way around workmen bobbing on air hammers and leaning on power drills. Live wires hung from gaping holes in ceilings, and piles of dust, broken concrete, cardboard boxes and rubbish were everywhere. Furniture was months late in arriving. There were serious floods from vandalized plumbing. And much idealism, couched in the form of imagery about pitching in to sweep the floor, was frustrated.

Rochdale's soaring concrete tower could be just another high-rise apartment with red curtains flapping from windows in the soft breeze. It stands on the rim of the stylish Bay-Bloor district of boutiques, fur salons and expensive shops, overlooking the University of Toronto's Varsity Stadium and the well-heeled Medical Arts Building. There are a bank branch and some offices on the main floor. But Rochdale's outer lobby is usually peopled with an assortment of beings groomed and dressed suitably for roles in the hippie party scenes of the movie *I Love You, Alice B. Toklas*.

The "communications desk," a big wooden affair in the inner lobby, comes and goes. When functioning, it is covered with papers and handbags. Two harried souls answer an endless stream of questions: *Where can I find Mary so-and-so?* and telephone calls: *Is Mary so-and-so there?* Of an evening, a permanent crowd of twenty adolescents, youths and adults, two infants and three pets waits at the four elevators, one of which is evidently out of order. The three functioning lifts pause for mysteriously long intervals at each floor. A happy young man in buckskin plays a guitar, singing tolerably well.

On the second floor is a lounge wherein take place council meetings, folk concerts, visits from Jerry Rubin and Marshall McLuhan, and lounging. Here also is the LBJ Suite, which derives its name from the first-name initials of big-mustached former manager Bernie Bomers, his practical former assistant, Linda Bomphray, and clean-shaven, business-suited former registrar Jack Dimond. Rochdale goes into the current school year with no one assigned these jobs.

On the walls are painted messages: Rochdale Doesn't Like Weekend Slobs. Are You A Slob? Wandering through the building is a young man with flowing blond hair and tight blue jeans whose head is twitching; he is on a "speed trip" induced by an overdose of methedrine. A girl with long straight black hair paces like an animal back and forth on a stair landing. The smell of marijuana is strong on weekend evenings, and the red carpeted halls are commonly strewn with cigarette butts. The music is mainly acid rock, although one occasionally hears Bach on record or, here and there, live. Music is one pursuit that is alive and well and living in Rochdale.

Into Rochdale's beginning last year plunged about four hundred University of Toronto students, perhaps fifty from the New School of Art and the Ontario College of Art, one hundred to one hundred and fifty students from Ryerson Polytechnical Institute and about the same number of full-time Rochdale members. Mingled in were a dozen "resource persons," the Rochdale equivalent of faculty. Two of them, English honors graduate Dennis Lee and Anglican minister Ian MacKenzie, were full-time and paid as such. Eight to ten other resource persons got $2,000 to $7,000 in the form of rent rebates or cash. "They tended to get what they said they needed," Lee says.

Jim Garrard, for instance, head of Rochdale's promising dramatic endeavors, was (and is) excused from paying half his rent. Stan Bevington, head of artistically-prestigious Coach House Press, is affiliated with Rochdale by virtue of an arrangement under which he does all the college's printing for a price which includes the cost of paying off his machines. He invites some students interested in graphic design and printing to work with him. Other resource people—photographers, psychologists, weavers— are helped with room or board, get small bursaries or raise funds for themselves. Each case is considered personal and unique. "It's very messy and unsatisfactory," Lee says. "But if you step back a pace it's attractive in principle. We just don't know how to make it work yet."

Rochdale's first wave of inhabitants was attracted by a variety of fare. Some were familiar with Campus Co-op and visualized a great big happy modern cooperative residence. Some were fed up with the ways and content of traditional university education and visualized self-starting seminars of intellectually-committed people growing together. Some, like high school teachers Joan Doiron and her husband Henri, sought respite from the massive, persistent conformism of their middle-class suburban schools. Ryerson journalism student Arnold Rapps, twenty-six, says many came because they were lonely; like Arnold, they had a vision of experimental living. Many were university students breaking away from stultifying backgrounds. "They saw Rochdale as a little Europe in Toronto where they could get away with a lot of things," Rapps says. *Freedom.* All hoped Rochdale would be different from the world they knew.

Dozens, perhaps more than one hundred, are Americans. One of them is Jennifer Michaels, twenty years old and a cool-eyed blonde. A native of Chattanooga, her husband so far has avoided the American Selective Service System. She wants to model and found that Toronto, as a fashion center, is now giving New York City competition. A fashion photographer and other people she met "and would be friends with anyway" were living at Rochdale, and so she and her husband decided to move in.

Initially, high expectations characterized the Rochdale mood. But as the long gray winter set in, as physical problems with the building continued and as interpersonal problems emerged, Rochdalers were forced to examine themselves and their new institution. "It's positively beautiful to see the initial euphoria," Lee recalls. "But then people run into difficulties. There are junctures which are enormously painful. A number who leave, leave at these junctures, seeing the distress as the end of their hopes. To others the distress is just a beginning." Lee himself moved out, "not by choice but to preserve myself. I just couldn't spread myself as thin as the situation was forcing me to." And in May he resigned from Rochdale, as a number of the founders have.

Most of those who moved out were students from the universities and colleges who couldn't stand the dirt, noise, frustrations, lack of privacy, way of life or the other Rochdalers. Art Hendricks, an ex-Rochdaler studying journalism at Ryerson, remembers Rochdale as "lousy—people decide what they want to study and then get a group together to form a seminar. They only study what they agree with, they never meet opposing views, and education degenerates into nothing more than the reinforcement of what they already think and believe." By the end of February—after the equivalent of one semester—the turnover rate was 6 percent a month.

Moves within the building, from room to room and floor to floor, reached a similar pace. I met one youth who was badly dissatisfied with his life in a fifteenth-floor Ashram Suite (eight rooms whose residents share a common lounge, kitchen, toilet and bath) [4] and who said he was "getting out." I asked where he was going to escape. "Down to the thirteenth floor," he replied. If Rochdalers don't find Utopia on one floor, they look for it on another. Some have shifted as many as six times, like human sand.

The replacements for those who have left altogether have been mostly young working men, typically high school dropouts with $55-a-week jobs driving bakery trucks. The average age and level of education thus is dropping, as is the proportion of women students. The turnover has vitiated Rochdale in two ways, by downgrading its population and by robbing it of an effective collective memory, thereby lowering the level of intellectual exchange that does occur and stretching out the period Rochdalers require to arrive at a consensus on major problems. Trial-and-error solutions are applied to continuing problems, such as whether to keep out "crashers"—uninvited guests—and if so, how. Even repetitive exercises are carried out with strain and strife because almost every new Rochdaler goes through months of fanatically rejecting or avoiding every whiff of organization or authority. Rochdale's governing councils have oscillated between stalemate and issuing unrealistic *diktats*. Example: Writers intending to write about Rochdale *must* contribute money to the college. (A *Time* man was "ordered" to pay $3,000.) The council governs only insofar as those who happen to learn of its legislation happen to agree with it.

The most persistent and severe problem is that of "crashers" who, in the winter, stream to Rochdale for food and shelter. Runaways, mainly teen-aged girls from the suburbs, are a year-round phenomenon. And by mid-April the good-weather wanderers present themselves at the communications desk in the lobby: young men in leather jackets who motorcycled from Nova Scotia, British Columbia or the United States. All of these are "crashers." Slight, red-mustached Peter Turner, twenty-three, a well-liked and respected American who worked for a year on Eugene McCarthy's national committee, told of the "crasher" problem:

"Thirteen [the thirteenth floor] had a 'community.' At the beginning of last year there were all these extremely enthusiastic people on thirteen. It was totally idealistic. There weren't really any hassles to be resolved. A few people had pets and they got adopted by everybody. And if a couple of people did things, others would come along and pitch in. And everybody would sit up until all hours. . . .

"And then there started to be a lot of people crashing. It started in the middle of October. To the end of October, idealism prevailed to the extent that everybody agreed that the kitchen shouldn't be locked and no doors should be locked. Then it was decided that crashers couldn't take food from the kitchen. One group felt crashers are a group that has been rejected by society and must be helped. *Society has failed. These are children; be friendly to them.* It is part of the *raison d'être* of Rochdale. Another group didn't want crashers because they thought they'd be detrimental to Rochdale. When crashers come in it disrupts the whole feeling of community. You come in to eat breakfast in the morning and here are these ten bodies all stretched out on Chesterfields.

"It was then decided that crashers would have to find places to sleep in people's rooms if they wanted to stay for the night. This was decided in the second week of November. [But] there were a lot of crashers who were 'speed freaks' who would just sit around for hours like this—just sitting—not making any attempt to involve themselves with the residents. So it was decided that crashers who were people's guests would be allowed, but people who just sat there would be kicked out. Then people started locking doors. . . ."

By early last summer a consensus had hardened in the building that a screening and "crasher" policy was necessary. Much rent was going uncollected, although a $31,000-plus monthly mortgage payment had to be met. Rochdale was housing drug pushers, "greasers" (those from tough neighborhoods where violence, cheating, theft, manipulation and endless excuse-making are accepted ways of life) and "bikers" (those with motorcycles and leather jackets). The concerns of these groups cannot be construed as educational if the word is to have any semblance of meaning. Among the pushers were "big dealers" who got "ripped" (had their "stuff" stolen or strong-armed away). "Ripping" led pushers to arm themselves, which made Rochdale residents uneasy because it led to the presence of armed "rippers."

In the public mind, sex, too, is closely associated with Rochdale, which has a strictly-no-questions-asked policy about relations between the sexes. The Ashram Suites consist of three double rooms and five single rooms, a kitchen, common lounge and bath, with no segregation by sex. One survey, by a University of Toronto sociology student living at Rochdale, found that of thirty-two persons questioned, 80 percent preferred relations with the one person with whom they were deeply involved (regardless of his marital status); 10 percent were less selective in choosing sexual partners; the rest were living with prospective mates or were refraining entirely. Details on the city's venereal disease clinics are posted in the Rochdale lobby.

Over the summer a "get-tough" council took charge, so far as it could. Many "heavies" were ejected. "Speed evicting parties" were held; according to Mr. Bomers, sixty-five speed freaks have been "permanently graduated." Some were charged with trespassing when they tried to return. Informers are paid to put the finger on speed and heroin pushers, and informers are no longer timid about coming forward. Rental and rent collection procedures have been tightened; food is being made less accessible to wanderers; the cafeteria and restaurant are being turned over to a private catering firm. Guns are required to be deposited in a safety deposit box. An agreement has been reached with the local police, under which the police are called in for particular disturbances but not for general surveillance.

Signs printed in bright red over every fire alarm box in the college read: "Anyone guilty of knowingly submitting a false fire alarm with this device will be required to await questioning by legal authorities and will vacate Rochdale within twelve hours of the offense." A new fee and admission policy acts somewhat as a screen. There is a trial membership of two to four months which costs $10. If the member is judged acceptable by the council, he pays a minimum of $25 for the school year (toward which the $10 is counted), plus any combination of $40 or forty hours of work (cleaning, manning the communications desk, and so on).

One gets the impression that nothing by way of education takes place at Rochdale, but this is inaccurate. The most invisible activities, such as a seminar on violence and a printing group, are comprised of members who are happy with their numbers and composition, and who therefore do not advertise themselves.

A nursery school, Indian Institute, Theatre Passe Muraille and weaving classes have exhibited staying power. The Indian Institute, subsidized by a federal grant, is an educational-residential center where Indian people can study and teach in their own languages. The theater group produced *Futz* at the downtown Central Library Theatre last spring. Before morality officers arrested the producer, director and complete cast—a first for Ontario—the play received fine reviews. Over the summer, an arts festival was staged. The performances, seminars and displays were well-received and well-reviewed. An intimate theater is being constructed inside a ground-floor office of the Rochdale building.

Other learning activities which have taken place with some continuity include the history and theory of jazz, classical music theory, folk singing, folk and pop song-writing, yoga, poetry, life drawing, Judaism and religious existentialism, cosmic history, the drug seminar, social journalism, a magic school, an outing society, Jungian psychology, sculpture, primitive religions, painting, films, ceramics, Confucianism, a seminar on revolution, silk-screen processing, and sensitivity training. A clearing house for information on the interests and skills of Rochdale people and scheduled activities was established this year. A library has taken shape, its backbone consisting of a collection of science fiction donated by Judith Merril, the American writer.

Affiliated with Rochdale—affiliation meaning there is a relationship ranging from sympathy to cooperation—are the House of Anansi (Dennis Lee's publishing house, which made a name for itself with *The University Game*) , the Modern Dance Theatre of Canada, Superschool (a "free" school for about thirty students between the ages of three and twenty) , the Coach House Press, and the Centre for the Study of Institutions and Theology (which conducts the violence seminar) .

Rochdale is a magnet for the alienated. Will their gropings illuminate new paths for the university and society? The lack so far of social commitment at Rochdale—beyond "legalize marijuana" petitions—is curious, for one of the failures of North American society in the eyes of its alienated is an insufficiency of social commitment. Perhaps nascent in Rochdale are leaders who will inspire some of their fellows to use their freedom in socially-relevant ways. Or is inspiration unacceptable to the alienated and therefore unworkable? Certainly the Rochdale ethos leaves little room for the "great leader."

Rochdale may simply be a partial vindication of McLuhan's aphorism that "the future is with us," and it may prove only that significant numbers of the young generation would rather try primitive freedom and suffer degrees of chaos than suffer even reformed campuses. One cannot evade the hope, however, that out of this maturation cell called Rochdale will come a few Real People who will be able to show what lies beyond alienation. Such young citizens of the future may recommend against further Rochdales. If their views spring from their Rochdale experience, then Rochdale will have served a noble purpose.

*Notes*

1. *Aim of the Project*
"The aim of the education program is to provide an environment where individuals and groups of people can create their own educational experiences —experiences relevant to the individuals involved and fashioned by them in regard to both form and content."
*Principles of the Project*
"Education at Rochdale will be democratic and community oriented. Decisions regarding education within Rochdale will be made by the people directly involved in the education project.

"The character of education at Rochdale will not be that of isolation from society but, rather, that of involvement with the extended community in a manner to be determined by those participating in the program. The Rochdale member is necessarily a member of a larger society, and no rigid distinction is made between his role as 'student' and as a 'social being.' "
*Approach to Education*

"Essentially, Rochdale will be a centre of imaginative intellectual and creative activity and will appeal to potential members on this basis. . . ."

2. *Objects of Rochdale College*

"a)   To advance learning and the dissemination of knowledge;

"b)   To promote the intellectual, social, moral and physical development of the members . . . and the betterment of society;

"c)   To establish an education-residential institution in which participants determine the form and content of their own education and the direction and intensity of their involvement;

"d)   To establish and maintain a library;

"e)   To establish and conduct seminars, lectures and correspondence courses and to publish a journal and such other scholarly material as shall be relevant to the educational purposes of the Corporation. . . ."

3. The sum of $5,038,200 was loaned to Campus Co-operative Residence Inc. by Central Mortgage and Housing. The remaining 10 percent of the cost of the $5,713,000 building came from Rubin Corporation, the developer ($430,000 at 7 percent interest), past earnings of Campus Co-op ($124,800), and from a college fraternity ($120,000). The long-term CMHC mortgage at 5.875 percent interest requires equalized payments averaging $31,275 monthly. There are also other interest and repayment costs. The building budget for the 1968–69 academic year was $586,430. Income is mainly from rents from the building, which theoretically accommodates 850 persons.

4. There are five types of rooms or suites at Rochdale. Besides the Ashram Suites, other living units are Aphrodite Suites (living room, bedroom, kitchen and bath), Franz Kafka Units (a single room and double room, sharing a common bath), Gnostic Chambers (the same as Franz Kafka units, but with a kitchen) and Zeus Suites (a huge living room, two bedrooms, kitchen and bath). Costs range from $250 a month for a Zeus Suite down to $17 a week if you double up in a Gnostic Chamber.

# 6

## EPILOGUE

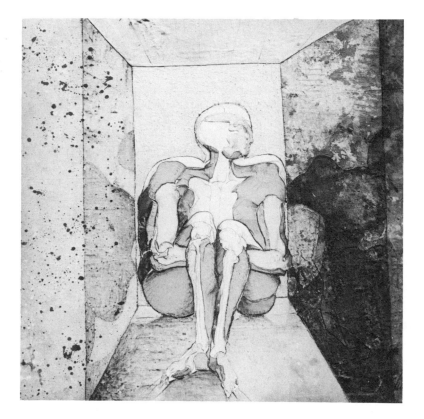

*You may please all of the students some of the time; you can even please some of the students all of the time; but you can't please all of the students all the time.*

(With thanks to Abraham Lincoln)

# Dr. Johns Wants Us
# to Do Our Own Thing

*Bill Peterson*

*The following news article was written by Bill Peterson, staff writer for the Louisville, Kentucky* Courier-Journal, *on October 28, 1968. The college is located in Pikeville, Kentucky. Dr. Johns is no longer president.*

In a year when liberal college students across the nation are rebelling against conservative administrators, the inconceivable is happening at Pikeville College—conservative students are accusing their administration of being too liberal.

The students haven't taken to the streets. Nor have they threatened to take over the college administration bulding.

But the signs of a liberal-conservative conflict are unmistakable at the campus, which is dug into a mountain slope high above this Eastern Kentucky city of 5,800.

The issues in the split are the same as on many campuses: free speech, freedom in the classroom, the college's involvement in social problems, the impersonality of the education system, student dress and activities, and the college's response to change.

However, the sides are the reverse of what they are at other campuses—with students taking a conservative position on almost every issue and the administration taking a liberal one.

Senior Dave Cleavanger, who classes himself as a conservative, put it this way: "We must have the only right-wing student protest movement in the country."

The student conservatives, who seem to have a numerical upper hand in the 1,200-member student body, strongly support the Vietnam war and the draft.

As for the college, they feel that the administration of Pikeville's 37-year-old president, Dr. Thomas H. Johns, is too liberal and that Johns is attempting to change the institution too fast.

Administrators at other colleges, Johns said, are baffled by the conservative revolt on his campus and are "amazed at what we're doing here."

"We're taking education out of its box," he said. "We're addressing it to the 20th century."

Conservatives at this Presbyterian-affiliated institution aren't impressed, although they are careful to note that they aren't against change, as such.

In often defiant tones, conservative students have accused Johns of ousting elderly faculty members and replacing them with teachers who have "leftist" leanings. They also complain that Johns is placing too much emphasis on sociology and psychology in the curriculum.

Some have questioned his contract and tenure. And one group actually considered trying to impeach the college president.

The college Board of Trustees has given Johns a vote of confidence but opposition by the conservatives continues. Said Student Council president Robert Ford, "We're not satisfied with the investigation, we're going to have to have more."

Ford and a group of other conservatives are particularly concerned with what student newspaper editor John Mays described as "left wing extremists" on the campus faculty.

President Johns said he's willing to do everything possible to cooperate with the students, but that he won't budge from his policy of "freeing kids' minds."

Johns said his administration has given students new freedom to speak out in their classrooms, put them on faculty and college trustee committees and repeatedly encouraged them to "do your own thing."

These moves would have made him a campus darling at Berkeley or Columbia—but not at Pikeville, where many students still are asked to sign a pledge that they won't drink alcoholic beverages.

"We don't know what our thing is," remarked one sophomore. "And even if we did we don't know how to do it."

Another student, a senior biology major, said that Johns urged him to investigate water pollution in the Pikeville area as "his thing." The student replied that he wasn't qualified to do so.

"What they're doing is asking students who aren't educated to solve problems educated people can't solve," this student said, adding, "this whole involvement, learning by experience—it's threatening the stability of our school."

At many other campuses, students complain that the faculty is too distant. At Pikeville, conservative students complain that faculty members are too chummy.

"I think too many faculty members try too hard to be on our level," said junior Holly Bowling. "I just don't want my professor to be a pal."

At many other campuses, students complain that they are required to dress too formally. At Pikeville, conservative students complain that some teachers dress too casually.

Miss Bowling's roommate, Mary Ann Close, said the skirts of some women teachers are too short and that the hair of some men teachers is too long. She also deplored the fact that some faculty members wear turtleneck sweaters and not neckties.

Not all the students are conservative. There is a small, but increasingly vocal, group of campus liberals, and the conservatives fear that the liberals are gaining support "by leaps and bounds."

Liberal spokesman Marvin Rudnick, a transfer student from Syracuse University, disagreed. "We're a minority," he said. "We've been grossed out."

Rudnick said the liberals, most of whom grew up outside Kentucky, would be considered moderates on most campuses and that they are incorrectly labeled radicals in Pikeville.

Liberal activities at the college, he said, have included supporting the presidential candidacy of Sen. Eugene McCarthy and staging a "spontaneous" sit-in two weeks ago to protest the halting of an outdoor record hop by Pikeville police.

President Johns said he believes the skirmishing between liberals and conservatives is healthy.

"Peaches and cream doesn't bring dialogue. Confrontation does," he said. "Education is the polarization of ideas and confrontation. People finally have to be made aware of their thinking."

# APPENDIX

# A Personal Bibliography
# on Higher Education

*Phillip Werdell*

*In this open letter to students, Phillip Werdell asks, "What good are bibliographies?" The author's long experience with student-initiated educational reform includes working for the United States National Students Association as consultant on over 200 campuses and setting up the Association's Center for Educational Reform. Werdell has worked in New Haven and Manhattan, Kansas communities organizing educational alternatives outside the school establishment. Presently he is Associate Coordinator of the Master Plan of the City University of New York.*

*If you like, you are welcome to reproduce and distribute this letter for your own purposes BUT please do not allow it to be copyrighted in any form. This will assure that others have free access to this material for their purposes.*

November 15, 1967

Dear friends,

A number of students have asked me to suggest articles and books which might help them in their efforts towards reforming higher education. This is my own effort to sort through what I have read to date and place it in a personal and political context:

personal context to make my own judgments as clear as possible and political context to make an attempt to show the possible relevance to actions which students might take. It is, as Roger Landrum recently put it, "attempting to write from the personal and political stance of creating future history."

Just to suggest articles and books which a student might read is to assert that there is a firm intellectual tradition upon which future intellectual history can be built. Moreover, this letter—which is a conscious experiment in creating a more effective bibliography—builds upon my past efforts to suggest articles and books on education that students might find helpful. Since all these suggestions to date have been somewhat successful and since all my recent efforts have been oral, I will begin by sketching each of these in a general and concise form.

*The "First, what do you mean?" response:* It is impossible to give you a simple list of articles and books on higher education. *I* assume that teaching (for example, prescribing a bibliography) must be made relevant to each individual student. An exhaustive bibliography is most likely to be confusing, to frighten a student, to imply that he will not be able to deal with me (the bibliography maker) until he has read all the books, to leave him powerless and fundamentally unhelped, possibly even temporarily disabled. On the other hand, it is my experience that when I suggest four or five articles or books (that is, a manageable suggestion), my suggestions are most frequently off the mark, not immediately relevant to the student, not likely to be sufficiently helpful that he will come back later to talk about what he read or ask for more suggestions or give me some suggestions from his further reading, almost never sufficiently stimulating to encourage the student to write about education himself, much less act. What good are bibliographies? I assume that learning (for example, acquiring a better understanding of the possibilities of higher education) has no limits, that everything is potentially relevant, that every book is worth reading. Moreover, I have found that I learn more from doing something than from reading about it, more from talking with someone who has direct experience in something than from reading books and articles that were important to him, more from reading books or articles which *I* felt were going to be relevant than from taking the arbitrary suggestions of others.

*The "Well, some people who are doing what you seem to want to do have short annotated bibliographies available" response:* There are at least three short book lists which you, as a student with a fairly new interest in educational reform, might find helpful.

First, you might write for a copy of issue number 196 of *Moderator* magazine (1738 Pine Street, Philadelphia, Pa. 19103). In a section entitled "Bookshelf" there is a short list of books on education recommended by Harold Taylor. Taylor is one of the few adult educators with whom students interested in educational reform have been able to continually have a mutually instructive and free-flowing conversation. He was President of Sarah Lawrence College long before the practices of the college were out of disfavor with the Educational Establishment. He has since gone on to involve himself in a number of even more experimental educational ventures including a model international college which holds most of its classes on board a ship or wherever the ship might dock, and an ambitious study searching for practical ways to give students in teacher education programs experience in a foreign country and foreign teachers experience in American primary and secondary classrooms. Not only does Taylor bring an international perspective often lacking in educational thinking and work in America, but he spends a great deal of time with students who are interested in educational reform. Thus, there is a good chance that he has had some helpful insights regarding which books that he has suggested to students have been most beneficial.

Second, you might write the United States Student Press Association (1770 Church Street NW, Washington, D.C. 20036) for the bibliography they use in their Higher Education Program. One of the major elements of this program is a summer seminar in which student editors who have a strong interest but little background in educational reform come together to learn as much as they can before they go back to issue their educational community's newspaper. Student editors are busy people and learn quickly to be discriminate in what they read. They need a broad and diverse background, but they search out material which is as concise and practical as possible. Since there have already been three summer seminars, it is likely that they have forced the USSPA staff to make some serious decisions about recommended reading. The original bibliography prepared by Laura Gadowsky and Rita Dirschowitz (the only one I have seen) contained about twelve books with an unusually insightful paragraph judging the relevance of each.

Third, you might write the United States National Student Association (2115 S Street NW, Washington, D.C. 20008) for any bibliographies on education which they might have. There are over a dozen full-time staff members working on a wide variety of educational reform programs, each certainly developing a list of articles and books which he recommends to students interested in his particular program. As a general, annotated, and short bibliography, I still find an article I wrote for the Summer 1966 *Student Government Bulletin* most helpful. The article, entitled "Building a Base for Educational Reform," suggests about twelve general areas to which a student interested in educational reform should be exposed, a variety of ways in which formal and informal educational experiences might be structured to pursue these questions, and the books and articles which I then felt were most relevant and helpful to students investigating each of these areas afresh. A number of students have mentioned to me that this article provided a helpful context in which they could decide on the book or article which would be most relevant for them to choose to read first. There have also been a number of seminars and internships on educational reform set up by students which have used some of the suggestions in this article.

Possibly most important, you might write to the national offices of a wide variety of student organizations, e.g., University Christian Movement (P.O. Box 399, Madison Square Station, New York, New York 10010), or young Americans for Freedom (1221 Massachusetts Ave. NW, Washington, D.C. 20005). You might ask for their publication list *and* for the recommendations of one of their officers or staff members regarding further articles or books on higher education. Most student organizations are entering the questions of analysis and reform of higher education from a very independent stance. The three particular bibliographies which I suggested reflect the "prejudices" of my own experience and work. You might find the "prejudices" of one or more other student organizations much more stimulating and helpful. Also, by taking into account the recommendations of a number of diverse groups, you are likely to gain a good deal of perspective which I cannot pretend to be able to offer.

*The "Say, why don't you try an experiment and create a bibliography suited to your own unique situation?" response:* Especially if you already have some fairly clear ideas about educational reform, you might begin a more rigorous study by finding out what various elements and constituencies of the academic community are reading about education. Not only will you come up with a fairly unique bibliography, but also you will have some first hand experience regarding the educational thinking of men who affect the educational policy on your campus, you will have someone to talk with about various books or articles that you read, and you will begin to have some idea of whom you are (and are not) up against when you choose a particular course of action. Moreover, you will have developed the beginnings of good relationships with people who might be able to help you, and you may have a better idea of the most effective arguments for dealing with people who decide not to help you. (Wouldn't it be nice to have a list of quotes from the speeches your college president has made over the last few years, even the goals and policies suggested in writings which he highly recommended?) To be specific, I would suggest that you ask a number of people to recommend articles and books on higher education which you should read: your college president, your deans, your own faculty members, the chairmen of various academic departments, members of your board of Trustees or Regents, leaders of various factions on educational issues in the state legislature (especially if you come from a public institution), a number of ordinary citizens with very different attitudes toward your campus, a couple of members of the local press, radio and TV stations including editorial and education writers, and, most certainly, your parents. (Warning: most of the people you talk to, even crucial policy makers, do very little reading about education—if any. *Do not threaten* them by even implying that they should be able to give you a long or perfect list of things to read. Many will feel that they are experts on education without having read a thing, a very democratic notion. Others will want to suggest pamphlets or periodicals which may have little to do with education, in *your* mind. Or, they will suggest that you read a book or an article which they have not read themselves, and, this is crucial, remember that *you* have not read most of the books which you think are probably very important. At least, *I* haven't.) . . .

COPYRIGHTS AND ACKNOWLEDGMENTS (*Continued from Page iv*)

THE DIAL PRESS for "A Dog in Brooklyn, A Girl in Detroit." Copyright © 1962 by Herbert Gold. From *The Age of Happy Problems* by Herbert Gold. Reprinted by permission of the publisher, The Dial Press.

DOUBLEDAY & COMPANY for "Elegy for Jane" from *The Collected Poems of Theodore Roethke* by Theodore Roethke, copyright 1950 by Theodore Roethke. Reprinted by permission of Doubleday & Company, Inc. For excerpt from *Sexual Politics* by Kate Millett, copyright © 1969, 1970 by Kate Millett. Reprinted by permission of Doubleday & Company, Inc.

MARION DUNHAM for "Truth, Beauty and Sour Grapes, or: Is Gold Getting Rich Telling Us What Rotten Shape Society Is In?"

E. P. DUTTON & COMPANY for excerpt from *Ghosts*, from the book *Ghosts, An Enemy of the People, The Warrior of Helgeland* by Henrik Ibsen. Trans. by R. Farquharson Sharp. Everyman's Library Edition. Published by E. P. Dutton & Co., Inc. and used with their permission.

FABER AND FABER LTD. for "Talking in Bed" from *The Whitsun Weddings* by Philip Larkin. Reprinted by permission of Faber and Faber Ltd.

FAMILY CIRCLE MAGAZINE, March 1971 issue, for Maria Wilhelm, "An Interview with David Riesman."

FARRAR, STRAUS & GIROUX for "Down & Back." Reprinted with the permission of Farrar, Straus & Giroux, Inc. from *Love and Fame* by John Berryman, copyright © 1970 by John Berryman.

FORTUNE MAGAZINE for "The Prince of Creation" by Susanne K. Langer. Reprinted from the January 1944 issue of Fortune Magazine by special permission; © 1943 Time Inc.

OTTO FRIEDRICH for "There Are 00 Trees in Russia," copyright © 1964, by Minneapolis Star and Tribune Co., Inc. Reprinted from the October, 1964 issue of Harper's Magazine by permission of the author.

HARCOURT BRACE JOVANOVICH for excerpts from *Language in Thought and Action*, First Edition, by S. I. Hayakawa. Reprinted by permission of the publisher, Harcourt Brace Jovanovich, Inc.

HARVARD UNIVERSITY PRESS for excerpt from *The Uses of the University* by Clark Kerr. Reprinted by permission of the publisher, Harvard University Press.

ROBERT S. HOOVER for "Nairobi College" by the Planning Committee of Nairobi College.

HOUGHTON MIFFLIN COMPANY for "The Conversion of the Jews" from Philip Roth's *Goodbye Columbus*. Copyright © 1959 by Philip Roth. Reprinted by permission of the publisher, Houghton Mifflin Company.

THE HUMANIST for "Toward an Ideal College" by Judson Jerome. This article first appeared in *The Humanist*, March–April 1969, and is reprinted by permission.

SUSANNE K. LANGER for "The Prince of Creation."

SEYMOUR LIPSET for "Violence and Power on Campus: A Debate" by Morris Abram, Seymour Lipset, Michael Rossman, and Michael Vozick.

LOOK MAGAZINE for excerpts from "Motherhood: Who Needs It?" by Betty Rollin, *Look*, September 22, 1970.

THE STERLING LORD AGENCY for "Why We're Against the Biggees" by James S. Kunen, *The Atlantic*, October 1968. Copyright © 1968 by James S. Kunen. Reprinted by permission of The Sterling Lord Agency, Inc.

EDWIN H. MORRIS & COMPANY for *Carmen Ohio* by Fred A. Cornell. Copyright © 1916 by Ohio State University Association. Copyright renewed by Ohio State University Association. All rights controlled by Edwin H. Morris & Company, Inc. Used by permission.

THE NEW REPUBLIC for "The Talker" by Mona Van Duyn. Reprinted by permission of *The New Republic*, © 1971, Harrison-Blaine of New Jersey, Inc.

HAROLD OBER ASSOCIATES for "Theme for English B" from *The Langston Hughes Reader*, published by George Braziller, Inc., 1958. Reprinted by permission of Harold Ober Associates, Incorporated. Copyright 1951 by Langston Hughes. For "Space for Something Else: Bensalem" by Elizabeth Sewell. Reprinted by permission of Harold Ober Associates, Incorporated. Copyright © 1968 by The New City Foundation.

OXFORD UNIVERSITY PRESS for "Experiment at Berkeley" from *Experiment at*

COPYRIGHTS AND ACKNOWLEDGMENTS (cont.)

*Berkeley* by Joseph Tussman. Copyright © 1969 by Oxford University Press, Inc. Reprinted by permission.

LAURENCE POLLINGER LTD. and THE ESTATE OF THE LATE MRS. FRIEDA LAWRENCE for "Cocksure Women and Hensure Men" from *Phoenix II: Uncollected, Unpublished and Other Prose Works by D. H. Lawrence* edited by Harry T. Moore, published by William Heinemann Ltd., London.

QUINTO SOL PUBLICATIONS for "The Immigrant Experience" by Richard Olivas, from *Voices: Readings from El Grito* edited by Octavio I. Romano, published by Quinto Sol Publications, Inc., 1971.

RAMPARTS MAGAZINE for excerpts from "Why Women's Liberation?" by Marlene Dixon, *Ramparts,* July 1969. Copyright Ramparts Magazine, 1969. By permission of the Editors. For "From Cornell: A Black Radical's Report on His Campus Struggles" by Michael Thelwell, *Ramparts,* December 1969. Copyright Ramparts Magazine, 1969. By permission of the Editors.

RANDOM HOUSE for "Talking in Bed." Copyright © 1960 by Philip Larkin. Reprinted from *The Whitsun Weddings,* by Philip Larkin, by permission of Random House, Inc. For "The Present Moment in Progressive Education." Copyright © 1969 by Paul Goodman. Reprinted from *New Reformation: Notes of a Neolithic Conservative,* by Paul Goodman, by permission of Random House, Inc. For excerpt from *The Closed Corporation* by James Ridgeway. Copyright © 1968 by James Ridgeway. Reprinted by permission of Random House, Inc.

MICHAEL ROSSMAN for "Violence and Power on Campus: A Debate" by Morris Abram, Seymour Lipset, Michael Rossman, and Michael Vozick.

ROUTLEDGE & KEGAN PAUL LTD. for "University Examinations in Egypt" from *The Laughing Hyena and Other Poems* by D. J. Enright, published by Routledge & Kegan Paul Ltd., London, 1953.

SAN FRANCISCO EXAMINER for excerpt from "Crisis at SF State" by Harvey Yorke.

SATURDAY REVIEW for "Leslie Aumaire" by Harold Witt, *Saturday Review,* November 19, 1966; copyright 1966 Saturday Review, Inc. For "Status-Seeking in Academe" by David Boroff, *Saturday Review,* December 19, 1964; copyright 1964 Saturday Review, Inc. For excerpts from "Without Law, the University Is a Sitting Duck" by Harris Wofford, Jr., and Theodore M. Hesburgh, *Saturday Review,* April 19, 1969; copyright 1969 Saturday Review, Inc.

STEIN AND DAY for excerpts from the book *Waiting for the End* by Leslie Fiedler. Copyright © 1964 by Leslie A. Fiedler. Reprinted with permission of Stein and Day, Publishers.

THE TIMES OF INDIA for "Top Scholars Urge Inquiry into Calcutta 'Orgies.'" Courtesy: The Times of India, Bombay, India.

UNITED STATES NATIONAL STUDENT ASSOCIATION for "A Personal Bibliography on Higher Education" by Phillip Werdell.

UNITED STATES SELECTIVE SERVICE SYSTEM for excerpt from "Channeling," U.S. Government Printing Office, Washington, D.C., 1967.

THE UNIVERSITY OF CHICAGO PRESS for "The 'Cooling-Out' Function in Higher Education," reprinted from Burton R. Clark, "The 'Cooling-Out' Function in Higher Education," *American Journal of Sociology,* LXV (May, 1960), 569–76, with the permission of the author and the editor. Published by The University of Chicago Press, © 1960 by The University of Chicago. All rights reserved.

THE UNIVERSITY OF MISSISSIPPI for excerpts from the 1970 General Catalogue of The University of Mississippi.

THE VIKING PRESS for "Cocksure Women and Hensure Men" from *Phoenix II: Uncollected, Unpublished and Other Prose Works by D. H. Lawrence,* edited by Harry T. Moore. Copyright 1928 by Forum Publishing Company, copyright © renewed 1956 by Frieda Lawrence. Reprinted by permission of The Viking Press, Inc. For "Of This Time, Of That Place" by Lionel Trilling. Copyright 1943, copyright © renewed 1971 by Lionel Trilling. All rights reserved. Reprinted by permission of The Viking Press, Inc.

AUSTIN WARREN and TONY STONEBURNER for "There Is Nothing I Can't Use in My Teaching" by Austin Warren, from *A Recognition of Austin Warren* edited by Tony Stoneburner. By permission of Austin Warren and Tony Stoneburner.

MARIA WILHELM for "An Interview with David Riesman."

HAROLD WITT for "Leslie Aumaire."

HARVEY YORKE for excerpt from "Crisis at SF State."

COPYRIGHTS AND ACKNOWLEDGMENTS (cont.)

MARY YOST ASSOCIATES for "Life in the Yellow Submarine" by Barbara Probst Solomon, *Harper's*, October 1968. © Barbara Probst Solomon.

BARRIE ZWICKER for "Rochdale: The Ultimate Freedom." Copyright © 1969 by Barrie Zwicker.

*ILLUSTRATION CREDITS*

Page 1: William Blake, *Glad Day*. Courtesy of The British Museum, London.

Page 5: John and Faith Hubley, cover illustration for *Zuckerkandl* by Robert Hutchins (New York: Grove Press, 1969).

Page 91: Wide World photo.

Page 95: Photograph by Michael D. Sullivan.

Page 181: Photograph by Ben Martin.

Page 223: Saul Steinberg, *Abundance*. Reprinted by permission of Julian Bach Literary Agency, Inc. © 1954 by Saul Steinberg.

Page 227: Saul Steinberg, *Pen in Hand*. Reprinted by permission of Julian Bach Literary Agency, Inc. © 1960 by Saul Steinberg.

Page 269: Wide World photo.

Page 289: M. C. Escher, *Relativity*, from the Collection of C. V. S. Roosevelt.

Page 355: Jan Stussy, *Life in a Box Depends on How You Sit*. Collage, 48" x 48". Courtesy of Esther-Robles Gallery.

A
B
C 2
D 3
E 4
F 5
G 6
H 7
I 8
J 9

1497

86